Eugenio
Montale

10/13/81

Eugenio Montale: Poet on the Edge

Rebecca J. West

Harvard
University
Press
Cambridge,
Massachusetts
and
London,
England
1981

Publication of this book has been aided by a grant from the
Andrew W. Mellon Foundation

Library of Congress Cataloging in Publication Data

West, Rebecca J., 1946–
    Eugenio Montale, poet on the edge.

    Includes bibliographical references and index.
    1. Montale, Eugenio, 1896–   —Criticism and
interpretation.   I.   Title.
PQ4829.O565Z95   851'.912   81-4119
ISBN 0-674-26910-1   AACR2

To
My
Mother
and
My
Father

Preface

THIS book is the result
of what Dante, in referring to his great master Vergil, called *lungo studio* and *grande amore*. I intend no comparison between that infinitely
rich partnership and my own involvement as student, reader, and critic
with Montale's poetry, except insofar as in both cases *study* and *love*
contain, in their exquisite simplicity, a world of intellectual and human
experience. I have studied and loved Eugenio Montale's poetry and
have been enormously enriched by it in my life and my work for more
than a decade. My hope is that this book will encourage others to read
him; or in the case of those who have already done so, I seek to add my
experience as reflected here to their own insights into the wealth and
complexity of his poetry. I have written this study especially for those
non-Italian readers who know something of the Italian lyric or of modern and contemporary poetry in general but who may not feel confident
enough of their Italian to approach Montale and the Italian criticism

surrounding his work without some mediation in English. This is not, however, a basic introduction to Montale; several American scholars and others writing in English have produced books and articles that more than satisfy this need, and my indebtedness to them is evident throughout this book. Rather I have focused on certain aspects of theme and style and on the underlying poetics of Montale's six collections as well as on the meditations of many recent Italian critics of his oeuvre in an attempt to penetrate more deeply into the meaning and beauty of this poetry.

I have translated into English all Italian materials. Unfortunately, complete and definitive English versions of all six collections of Montale's poetry do not yet exist; but the reader who feels the need for further translations will find readily available several collections of selected poems and prose in English. I have provided a partial list of such sources, including critical materials in English, in the notes to the introduction.

It is no doubt true that poetry can never be adequately translated, and it is certainly true that criticism cannot ever fully explain poetry, with or without the aid of translated versions. The English translations I provide are literal; in my readings of the poetry I seek, above all, to translate to the reader my sense of the infinitely unexplainable and yet perpetually compelling mystery of their greatness. My main and constant aim is to untangle the many threads that come together to form the Montalian weave. I focus more on detail than general theory, on text rather than context. This close attention to seemingly minimal or minor details is dictated in great part by the very nature of Montale's poetry, perhaps the greatest lesson of which is that of recognizing limits and of neither exalting nor demeaning one's position within them.

Acknowledgments are made to the following publishers for their generous permission to quote, reuse, and/or translate materials controlled by them: excerpts from Eugenio Montale's *Auto da fé*, copyright © 1966 by Casa Editrice Il Saggiatore, reprinted and translated by permission of Casa Editrice Il Saggiatore; excerpts from Eugenio Montale's *Auto da fé* and *Sulla poesia*, translated by the author with the kind consent of Antaeus–The Ecco Press, which will publish *Selected Essays* of Montale translated by Jonathan Galassi; excerpts from Eugenio Montale's *Sulla poesia*, *Farfalla di Dinard*, and *Tutte le poesie*,

Preface

To all those who have sustained me in this work I offer thanks. Specifically my gratitude goes to Eugenio Montale both for his poetry and for his warm personal hospitality to me during our meetings; to Cesare Segre, who facilitated my first meeting with the poet and whose scholarship and friendship are deeply valued; to Guido Almansi, whose work on Montale has truly taught me invaluable lessons and whose vivacity and generosity I most emphatically treasure; to Rachel Jacoff, my *prima amica* and best ear; to Glauco Cambon, Luciano Rebay, Emerico Giachery, Paolo Cherchi, John Peck, Jonathan Galassi, and William Arrowsmith, as well as other scholars, translators, poets, and colleagues too numerous to name, whose work on Montale and direct or indirect involvement with my own work made the writing of this book a human as well as an intellectual adventure. Although not directly involved in this project Thomas G. Bergin has been a constant source of practical and spiritual aid and an inimitable model of all that is best in the academic profession. To him and to all my past teachers of Italian, many thanks for your patient guidance.

I also wish to thank the American Academy in Rome, the National Endowment for the Humanities, and the University of Chicago for providing me with a year's leave, during which, as a Fellow at the Academy, I had the peace and solitude necessary for writing much of this book. My love and gratitude go to my family for always believing in me and to my husband for knowing when to be there and when to leave me to my solitary meditations.

Preface

Finally, loving thanks to my *custodi silenziosi*, those omnipresent recondite friends, whose insights, truths, harmonies, and meanings often resist expression. Without them even a year-round residence in the *cittd eterna* would not have been enough.

Rebecca J. West

Chicago
February 1981

Contents

Eugenio
Montale

Introduction

Eugenio Montale
has enjoyed copious and extremely serious critical attention in his own
country since the very beginning of his career as a published poet in
1925, when his first collection, *Ossi di seppia* (Cuttlefish Bones), appeared. In the United States attention to his work has been a much
more recent phenomenon, manifested in selected translations of his
poetry and prose, introductory articles, and finally in some few longer
critical studies.[1] Since 1975, the year in which Montale was awarded
the Nobel Prize for Literature, his name and work have become somewhat better known outside Italy and Europe, but that knowledge tends
to be partial and its expansion inhibited by the dearth of complete
translations of his six collections of poetry.[2] Modern Italian authors
have never been as generally accessible to the American public as
French or, more recently, Latin American ones, partly for rather com-
plicated historical reasons and partly for the simple reason that they
have been less frequently translated and less publicized outside their

1

Introduction

own culture. In Montale's case the poet's own insistence on privacy, and the very real difficulties of his poetic language and style, difficulties that even Italian critics have recognized, have increased his inaccessibility.

By learning something of the man and of the times in which he has lived and written, we can learn something of the origins and significance of his dogged privacy and his so-called literary hermeticism. I have gathered information for the most part from Italian and other secondary sources,[3] for Montale himself is stubbornly laconic about what he has called his *fatti* and *nonfatti* (events or facts and nonevents), preferring to give partial or even somewhat untrue information rather than reveal the intimate details of his life. He insists that there is little of real interest to be known; if life is, in his words, a "labyrinth," he comments that he has passed through its "innumerable small paths without sustaining serious harm."[4]

Montale's passage through the labyrinth began on October 12, 1896, in Genoa. He spent his childhood summers in the area of the Cinque Terre, a beautiful, rugged coastal area south of Genoa, where his family had a vacation residence. In 1915 at the age of nineteen Montale decided to dedicate himself to the study of bel canto and did so with the old maestro Ernesto Sivori until Sivori's death in 1916. The poet wrote a prose piece years later—"In the Key of 'F,'" now included in the volume *Farfalla di Dinard* (Butterfly of Dinard), a collection of fictionalized autobiographical stories—in which he recounts something of his experience with Sivori. The young aspirant was particularly impressed by Sivori's comment that much more than a good voice a singer needs a certain fire, called *l'axillo*, or a "spur" to success. Montale was never able to determine if he possessed the needed fire, for upon Sivori's death "the magic, if not singing itself" (l'incanto, se non il canto) was finished for him.[5] Nonetheless his continued interest in and love for music is evident throughout his poetry and prose; throughout his life he has continued to sing for the pleasure of friends and family. In spite of the fact that he never became a professional singer, Montale recognized the utility of his early training, writing in his "Imaginary Interview" of 1946 that "the experience was useful [for] there exists a problem of pitch even outside of singing, in every human enterprise."[6]

In this story Montale calls himself a "miserable bookworm" (gramo topo di biblioteca). Although indeed a lover of reading he never studied for a university degree, instead teaching himself by an eclectic consumption of various literary and philosophical materials, eventually learning enough French, Spanish, and English to be able to earn his living later as a translator and reviewer of many non-Italian texts. He started to write poetry at a very early age, even before studying voice, verses he later called *fantaisiste* and naïvely futuristic. They were never published. His first poem, which the poet describes as "tout entier à sa proie attaché," was "Meriggiare" (Nooning), written in 1916 and included in the first collection, *Ossi di seppia.* In 1922 the journal *Primo Tempo* published his suite of seven poems entitled "Accordi" (Chords), in which Montale sought to recreate in words the sounds of various musical instruments. Only one of these poems—"Corno inglese" (English Horn)—was included in the 1925 volume. But between the study of voice and the beginnings of a career as published poet, war intervened. From 1917 to 1919 Montale served as a soldier, mostly in the Trentino area and in and around Genoa. Unlike his great contemporary Ungaretti, whose poetry makes great use of his wartime experiences, Montale never wrote much about those years as a soldier; it was the Second World War, with its physical and metaphysical hardships, that was to affect Montale's poetic voice, even though he was not an active military participant in it.

After 1919 Montale returned to his family home and continued to write poetry and to frequent the literary circles of Genoa and Turin, where he formed important friendships with such critics and poets as Angelo Barile, Camillo Sbarbaro, and Adriano Grande. In 1922 he met the antifascist intellectual Piero Gobetti, who was to publish Montale's first book of poems in 1925. *Ossi di seppia* is in its early editions filled with dedications to friends "to whom [the] poems owe so much," friends such as Grande, Sbarbaro, Emilio Cecchi, Bobi Bazlen, and Sergio Solmi. But these many names were deleted from the fifth edition (Einaudi, 1942) "in order to make this edition more in line with that of *Le occasioni,*" the second collection, published in 1939 by Einaudi, "which is a book filled with silent dedications."[7] In the same year, 1925, Montale published "Homage to Italo Svevo," which greatly advanced the Italian and European discovery of the then obscure Triestine novelist. These two events—the publication of the "Homage" and of *Ossi*—established Montale's reputation as a writer worthy of critical note, and it was shortly thereafter that important critics such as Alfredo

Introduction

Gargiulo and Gianfranco Contini began to write of the poetry. The second edition of *Ossi* (Ribet, 1928) included Gargiulo's now classic introduction to the volume, in which he wrote of the "scathing criticism of existence" at the heart of the poems.[8]

It was not until 1927 that Montale left home to take up his first real job in Florence, first as an editor for Bemporad Publishing and then, in 1929, as director of the Gabinetto Scientifico Letterario Vieusseux, a research library. During his Florentine years the poet met many more writers, journalists, and critics and contributed articles to several of the literary journals of the time, especially *Solaria*. Two café restaurants figure prominently in the intellectual life of Montale in those years: the Giubbe Rosse and the Antico Fattore. They were the meeting places for intellectuals and artists who sought to combat the stifling atmosphere created by Fascism with a quiet dedication to the free exchange of ideas. Not that these were gatherings dominated by politics; the little *cenacolo* (dinner club) formed at the Antico Fattore in 1932, and which survived for ten years, was not in any sense openly political. Of it Montale wrote many years later that "the dates 1932–1942 are eloquent. If we had been something like *carbonari* or conspirators the club would not have had a long life. Actually politics never entered into our discussions."[9] Musicians, writers, painters, artists of all sorts, gathered to discuss their art and to provide mutual encouragement. In 1931 a literary prize was established to be awarded by the nonwriters of the group; Montale won it with his poem "La casa dei doganieri" (The Customs House), which was subsequently included in the small collection *La casa dei doganieri e altri versi*, published by Vallecchi in 1932. Recalling a typical gathering, Matilde Nannetti, who along with her husband, Vieri, opened her home for Sunday circles, said: "Rosai would draw off in the corner; we would be talking; Vieri would get excited, as would Franchi; Montale would maintain his imperturbability; his silences enriched those hours, made them more alive than the voices of others!"[10]

Certainly the maintenance of a quiet, unobtrusive façade was one way of surviving the censorship and blatant harassment of the prevailing regime; but Montale's silences were perhaps also an indication of his perennial sense of alienation, his constitutional maladjustment to whatever ambience he found himself in.[11] He later wrote of those Florentine years: "Until I was thirty years old I had known scarcely anyone, now I saw even too many people, but my solitude was not less than that of the period of the *Ossi di seppia.* I tried to live in Florence with the detachment of a foreigner, of a Browning; but I had not taken into account the 'mercenaries' of the feudal regime on which I depended."[12] Here, the poet is certainly referring to his experience with the official government, which in 1938 relieved him of his post as director of the Vieusseux, which was itself being transformed into a propaganda center. This episode is recounted in fictionalized form in the story "Il colpevole" (The Guilty One), included in the volume *Butterfly of Dinard.*[13]

Montale's second collection of poetry, which included the poems of the small volume *La casa dei doganieri e altri versi* and many new poems, appeared in 1939 with the title *Le occasioni* (Occasions). The poems, all written between 1928 and 1939, represent what is generally thought of as the most hermetic period of Montale's development, concentrating as most of them do on a personal and private search for salvation through love. In them we sense a conscious avoidance of dangerous public or political themes, for Montale was as aware as any other writer of the unspoken limits imposed by the prevailing regime. Yet it is equally and perhaps finally more accurate to concentrate on the poet's unpolitical insistence on what Guido Almansi and Bruce Merry have called "the private language of poetry."[14] In his own comments on the writing of *Le occasioni,* the poet speaks of his search for "another dimension in [the] heavy polysyllabic language" in which he wrote: the Italian that he often cursed for its unsuitability to his ideal of a poetry containing tacitly within itself its own motivations.[15] From the beginning of his career as poet Montale has always insisted on the solitary, very nonpublic nature of poetry's birth and continued life.

During the Second World War Montale lived on translations and short articles published in the numerous literary journals that sprang up and continued to flourish during those hard times. It was also during his years in Florence that the poet met Drusilla Tanzi, then the wife of the art critic Matteo Marangoni. She was to become his close companion and, many years later, his wife. In 1943 Montale again published a short volume of poetry entitled *Finisterre.* It appeared in a Swiss edition (smuggled out of Italy by the critic Gianfranco Contini), for, as Montale commented in his "Imaginary Interview," it was unpublishable in Italy. He prefaced it with an epigraph from D'Aubigné that made clear the poet's appraisal of the regime in power: "Les princes n'ont point d'yeux pour voir ces grand's merveilles; leurs mains ne servent plus qu'à nous persécuter."[16] These poems are no more openly political in motivation or theme than the preceding collections, in spite of their rather daring epigraph. It was in this period that Montale's lack of active engagement first began to leave him open to what would become a harsh reassessment of his excellence by many more politically- and socially-minded writers and critics. Montale's understated yet constant opposition not only to the more blatant injustices and atrocities of Fascism but also to the spirit of collective and faceless brute force underlying its implementation and growth was simply not enough for those who were more directly involved in opposing it. Many of Montale's recent poems, in *Satura* especially, directly or indirectly address this so-called failing, for the poet could never again assert his essentially apolitical stance without being aware of its polemical, highly public implications.

Between the publication of *Finisterre* in 1943 and the appearance of his third collection of poetry, *La bufera e altro* (The Storm and Other Poems) in 1956, Montale made many translations of T. S. Eliot, Yeats, Dylan Thomas, Shakespeare, and others, a selected number of which are now available in the *Quaderno di traduzioni* (Notebook of Translations), first published by Mondadori in 1948. The poet's professional life was still unsettled in the mid-1940s, however, at a time when he himself was approaching fifty. His poetry had enjoyed critical success, but he had no fixed post and could not live on royalties alone; and Mosca ("Fly"), as Montale now affectionately called Drusilla, was seriously ill. It was during this postwar period that he took up painting as a pastime, using wine, coffee grounds, toothpaste, and cigarette ashes to blend his colors, averse as always to more noble materials. (Similarly, Montale would compose many of his poems on bus tickets and candy wrappers, which he then left in his coat pockets and which the maid would habitually dump into the garbage.) Today a couple of the most whimsical of his watercolors serve as covers for his prose books *Farfalla di Dinard* and *Fuori di casa* (Away from Home). But painting was a hobby; what he needed was a job.

Finally in 1946 he was hired as a theater critic by the Milanese daily newspaper *La Corriere della Sera*. He did much of his journalistic work from Florence, moving to Milan only in 1948 when, thanks to a fortuitous occasion, he was hired as a full-time contributor to the newspaper.

Introduction

The poet happened to be visiting the chief editor's office one day in 1948 when notice of Gandhi's death was received. The editor needed a cover story immediately. Montale sat down and pounded out a piece so pleasing to the boss that, according to at least one version of the incident, the poet was hired on the spot. His assignment consisted of writing five articles of general interest a month as well as doing any needed translations. In this way were born the prose pieces eventually collected in *Butterfly of Dinard* and *Fuori di casa*, the latter a collection of Montale's travel articles describing his experiences in Syria, Portugal, and England, and his ninety hours in New York. In his travels Montale often met and interviewed famous people, and the short pieces he wrote on such literary figures as Eliot, Malraux, and Pound are now collected in the volume *Sulla poesia* (On Poetry), published by Mondadori in 1977. The poet never moved from Milan after his transfer there in 1948. His association with the *Corriere* continued well into the 1960s; in 1955 he shifted slightly from his initial post to that of music critic for the *Corriere d'Informazione*. His old love of music and especially his vast knowledge of opera were put to active use in that role. According to Almansi and Merry, Montale's enthusiasm and dedication were such that "for the next twelve years [after 1955] . . . he is reputed never to have missed a first night at La Scala."[17]

The year 1956 saw the appearance of Montale's third collection of poetry, *La bufera e altro*, which included the poems of *Finisterre* as its opening section. The storm of the title refers both to the chaos of the war and to the sense, more intense than ever before, of a personal and essentially spiritual turbulence centering around the beloved, Montale's poetic lady Clizia. Some of the most powerful and unforgettable poems of all of Montale's production are to be found in the "Silvae" section of this collection.

The next decade was to encompass the most active period of public recognition of the poet. In 1961 Montale was awarded honorary degrees from the universities of Rome, Milan, and Cambridge; many of his journalistic pieces were gathered into the volume *Auto da fé*, published by Il Saggiatore in 1966. In 1967 then President of the Republic Giuseppe Saragat named the poet *senatore a vita* (an honorary membership for life in the Italian Senate). It was also during this period that Montale suffered his greatest personal loss, for Mosca died in 1963 after many years of ill health. By the close of the sixties Montale's reputation

Introduction

was firmly established; with the three great collections behind him, and the many honors accorded him, he had become a living classic. Few if any of his readers expected that he would publish any further collections of poetry, for he was past seventy and had never been a prolific publisher of verse. The surprise was great, therefore, when in 1971 Montale brought out his fourth collection, *Satura*, and surprise modulated into something like astonishment when two more collections, and thick ones at that—*Diario del '71 e del '72* (Diary of '71 and '72) and *Quaderno di quattro anni* (Notebook of Four Years)—followed in 1973 and 1977, respectively. Montale won the Nobel Prize in 1975. In 1977 Mondadori published a volume of his collected poetry entitled *Tutte le poesie* (Complete Poems), and in 1980 Einaudi brought out another edition of the complete poems, edited and with notes by Contini and Rosanna Bettarini, in which are included several hitherto unpublished poems.

As Montale's worldwide reputation has grown, so too has the number of critics, translators, and admirers who seek his company, making his advanced stage in life the least solitary of all for this lifelong advocate of solitude and privacy. He is a courteous and charming host, yet the core of reticence and even mystery that remains in his poetry is characteristic of the man also, with the result that there are as few who can claim to have known Montale as to have mastered fully the challenge of his compellingly complex poetic universe. Montale's insistence on privacy is in part the result of his belief in the absolute uniqueness and inexplicability of the individual in life and in art. In this sense both his literary and his personal hermeticism are tacit critiques of the push toward the public and collective mode of life and of art that has become more and more inevitable in our publicity-drenched age. Montale has called poetry "the most discreet of the arts" and lyric poetry "the fruit of solitude and of accumulation."[18] There is, therefore, a sort of rich irony in his own life; for this solitary man, perhaps the most unwilling of all of his Italian contemporaries to assume the mantle of Poet, has ended up living out his last years as Italy's greatest living poet—an irony not unremarked by Montale himself, as evidenced in many of his most recent poems.[19]

If Montale's external, documentable life has been uneventful, his poetry is deeply reflective of the eventfulness and complexity of his inner life. Although the biographical and broader historical and cultural real-

Introduction

ities of Montale's more than sixty-year career are undeniably useful in understanding his poetry, I prefer to concentrate on various textual issues, the what and how of the poems themselves, that originate in the poems and inevitably return to them for their clarification and provisional resolution. Nor are these topics of study unconnected to the history of Montalian criticism as it has developed over the last sixty years, for they have presented themselves as basic cruxes, much as allegory is inevitable to the Dantean or myth to the Joycean. These issues at the heart of Montale's poetry can be isolated, if artificially, as the following: first there is what has been called Montale's countereloquence, his often harsh and persistently understated voice, which is primarily a question of style but cannot be divorced from content or poetics; second there is the essential ambiguity that permeates Montale's poetry and saturates his work at every level, resulting finally in what might be called a poetics of doubt; finally, there is what I call Montale's marginality. By *margin* I mean an edge space, a real or metaphoric area of delineation that serves to define the limits or boundaries of an entity or concept. It is also quite obviously that which is not central, either spatially or literally. Throughout my reading of Montale's poetry one word repeatedly came to mind: the *edge*. Rather than expressing the fullness of a center or concentrating on completely realized spaces either physical or psychological in nature, the poet instead turns to those areas of thought, experience, and expression that can be designated as marginal. As I use this critical metaphor it subsumes both the understated quality of Montale's poetry and its constant recourse to ambiguity, both of which draw our attention to the two or more realms between which they mediate rather than to an unequivocal concentration on one clearly central element. Understatement points both to the inadequacies inherent in language that link it to silence and, at the same time, to full, confident statement from which it, in its attenuating capacity, deviates. Ambiguity is equivocal speech, open to two or more possible interpretations while fully asserting neither. Montale's poetry demands that we be aware of these and other forms of expression that emphasize that symbolic zone of betwixt and between, and that are themselves on the margins between fullness and emptiness, confident assertion and the defeat of such assertion by silence.[20] In other words, rather than privileging what is on either side of a margin, Montale points to the margin itself. His preference for the marginal, the understated, the par-

Introduction

tial is evident not only in his themes but in his stylistic choices and finally in his overall poetics.

Montale has described his life's work as "a scarce production," "an absolutely useless product," poetry written "by a poor wretch and not a professional man of letters." He has also called poetry "one of the so-many possible positivities of life.[21] His poetry asks us to pay attention to the interplay of such tensions, between what can appear to be the powerless futility of art and its great positive force in the life of those who create it and of those who enjoy its tenacious existence. The poems discussed herein are undeniably positive in the sense in which all great art, no matter how tragic or pessimistic in theme or philosophy, is fundamentally so. Montale's voice, coming to us first as "an understated comment from the edge of the picture,"[22] has moved into the very center of what constitutes the modern and contemporary experience of poetry's potential and achievement.

1
The Marginal: Readings of the First Voice

"I<small>N</small> Limine," the first poem of the first collection, *Ossi di seppia* (Cuttlefish Bones), is the threshold of Montale's poetic universe.[1] As such it is appropriately set off—printed entirely in italics, detached from the body of the collection—and thus privileged in its introductory function. Beyond this initiatory role, however, there is a further significance to the liminality suggested by the poem's rubric, one that establishes a particular attitude toward poetry and that serves to orient the reader as he begins the journey through this terra incognita. As with any journey, however, the full meaning cannot be understood until we reach the end; from this terminal point we can then look back at the beginning and the intermediate steps with an awareness of how much they determined the final point of arrival. In the context of Montale's poetry this final point is the totality of meaning created by all six collections, for Montale himself has emphasized the ultimate unity of his work, stating that he has written "one sole book, of which first [he] gave the *recto*, [then] the *verso*,"[2] a reference to the first and last triads. In another context the poet has asserted that there is "a certain continuity among the first three books ... in the succeeding ones there is [something] like the other side of the coin."[3]

The word *coin* is especially appropriate in describing the attitude I assume toward the collections discussed in this study, for it is within the closed circle beginning with *Ossi di seppia* and ending, for now, with *Quaderno di quattro anni* (Notebook of Four Years) that I primarily locate my investigation. I do not, however, seek to deny the importance of the open-ended linearity of twentieth-century history, both literary and general, to the comprehension of that circle. It is by now apparent that Montale's poetry contains many of the fundamental preoccupations of modernism, and any discourse concerning his art is inevitably a discourse on modern poetry understood collectively: its genesis, its strategies, its successes and failures. I do not, however, concentrate on this wider context but rather stay primarily within the boundaries of textual considerations. The object of study is, therefore, not a completely self-enclosed formal structure but a poetic microcosm. A deeper understanding of its essentially understated, ambiguous, marginal core leads to further consideration of the wider implications of these essential elements not only for modern poetry but also for poetic creation, itself one of the abiding and ultimately suprahistorical mysteries of human artistic activity.

This extremely general concern—poetic creation—leads us back to the first poem of *Ossi* and to the collection it introduces. In this first collection Montale seeks to create a unique poetic space, to forge a voice, and to confront the inevitable questions implicitly asked of all poets: What is poetry in general and this poetry in particular about? What does this poetry open out to the reader in experiential and epistemological terms? How might the reader best orient himself to and establish contact with this poetic vision? I am not suggesting that these concerns were completely or even partially conscious ones for Montale, for as he later wrote concerning the creation of his first voice: "I obeyed a need of musical expression. I wanted my word to be more adherent than that of other poets whom I had known ... And my desire for adherence remained musical, instinctive, unprogrammatic."[4] This desire for adherence resulted first in the toning down of the poetic voice. As Gianfranco Contini, one of the earliest and most perceptive of Mon-

13
The
Marginal:
Readings
of the
First
Voice

tale's readers, noted, "Montale's discourse is a discourse with a 'familiar' tone and timbre," a subdued, "domestic" voice that "presupposes, moreover, [the presence of] a very close interlocutor."[5] He refers, of course, to the well-known *tu*, or informal "you," of Montale's poetic dialogues, of which the poet wrote many years after its initial appearance in "In Limine," "I critici ripetono, / da me depistati, / che il mio *tu* è un istituto"[6] (the critics repeat, / by me put off the track, / that my *you* is an institution), thus effectively precluding any further such critical pronouncements. Institution or not, the imagined interlocutor is one of the lexical and psychological constants of Montale's poetry. It determines to a great extent the intimate and even conversational quality of so much of the poetry as well as the sense of direct communicative thrust, as the reader feels himself to be personally addressed, called to, warned, and counseled by the informal imperative form in which the *tu* is most often contained.

"In Limine" opens with just such an address—"Godi" (Enjoy)— followed by a crescendo of imperatives in the final stanza: *cerca* (seek); *balza fuori* (jump out); *fuggi* (flee); *va* (go). These imperatives tell us to enjoy, but we are also warned to flee, to go away from the space created in the poem. Thus, as Almansi and Merry so incisively point out, "the 'tu' is the reader himself who has to find a way out from the white space at the end of a poem. The adventure begins in the types that form the printed composition, but the final solution lies beyond them."[7] Of course, the *tu* is also and perhaps primarily a dramatic presence in the poem, the "other" for whom escape is urged. But if we read the poem as a poem about poetry's emergence as well as about experience that is beyond literature, then it is accurate to call it "a self-questioning poem"[8] conscious of its own status as poem and implicitly confronting the question of its relationship with the reader.

In order to pursue this self-questioning it is first helpful to describe the immediate or literal dramatic situation created in "In Limine." The first-person speaker, enclosed in a static garden (pomario) filled with "a dead/tangle of memories" (un morto/viluppo di memorie), is touched by the stirrings of wind and change he senses outside the garden walls. Unable, however, to escape these boundaries, he urges that the other, who is not named or specified in any way, attempt salvation by getting beyond the walls, while he will stay behind, comforted by the thought of her breakthrough.[9] The poem can bear a less literal reading, however.

Where, in fact, is the *I* of the poem speaking from? The wind enters into a garden, called variously *pomario, orto,* and *lembo di terra* (orchard, vegetable garden, strip of earth). It is also called first *reliquiario* (reliquary) and then *crogiuolo* (crucible). This is a space not untouched by extraliteral associations; it is soon recognizable as a literary garden not only because the *topos* inevitably comes to mind but because the poet himself invests it with multiple transforming and transformed identities: garden to reliquary to crucible.[10] Although the word *orto* will ultimately take on particular symbolic resonance in Montale's poetry (it is one of the lexical leitmotifs of *Ossi*),[11] it is more fruitful in this instance to consider further the words *pomario* and *lembo.*

One Italian critic of Montale has suggested that there is "a strict affinity between *pomario* and *pomerium (pomerio)* (and between *lembo* and *limbo*)."[12] This affinity is etymologically determined: the first two words refer to spaces behind or near walls, the second two to edges or borders. Pursuing this suggestion, we find that *pomerium* is the Latin term designating "the boundary line of the site destined for a city, which site, according to the rules of augural procedure, was inaugurated as a *templum* or rectangular area, within which auspices could be taken."[13] It was a consecrated space, usually running along both the inside and outside of the city walls, which had to be left free of buildings; it was, in short, a marginal space or edge that belonged neither to the undefined area outside of it nor to the daily life of the city within but that allowed for the delineation of the concepts of in and out, profane and sacred, structured and wild. Similarly, *limbo* is that space designated for those neither fully damned nor fully beatified, an in-between space that in Dante's *Commedia* is the place of "gente di molto valore" (people of great esteem), specifically the poets, among them Vergil, Homer, Horace, Ovid, and Lucan. This limbo is "cerchiato d'alte mura" (surrounded by high walls) in Dante's portrayal, much as Montale's "lembo di terra" is surrounded by an "erto muro" (steep wall).[14]

I do not mean to imply with these last comments that there is a strict correspondence between the initiation into Dante's poetic universe and that of Montale, although Silvio Ramat speaks of "In Limine" as "like words sculpted on a door that might lead to Hell."[15] Nor am I insisting on any explicit connection between the edge spaces of the *pomerium* and the limbo and Montale's *pomario* and *lembo.* The points of contact are general rather than being specifically determined by some con-

15
The
Marginal:
Readings
of the
First
Voice

scious imitation of Dante or direct recourse to the etymological reso-
nances of words; but they nonetheless suggest a useful critical direction.
They are the result of an analogous response to the issues raised by the
creation of an imaginary space that both speaks of poetry and is poetry
at the same time. It need hardly be argued that Dante's *Commedia* is as
much about itself as poem as it is about divine revelation and the
human goal of eternal beatitude. Similarly Montale's poetry is always
imbued with self-reflexive commentary, and this is especially so in this
opening poem. It is quite literally on the edge—on the threshold of a
poetic undertaking that is still in the process of defining itself.

The Montalian critic Emerico Giachery reminds us of the judgment
of Giorgio Orelli, who "associates the impression of a reading of 'Godi
se il vento' [In Limine] to that which can come from the initial cantos
. . . of the *Comedy*, the latter springing from exigencies of *montage*
above all, and not yet fully pervaded with the poetic dynamism that is
slowly born in the work, [a work] that, as Valéry had it, reveals itself to
itself bit by bit in its own process of being made, and grows along with
the author."[16] These words recall in turn Montale's own comments on
the elaboration of the *Commedia* in words applicable to his own poetry:
"there is no doubt that the ideation of [Dante's] poem, its very structure, had not already been fixed from the first line, and instead pro-
ceeded by modifying and enriching itself . . . during the elaboration and
hypothetical revision of the work."[17] This dynamism is the first meaning I would assign to "In Limine's" liminality or marginality; its own
symbolic space as initiatory poem is on the edge not simply because it
introduces us into the poetry to follow but because it, as the beginning
of a new poetic discourse, is inevitably precarious, located between the
known poetry preceding it and the unknown and uniquely new discourse it precedes. In this sense it functions as any preface does; that is,
it serves to carry us over into the alien space of the book we are about to
read as a mediation between the reality without and the one within.

If we accept that the garden in which the speaker is dramatically
placed is also a metaliterary space, or poetry itself, we see that this space
is not untouched by temporal concerns. That is, it is not some fixed
garden of pure aesthetic delights entirely divorced from time but rather
a space that is transformed (si trasforma) from reliquary to crucible,
from the static coldness of a container of dead relics to the seething heat
of a melting pot, the container of potential new forms. The reliquary is

clearly linked to the past in that it holds "a dead / tangle of memories" and "the stories, the acts / canceled out by the game of the future." The term *reliquiario* is again used many years after the writing of this poem in Montale's short story entitled "Reliquie" (Relics) to describe "a box where [were kept] newspaper clippings, old letters tied up with a ribbon, and some little saints that [he dared not] destroy . . ."[18] These are lifeless objects representing once living and lived moments; they are, in short, tangible memories, memories being the most private form of history. They remain lifeless and useless unless brought back to some new form of life. Montale's raw material for his future poetry will in great part be these relics, or personal memories, transformed and resuscitated through poetic creation.

But poetry cannot rely on private history alone; the past to which this poem alludes is also the collective inheritance of past literary achievement as well as what might be designated as *langue*, the shared linguistic code from which the poet forges his own *parole*, his unique language. Montale, like all poets, must move between them in order that his art emerge. It is on the word *between* that I wish to place emphasis. A search for total newness is futile, just as a clinging to the already accomplished is fruitless; art must find its *juste milieu* in order to be authentic, gripping, and real. As the *pomario-lembo* can be seen as the emblematic space of Montale's emerging art, so the symbolic space and time of poetry is between past and future, tradition and innovation, established linguistic and artistic codes and individual transformations of them. This is the second sort of marginality I would ascribe to the concept of poetry elaborated in "In Limine." The poetic speaker, and more importantly the poet himself, cannot escape the edge space in which he is both spatially and temporally trapped, for it is the very space of art, which is always between past and future, between aesthetic self-enclosure and meaningful integration into the nonartistic process of life outside, and into which it will inevitably be drawn.

It is equally clear from this first poem that Montale assigns no revelatory or salutory function to poetry. The other is urged to seek the phantom who might save her somewhere outside the confines of the garden. The edge is a dangerous place to be; it holds out no certainties and offers minimal comforts to the one poised on it—"ora la sete / mi sarà lieve, meno acre la ruggine . . ." (now thirst / will be mild for me, less sharp the rust). What is implicit in this poem will become explicit

17
The
Marginal:
Readings
of the
First
Voice

in succeeding poems: to be in an edge space is to accept fully the ambiguities, the double-edged uncertainties of such a position. What is here suggested as a general attitude toward poetry later becomes the very stuff of which Montale's poetry is made, thematically, stylistically, and philosophically. Thus the critical metaphor of marginality can be more widely applied to an understanding of what Avalle has called the "equivocal structure"[19] of so much of Montale's writing.

There is both a positive and a negative side to the concept of poetry as partaking of a betwixt-and-between status.[20] In *Ossi di seppia*, the sense of an emerging poetry in the process of defining itself is especially positive. At this point poetry is seen as a potentiality not for the attainment of ultimate truth or revelation but as a tool for excavating meaning and creating significant new experience both for the poet and the reader. Later, Montale's awareness of the fundamental ambiguities of all literary discourse threatens even his minimal faith in the power of words to mediate between the self and others and the self and the world. At this point the negative aspects of being on the edge come to the fore, especially in the two most recent collections, *Diario del '71 e del '72 (Diary of '71 and '72)* and *Quaderno di quattro anni (Notebook of Four Years)*, and the balancing act is more and more permeated with a sense of the abyss of meaninglessness yawning below. This negative aspect is not, however, an essential part of the first voice, filled as it is with a tenuous yet tenacious belief in poetry as "one of the so-many possible positivities of life."[21]

Limits, edges, margins—all are central to Montale's poetic imagination and to his evolving poetics; their importance is most clearly evident in *Ossi di seppia*, where the poet is involved in the creation of his first voice. The origins of this tendency to stay on the edges, to mute the poetic voice, to emphasize the concept of eccentricity may have been primarily psychological (Montale often speaks of a sense of disjuncture[22]) or perhaps cultural and historical (he felt the necessity in the early years of this century to avoid the siren's call of D'Annunzian vatic poetry and futuristic bombast) or most likely some combination of these and other factors. Whatever the source of Montale's attitude toward his emerging poetry, it is from the very first imbued with a sense of the limitations of poetic discourse understood not as the full lyric expression of captured truths expressed in a confident or prophetic voice but rather as the necessarily countereloquent and understated search for its own possible meaning. Poetry is "more a means of knowledge than of representation,"[23] a process, a "realm of pure possibility."[24] As we have seen, Montale identified his primary *motivi* (motives and motifs) as three: *il paesaggio* (the landscape), *l'amore* (love), and *l'evasione* (evasion, escape).[25] These moving forces behind the poetry and its major thematic centers can be seen to capture in various ways the interstructurability characteristic of the marginal, the betwixt-and-between status attributable both to the dramatic situations portrayed in these early poems and to the very concept of the art of poetry that they imply. In discussing them I seek to clarify the manner in which these *motivi* contribute to the quality of emergence and to the identification of poetic creation with "a process, a becoming . . . a pupa changing from grub to moth."[26] From this critical perspective, the edge upon which Montale balances can be understood not as a negatively marginal position but as a positive space of dynamic growth that exemplifies Gaston Bachelard's assertion that "poetry puts language into a state of emergence, in which life becomes manifest through its vivacity."[27]

In *Ossi* the landscape is, concretely speaking, Liguria—Montale's "Ligurian landscape, which is most universal . . ."[28] In more metaphorical terms, however, I would suggest that the landscape in which the poet situates his poetry is itself marginal. I have already indicated the symbolic suggestiveness of the "edge of earth" of "In Limine." Other instances of such edge spaces abound in the first collection, including "le viuzze che seguono i ciglioni" (the lanes that follow the brinks) in "I Limoni" (The Lemon Trees); "l'erbosa soglia" (the grassy threshold) in "Sarcofaghi" (Sarcophagi); "un rovente muro d'orto" (a scorching garden wall) in "Meriggiare" (Nooning); "[le] rocce che orlavano il cammino" (the cliffs that edged the path) in the poem in "Mediterraneo" beginning, "Scendendo qualche volta" (Descending sometimes); "l'orizzonte" (the horizon) in "Arsenio"; "l'orizzonte" and "lembo" (horizon, edge) in "Crisalide" (Chrysalis); and "riviere" (coasts) in "Riviere." These spaces all share the attribute of betwixt and betweenness, a being on the edges or margins that is quite explicitly physical although already endowed with metaphysical undertones. The threshold between outdoors and in, the wall between garden and nongarden, the horizon between sky and earth, the paths and cliffs that act as borders, the seashores between sea and land: all of these draw attention to the areas between which they mediate and to the lack of autonomy they themselves possess. The very landscape is thus imbued with the quali-

19
The
Marginal:
Readings
of the
First
Voice

ties of delimitation, dichotomy, and difference: within the garden is distinctly different from without; the sea is not the land; the edge is not the center.

There is created a very strong sense of here and there, with these typically Montalian spaces mediating between them. We come to understand that the poetic I is most aware of these in-between spaces because he partakes fully of neither of the two positively definable elements in any configuration but rather straddles them both from his marginal Archimedean point. In the poem "Falsetto" the speaker identifies himself with those "della razza / di chi rimane a terra" (of the race / of those who remain on land), but in the entire "Mediterraneo" suite he is a creature of the sea, or is at least desirous of such a merging. But finally he is not fully one or the other. His most typical alliance is with the interstitial, both poetically, as he asserts in "The Lemon Trees" that unlike the "poeti laureati" (poets laureate) he favors the humbler "lanes that follow the brinks," and existentially, as in the lines "Mia vita è questo secco pendio, / mezzo non fine, strada aperta a sbocchi / di rigagnoli, lento franamento" (My life is this dry slope, / means not end, road open to mouths / of rivulets, slow erosion) of the poem beginning, "Giunge a volte" (It comes sometimes), in "Mediterraneo." This tendency to establish a physical marginality for the speaker that can be described in terms of geographic space although not limited to geography can be seen throughout *Ossi di seppia*. The deeper spiritual and metaphysical significance of this landscape becomes manifest when understood as an aspect of the poet's general preference for the eccentric: that which is displaced from the center.

Turning next to the *motivo* of love we see that while not as fully developed in this first collection as it will be in subsequent ones, it is nonetheless discernible in these early poems "under the form of phantasms that *frequent* the various poems and provoke the usual 'intermittences of the heart.' "[29] Even in this definition provided by Montale himself, love is described as intermittent, or literally "that which is sent between." The phrase is, as Montale indicates, Proustian in origin and clearly emphasizes the psychological marginality of the love experience, its appearances-disappearances of which the poetic image seizes the evanescent moment designated by the hyphen. In temporal terms this expressive tendency can be thought of as past-future, with the present functioning in much the same manner as the edge spaces, for the Montalian speaker is most often presented as incapable of fulfillment in a present (or centered) love relationship. Instead he is suspended on the edge between what was and what might or will be. The emblematic verb of this psychological marginality is *attendere*[30] (to serve and also to wait for). In *Le occasioni* (Occasions) it appears in the introductory poem "Il balcone" (The Balcony)—another significantly marginal space—in the lines, "sull'arduo nulla si spunta / l'ansia di attenderti vivo" (on the arduous nothingness is sharpened / the longing to [serve and/or wait for] you alive), establishing from this initiatory moment the primacy of the service-vigil to the love poems that follow, especially those of the "Mottetti." Yet even in *Ossi*, a collection that does not emphasize an identifiable and named beloved as later collections do, we find several instances in which love is described as the paradoxical moment of dynamic appearance and simultaneous disappearance of the beloved, as in the "Osso" that begins, "Il canneto rispunta i suoi cimelli" (The canebrake once again pushes forth its tips), where we read: "Sale un'ora d'attesa in cielo" (An hour of waiting rises up in the sky). In this prestorm atmosphere, the beloved's absence-presence is painfully felt:

Assente, come manchi in questa plaga
che ti presente e senza te consuma:
sei lontana e però tutto divaga
dal suo solco, dirupa, spare in bruma.

Absent, how you are missed in these parts
that forebode you and languish without you:
you are far off and yet everything departs
from its groove, overflows, fades away in mist.

The entire "Osso" that begins, "Cigola la carrucola del pozzo" (The well's pulley creaks), dramatizes the tenuous, fleeting quality of concrete images of love in the shadow of a remembered face that shimmers on the surface of the water only to dissolve as quickly in the black bottom of the well: "Trema un ricordo nel ricolmo secchio, / nel puro cerchio un'immagine ride" (A memory trembles in the filled bucket, / in the pure circle an image laughs); "Ah, che già stride / la ruota, ti ridona all'atro fondo" (Ah, already shrieks / the wheel, it gives you back to the black depths). In both of these poems, the beloved is unseizable and the lover kept in a state of continued desire.

21
The
Marginal:
Readings
of the
First
Voice

The verbs *attendere* and *aspettare* (to wait) appear often throughout *Ossi*, and although in many instances these moments of suspension are not directly tied to the absent beloved, they do nonetheless represent the profound existential and philosophical importance of the wait, the moment of potentiality. Examples include: "La buona pioggia è di là dallo squallore, / ma in attendere è gioia più compita" (The good rain is beyond the bleakness, / but in waiting is most full joy) in "Gloria del disteso mezzogiorno" (Glory of the extended midday); "Era in aria l'attesa / di un procelloso evento" (There was in the air the wait / for a tempestuous event) in "Fine dell'infanzia" (End of Childhood); "esprime un suo burchiello che si volge / al docile frangente—e là ci attende" (it launches one of its barges which turns / in the mild breakers—and there it waits for us) in "Crisalide" (Chrysalis). Although neither verb appears in the poem "Meriggiare" (Nooning), it depicts perhaps most perfectly the moment of suspension, creating a time out of time through the infinitive verb forms and the images of unmoving circular motion: the eternal ebb and flow of the sea, the rows of ants, and so on. Critics have noted the importance for Montale of the immanent-imminent miracle.[31] I would suggest that a slight shift in attention from the waited-for event or person to the wait itself reveals the greater power of the latter in the poet's creative process. Images of waxing and waning, of tenuous emergences, and of fluid, dynamic states abound in the poems of the first collection and contribute to our sense of the intermittent, provisional nature of Montale's reality. Some of the most memorable images include: "Tendono alla chiarità le cose oscure, / si esauriscono i corpi in un fluire / di tinte: queste in musiche" (Dark things tend toward brightness, / bodies are erased in a flowing / of tints: the latter in music) from the "Osso" that begins, "Portami il girasole" (Bring me the sunflower); "Felicità raggiunta, si cammina / per te su fil di lama. / Agli occhi sei barlume che vacilla, / al piede, teso ghiaccio che s'incrina" (Happiness achieved, one walks / for you on the edge of the blade. / To the eyes you are a flicker that wavers, / to the foot, tense ice that cracks) from the "Osso" that begins with these lines; "Un albero di nuvole sull'acqua / cresce, poi crolla" (A tree of clouds on the water / grows, then collapses) from "Il canneto." The overwhelming sense is of a world of ever-shifting contours and of a sensibility attuned to the fragility of all experience.

It is not a simple task to locate and identify the speaker's position in these and other poems of *Ossi*, for the poetic voice's emergence into expression is as tenuous as the images that seek to fix and capture the location of observed or intuited occurrences, emotions, and objects. Returning to the love motif, we soon realize that it is not a question here or in later collections of an *amor de lonh* to which the lover is firmly rooted and thus existentially and psychologically defined by his single, obsessive desire for the one who is not present. Rather, as will become even more explicit in *Le occasioni*, and especially in the "Mottetti," the *I* of the *I-Thou* relationship is fundamentally threatened in his very being by the tenuousness of the wait, which makes of him an unformed, potential presence rather than a definable, fixed entity yearning toward another. He is marginal because the experience that occasions his birth into words is not in fact fully negative or fully positive but on the edges of both, in a gray space filled by the images of suspension, waxing and waning, appearance and disappearance. In later collections, as Montale develops his *canzoniere* to the beloved and as she takes on a more distinct and fixed identity and role, so does the poetic speaker become more definable, and so do the poetic images surrounding them both become more tied to clear-cut oppositions. This emphasis on unfulfilled, tenuous emotions and fleeting realities may be defined as Montale's psychological marginality.

The logical psychological resolution of a state of suspension is evasion: escape from and/or avoidance of a given place or person that produces the anxiety or tension. Montale describes his sought-for evasion as "the flight from the iron chain of necessity, the, let's say, lay miracle."[32] In "In Limine" the escape is urged for the other in the series of imperatives cited earlier, and there follow many poems that repeat such seemingly altruistic urgings. The best known are "il patto ch'io vorrei / stringere col destino: di scontare / la vostra gioia con la mia condanna" (the pact that I would want / to seal with destiny: to atone for / your joy with my punishment) in "Chrysalis"; "Vorrei prima di cedere segnarti / codesta via di fuga" (I would like before giving in to indicate for you / this path of flight) in "Casa sul mare" (House by the Sea); and "t'abbatti fra le braccia / del tuo divino amico che t'afferra. / Ti guardiamo noi, della razza / di chi rimane a terra" (you throw yourself into the arms / of your divine friend who grasps you. / We watch you, we of the race / of those who remain on land) in "Falsetto." The speaker's selflessness thus comes through in many early poems, if at

23
The
Marginal:
Readings
of the
First
Voice

times in a somewhat dangerously crepuscular tone of self-abnegation.

There is however another level at which the search for evasion functions, a level having more to do with the formal genesis of the poetry itself than with the human emotions of *caritas* or renunciation, which may or may not have occasioned the writing of the poems. When Montale wrote of the beginnings of his art in his "Imaginary Interview" he commented on the emotional and intellectual context of that genesis: "I seemed to be living under a bell jar, yet I felt that I was near something essential. A thin veil, scarcely a thread separated me from the definitive *quid*. The absolute expression would have been the rupturing of that veil, of that thread: an explosion, the end of the deception of the world as representation. But this was an unreachable goal."[33] If one considers the phrase "the absolute expression would have been the rupture of that veil, of that thread" in relation to such lines in the poems of *Ossi* as "Cerca una maglia rotta nella rete" (Seek a ruptured [broken] link in the net) from "In Limine" or "talora ci si aspetta / . . . il filo da disbrogliare" (sometimes we expect / . . . the thread to be untangled) from "I Limoni," the connection between formal expression itself and evasion becomes clear. It is not, or at least not only, an event, an epiphany, that Montale awaits—"the lay miracle"—that might save the beloved or reveal a truth but also, and perhaps primarily, a linguistic event that will free him too. Yet since, as the poet himself notes, such a moment of linguistic perfection is an unreachable goal, his desire will always remain unfulfilled and the impetus to write continuously sustained in the tension generated between what might ideally be written and what has already been imperfectly captured in words. This tension, or what might be designated metaphorically as the edge space between the "limbo of creative imagination"[34] and the fixed formality of realized art, is where I would situate the concept of literary marginality. This marginality informs all of the poetry with the vitalizing and dynamic quality of an essential commitment to process that is basic to the literary enterprise in its essence. It also permits us to consider the ontology of the lyric, which, as Hugo Friedrich has commented, "is a mystery, a zone at the extreme edge of the sayable, a wonder, a potential power . . ."[35]

These last comments bring me back to my point of departure: the first poem of *Ossi*, "In Limine." All three of the *motivi* are present in this poem, and we can discern their implications for an evolving poetics and for the future poetry that will embody certain attitudes toward the possibilities available to poetry. Keeping in mind the spatial marginality, we see that the dynamics of in and out, here and there are basic to the poem's structure. The wind "enters into the orchard"; the "raging" is "on this side of the steep wall" (di qua); the adverb *qui* (here) is used with an insistence on its separative function (here, not there) in the lines "qui dove affonda un morto / viluppo di memorie" (here where sinks down a dead / tangle of memories) and "si compongono qui le storie, gli atti / scancellati pel giuoco del futuro" (here are composed the stories, the acts / canceled out by the game of the future). The *you* is urged to jump out, to flee: "tu balza fuori," "fuggi." The speaker is, dramatically speaking, inside the garden, but the poetic consciousness is in fact not in or out, not here or there, but is rather mediating between the death implied by being within ("garden it was not, but reliquary") and the life existing *in potentia* outside the garden walls and beyond the net. Its space is on the edge straddling the two zones, one of enclosure—and, poetically speaking, of lifeness noncreation—the other of openness, freedom, and possible salvation, understood either existentially or literarily.

The love that motivates the desire for the other's escape is predicated on an implied preexistence of commitment to the well-being of the "you" as well as on a future of hope for her possible salvation. Yet the present moment of the relationship between the *I* and *thou* is void, for it looks only backward (to a "dead / tangle of memories") or forward (to the phantasm that might save the beloved), thus emptying the present of any real substance. Finally, the motive of evasion is basic to "In Limine," as the speaker urges the other to go beyond the limits in which they are both enclosed. Her escape is made possible by the process of transformation, which is the poem's very emergence from silence, as the dead memories are resuscitated and given new life in the crucible into which the garden has been transformed.

"In Limine" ends with both inwardly turned resignation and, at the same time, an implicit invitation to the reader to continue with the poet into the net of poetic elaboration as he states, "ora la sete / mi sarà lieve, meno acre la ruggine . . ." (now thirst / will be mild for me, less harsh the rust). Those three ellipsis points at the end of the last line lead us right over the threshold of this poem into the body of the collection with no more definite or positive promise than the slight allevia-

25
The
Marginal:
Readings
of the
First
Voice

tion of the thirst and corrosion that make up the poet's essential experience. Thus, in a typically paradoxical tactic Montale asks for our participation in the emerging poetry and simultaneously makes clear its radically limited and attenuated essence. The ultimate goal toward which this poetry will aim is absolute expression, the perfect expression of the definitive *quid* that would be the final breakthrough and escape. But this is a priori an unreachable goal. However hesitant it may be, the first step away from silence has been made, and Montale's commitment to the search for meaning, partial and flawed as it may be, is declared. By situating his poetry in the marginal space of emergence and dedication to self-defining process, Montale can remain balanced between the ultimate evasion—silence—and the final goal—perfected expression—implicitly showing throughout his future poetry the essential interplay of these two elements as his poetic structures bring to life the very dynamism that literary form is unavoidably destined to extinguish at least partially. How this poet survives the tension between what might be thought of as the eternal ideal of artistic perfection and completion and the necessary cognizance of art's imperfectibility can be understood only by following the path he cuts through his own language, culture, and literary inheritance throughout the sixty years of his poetic career. What is clear in this initial poem, however, is his awareness of the dilemma, an awareness that permeates all of his poetry with the compelling dynamism of all great art.

So far I have been discussing the concept of marginality in terms of themes or elements that are repeated throughout *Ossi*—geographic edge spaces, psychological margins, metapoetical considerations—all of which contribute to the elaboration of a poetics that both precedes and inhabits the poems themselves. This approach, however, may give the impression of a certain quality of repetitiveness or fixedness that the individual poems themselves belie. We see Montale's skill most clearly when we examine the dramatization of these identifiable motifs in each poem. This dramatization is particularly evident in two poems in which the qualities of potentiality, emergence, and ambiguity are brought to life with particular effectiveness through the poetic structures themselves. They are "Arsenio" and "Crisalide," both included in the section of *Ossi di seppia* entitled "Meriggi e Ombre" (Noons and Shadows). This section of *Ossi*, the penultimate of the collection, comes after the great and central "Ossi" and "Mediterraneo" suites and includes poems of longer and more dramatically sustained breath than those that preceded. "Arsenio" is one of the six poems added to the 1928 edition of *Ossi di seppia* (Turin: Ribet) and is dated 1927; a first version of "Crisalide" is dated spring 1924, and the poet himself tells us that "Meriggi e Ombre" "belongs to the period 1922–1924."[36] Giachery has quoted a letter by Montale dated August 24, 1924, in which the poet writes that he has "some bits of a certain 'chrysalis' that will come out one day or another,"[37] thus fixing the poem's final elaboration at some time between the summer of 1924 and the beginning of 1925. These two poems have often been linked by critics, although most often at the expense of the earlier "Crisalide," which has been judged by Forti, Ramat, and others to be inferior to the later poem.[38] Notable exceptions to this judgment have been voiced by Almansi and Merry and Joseph Cary. Almansi and Merry call it a "tougher poem precisely because it is less explicitly declamatory [than "Arsenio"], a more important poem because it is less apparently vital, in short, a more Montalian poem because however hard the reader squeezes this composition, he cannot extract from its text the juice of a clear or univocal message."[39] Cary refers to it as "a key poem which looks forward to the great achievements of the next five years . . ."[40]

To return to "Arsenio," the appearance of a named alter ego lends momentous weight to the poem, for the reader desires, perhaps unconsciously, such a personage throughout the reading of the collection, imbued as *Ossi* is with the compelling voice of one struggling toward identity. Yet in this poem the tables are radically turned, for the *I* to whom we have become accustomed becomes instead the *you* to whom the words are addressed, and it is no longer possible to separate one from the other. "Arsenio" does not answer the question of the exact identity of the poetic consciousness behind the words, even if critics seized upon him as an autobiographic *porte-parole* of Montale.[41]

The landscape in "Arsenio" is at once particular and universal: a seaside resort at the time just before a storm unleashes itself, that moment of immanence and of talismanic release from the limitations of self. It is a critical commonplace by now to speak of the importance of certain moments (especially noon) and of certain climatic conditions (storm, searing heat) in Montale's early poetry.[42] In drawing attention to such elements I want to emphasize the tie between the physical and the temporal, given the following implicit equation: heat, noon = past and / or present: storm = future. Only a few poems in *Ossi* make ex-

27
The
Marginal:
Readings
of the
First
Voice

tensive use of the future tense—"Quasi una fantasia" (Almost a Fantasy) and "Forse un mattino" (Perhaps One Morning) are two—and those that do are visionary, purely escapist poems that imply more a desired future of impossible realization than a true future.[43] Although "Arsenio" is written in the present tense, the sense of future is extremely strong, for it is a present moment straining toward a future completion, as the suspension of the prestorm world parallels the psychological and metaphysical suspension of the poetic character Arsenio.

Arsenio is urged to descend: "tu discendi," "discendi all'orizzonte," "discendi in mezzo al buio" (you descend; descend to the horizon; descend in the midst of darkness). The descent is clearly not simply physical but the same metaphysical plunge into self urged by Augustine or Dante.[44] He must move into a marginal space ("l'orizzonte") and fully accept the mystery of its undefinability if he is to assume a true identity, a being for himself that is full and nameable. The prestorm turbulence carries Arsenio into a mysterious world of new possibilities:

È il segno d'un'altra orbita: tu seguilo.
Discendi all'orizzonte che sovrasta
una tromba di piombo . . .

. . . fa che il passo
su la ghiaia ti scricchioli e t'inciampi
il viluppo dell'alghe: quell'istante
è forse, molto atteso, che ti scampi
dal finire il tuo viaggio, anello d'una
catena, immoto andare, oh troppo noto
delirio, Arsenio, d'immobilità . . .

It is the sign of another orbit: you, follow it.
Descend to the horizon that is crowned by
a leaden horn . . .

. . . make your step
crunch on the gravel and become entwined
with the tangle of seaweed: that instant
is perhaps, long awaited, when you'll escape
from the end of your voyage, link of a
chain, unmoving motion, oh too well-known
delirium, Arsenio, of immobility . . .

Arsenio is himself nothing in this moment of potentiality, poised as he is between the fixedness of his existential state of before (his unmoving motion) and the as yet undefined existence he might assume afterward. This new existence might be characterized by Arsenio's more profound comprehension of the ties that bind his solitary state to that of others:

e se un gesto ti sfiora, una parola
ti cade accanto, quello è forse, Arsenio,
nell'ora che si scioglie, il cenno d'una
vita strozzata per te sorta, e il vento
la porta con la cenere degli astri.

and if a gesture grazes you, a word
falls near you, that is perhaps, Arsenio,
in the hour that is dissolving, the sign of a
strangled life arisen for you, and the wind
carries it off with the ashes of the stars.

But it is only if Arsenio can accept the invisibility of this marginal moment that a new, positive existence might emerge; he must become lost (sperso), a reed among other plants, uprooted ("[you] reed that drags its roots along with it") and poised on the edge ("you tremble with life and extend yourself to a resonant void"). Alone, unseen in this landscape of opposites ("now rainy, now lit up," "the silent roar," "darkness that rushes down / and changes the noon into a night"), Arsenio must struggle to become as he descends, strains toward something, extends himself toward whatever might be offered to him. Between the symbols of his previously fixed sea-resort existence ("the hotels' sparkling windows," "limp awnings," "paper lanterns") and of the static communal life from which he needs to escape and the uncontrolled ferment of sea and storm, Arsenio seeks himself, his true self. The sense of a life poised on the edge and of language similarly poised pervades this poem, which is situated in the space of liminal potentiality so basic to Montale's developing poetic voice.[45]

The oxymoronic images that proliferate in this poem ("unmoving motion," "far-off seems the evening / that is near," "silent roar"), the placement of Arsenio between the security and fixedness of society (the sea resort from which he escapes as he moves toward the sea), and the uncontrolled, elemental sea and storm all emphasize the fundamental

29
The
Marginal:
Readings
of the
First
Voice

ambivalence that pervades the marginal zone. It is also a dangerous zone, for nothing, including the poetic protagonist, is either this or that, and there are no longer well-defined, nameable boundaries to offer protection. The danger in this case, as in others when the poetic voice is poised on the edge or the alter ego is about to assume a face, is that of dissipation of the potential positivity into sterile negativity and, for the poet, silence. As the anthropologist Victor Turner writes, "It is not a mere acquisition of knowledge, but a change in being"[46] to which the person undergoing a marginal process is subjected: the individual's ontology is at stake. In the case of Arsenio the outcome remains unresolved within the confines of the poem itself. Thus the negative aspect of marginality is at least partially averted. Arsenio has followed "the sign of another orbit"; he has entered into the frightening void where "the set trap . . . / of the ancient wave" (la tesa . . . / dell'onda antica) envelops him. This is truly the realm of the marginal, in which mysterious and powerful forces that reach far beyond the individual assail the passenger. Arsenio has become "a tabula rasa, a blank slate" and has learned that he, like all persons, is "clay or dust, mere matter," part of a cosmic experience of birth and death that unites men and stars.[47] Reading the last lines of the poem from this perspective, I would agree most emphatically with Almansi and Merry when they write that "Montale's 'white, bleached' hero (for this is the etymological meaning of the title) looks up at the storm and the stars with some of the confidence that comes from the desolate purity of cuttle-fish bones."[48]

By the end of the poem Arsenio is capable of seeing beyond the confines of his solitary life into the vastness of cosmic solitude. Whether reintegration into the limits and structures of society will be possible for him, given his new perspective, is impossible to say, for the poem does not bring him back but rather leaves him *raptus*, both "enraptured" and "transported" into a consideration at once illuminating and devastating. (To *consider* is to move with the *sidera*, or stars: here too, etymologies serve to bring to light deeper meanings at work.) The ending of this poem is, using Barbara Herrnstein Smith's term, "anti-closural,"[49] for it opens out onto a cosmic enormity that cannot be contained within the dramatic space created in the poem. The terrestrial dust (la polvere) of the first line has been transformed into the celestial ashes (la cenere degli astri) of the last; the "undifferentiated hours" (ore uguali) have become "the hour that comes undone" (l'ora che si scioglie). The "sparkling glasses," the "lit globes," the glimmers of the acetylene of trawlers—all these small human lights have been absorbed into the imponderable vastness of the stars themselves. And just as the landscape has been transmuted by the wild rains and winds, so too has Arsenio undergone a fundamental change in being reflected in the "visionary vocabulary"[50] of the last stanza. He is not, however, defined or fixed in his new state. As Forti notes, "The poem itself leads . . . the character to the threshold of a fully meaningful, creative and liberating gesture"[51]; and it is on the threshold that he remains. If, then, we identify Arsenio with the poetic consciousness that brings the poem into being (and not simplistically with the man Montale), the poem itself, like its marginal protagonist, remains on the threshold, and its primary message is that of the dynamism of its own emergence into form.

If Arsenio is a sort of poetic alter ego of the poet, the chrysalis of "Crisalide" is the poet's beloved for whose salvation he wishes. This chrysalis might be understood as falling somewhere between the *vermi* (worms) and the *angelica farfalla* (angelic butterfly) of Dante's *Purgatorio* (10. / 25). It is a creature that symbolizes most appropriately the neither-nor state of transformation, of intermediate being.[52] (Though this mediate creature is called by the *voi*, or less informal "you" form, she still represents the necessary other for whose escape the poet wishes, the *tu* of the insistent dialogue that permeates Montale's verse.) The season is spring, the time of rebirth and regeneration; the speaker observes this reflowering from his "remote garden corner" (questo estremo angolo d'orto), to which life comes intermittently in "impetuous waves" (impetuose onde):

Ogni attimo vi porta nuove fronde
e il suo sbigottimento avanza ogni altra
gioia fugace; viene a impetuose onde
la vita a questo estremo angolo d'orto.

Every instant brings you new foliage
and its awe surpasses every other
fleeting joy; in impetuous waves comes
life to this remote garden corner.

One is immediately reminded of the enclosed space of "In Limine"; there, the *orto* is filled with "a dead tangle of memories" and is touched

31
The
Marginal:
Readings
of the
First
Voice

by "the wave of life" (l'ondata della vita); here life comes in "impetuous waves" while the reflowering lady is threatened by a "surf of memories" (una risacca di memorie). The similarities are not simply incidental but are the result of a profound similarity in the poems' essential messages, which speak of emergence and of the possibilities available to poetry as a means of creation, or recreation, rather than of simple representation.

The lover observes the awakening of nature and of his beloved from an edge space separate and distinct from the warmth of April: "from this shadow," "this remote garden corner," "from [my] dark corner." In his study *The Poetics of Space* Gaston Bachelard devotes a chapter to a discussion of poetic corners; his remarks are helpful in commenting on Montale's corner. He writes that "every corner . . . every inch of secluded space in which we like to hide, or withdraw into ourselves, is a symbol of solitude for the imagination . . . the corner is a haven that insures one of the things we prize most highly—immobility . . . the corner is the chamber of being."[53] Montale is alone and essentially motionless in his corner, yet his position there allows him to partake imaginatively of the germinating life outside his own interior space. It is his mind that extends outward toward the essence of this moment of recreation:

. . . ed io
dall'oscuro mio canto mi protendo
a codesto solare avvenimento.

. . . and I
from my dark corner extend myself
to this solar coming.

In the line "dall'oscuro mio canto mi protendo" we see the absolute identification of the corner and the song-poem emerging from it (both meanings are attributable to the word *canto* in Italian). The enclosed dramatic space within the poem is, or at least allows for, the becoming of the poem itself as it extends toward realization, toward a life.

Both the observer-lover and the chrysalis-beloved are marginal characters, he because of his inability to experience directly the renewal of nature, she because of her intermediate, incomplete state. The hope of renascence expressed in the first three stanzas modulates into fear in the fourth, as the desired reflowering of the lady is seen as an illusion:

... ma l'ombra non dissolve
che vi reclama, opaca. M'apparite
allora, come me, nel limbo squallido
delle monche esistenze; e anche la vostra
rinascita è uno sterile segreto ...

... but the shadow does not dissolve
that reclaims you, opaque. You appear to me
then, like me, in the squalid limbo
of maimed existences; and even your
rebirth is a sterile secret ...

Nonetheless, outside the confines of the poet's chamber of being, the ferment of life speaks of salvation, even though it is illusory. The specific image of escape, "la barca di salvezza" (the boat of salvation), sends out a small craft, which waits to carry the hopeful two away:

... nel meriggio afoso
spunta la barca di salvezza, è giunta:
vedila che sciaborda tra le secche,
esprime un suo burchiello che si volge
al docile frangente—e là ci attende.

... in the sultry noon
sprouts the boat of salvation, it is arrived:
see it there as it laps among the shallows,
sends out one of its barges that turns
in the gentle breakers—and there it waits for us.

The verb used to describe this launching—*esprimere*—is especially resonant, for it draws attention to the metaliterary quality of this sending forth (the verb also means "to express"): the *burchiello* is both sea craft and word craft, the fruit of the generative act embodied in and by the poem itself.[54]

"The *It* is the eternal chrysalis, the *Thou* the eternal butterfly."[55] "Crisalide" is a poem about relationships: to self, to time, to the other. Almansi and Merry see its structure as antithetical, stating that "the text appears to oscillate between the illusion of fecundity and the disappointment of sterileness."[56] Cary emphasizes the dynamism of the emerging consciousness, writing that the poem "is the dramatization of

33
The
Marginal:
Readings
of the
First
Voice

the fortunes of a consciousness moving from an obsessional and lacerating sense of its own impotence to a commitment, *nevertheless*, to the well-being of another."[57]

In both these critical attempts to seize and describe the central meaning of this complex poem words having to do with motion are used: *oscillate*, a consciousness *moving*. I believe that another sort of structural rhythm can be discerned, one that is neither solely antithetical nor wholly progressive but rather both. The poem is made up of seven stanzas. The first three emphasize the separateness of the speaker; the fourth and central stanza effects a merging of the speaker with the other; and the last three again gradually reestablish the final and essential difference between the creating consciousness and the world of experience, both internal and external, that has been delineated throughout the poem. The separation of the speaker from that which he observes is established in the first three stanzas through the emphatic use of first-person pronouns ("per *me*," "ed *io* / . . . *mi* protendo") and possessive adjectives ("dall'oscuro *mio* canto," "la *mia* preda," "la *mia* parte," "la *mia* ricchezza)" as they are juxtaposed to the equally emphatic *voi* forms ("son *vostre* queste piante," "*vostro* cuore," "*voi* non pensate," "*voi* siete," "siete *voi*"). In the fourth stanza a merging is brought about first in the elided phrase *m'apparite* (you appear to me), followed immediately by the centrally placed *come me* (like me) and the highly charged *ci* (us) of the final phrase, "un prodigio fallito come tutti / quelli che ci fioriscono d'accanto" (a failed miracle like all / those that flourish around us). The first-person plural pronoun is used six times in the following three stanzas, and it is not until the final stanza that the poet returns to the separative forms, *yours* and *mine*. There is a violent shift between the fourth and fifth stanzas signaled by the change to the plural forms and intensified by the leap from flowering April to a parched "hour of fever" (ora di febbre) and "sultry noon" (meriggio afoso). The *voi* is also briefly transformed into a *tu* in the imperative *vedila* (see it) of the fifth stanza.[58] These changes reflect the fundamental change in emotional perspective on the part of the speaker; he now gives himself and the beloved over to the "agile [l'] illusione" (nimble illusion) that replaces the harsh reality of a failed miracle. It is within this dream of escape and renewal that the two can become united; outside its confines they remain inevitably separate. The beloved is finally named in the climactic sixth stanza:

Ah crisalide, com'è amara questa
tortura senza nome che ci volve
e ci porta lontani . . .

Ah chrysalis, how bitter is this
torture without name that surrounds us
and carries us far off . . .

In this stanza, the poet is both closest to and farthest from his goal of
absolute expression: close because of the great power and beauty of the
lines, far because what they express is the impossibility of final escape in
life and in art:

e noi andremo innanzi senza smuovere
un sasso solo della gran muraglia;
e forse tutto è fisso, tutto è scritto,
e non vedremo sorgere per via
la libertà, il miracolo,
il fatto che non era necessario!

and we shall proceed without budging
one single stone of the great wall;
and perhaps all is fixed, all is written,
and we shall not see rising up along the way
freedom, the miracle,
the fact that was not necessary!

The tension of emerging form implicit in the earlier phrases *mi protendo* (I extend myself) and *ci attende* (it waits for us) is maintained in
this stanza in which the words are linguistic events and yet deny the
possibility of full and free expression ("this torture / without name")
and of authentic release from either existential or literary determinism
("and perhaps all is fixed, all is written"). The last stanza intensifies this
recourse to silence in the phrases, "Il silenzio ci chiude nel suo
lembo / e le labbra non s'aprono per dire . . ." (Silence encloses us in its
edge / and lips do not open to say) and, "Penso allora / alle .tacite of-
ferte" (Then I think / of the silent offerings). As the illusion dissolves
the speaker once again underlines his essential difference from the lady:
"la vostra gioia" (your joy), "la mia condanna" (my punishment).

This antithetical movement between hope and despair and the

35
The
Marginal:
Readings
of the
First
Voice

progression toward significant expression are not denied in the final lines of the poem, for "il voto che mi nasce ancora in petto" (the desire that still is born in my heart) assures us that a birth or renewal is still possible, and the futurity of the completion of the line "poi finirà ogni moto" (then all motion will end) reveals that the dynamic sense of emergence that fills the poem has not reached any ultimate conclusion, even in the face of images that seem to give in to resigned silence:

> . . . Penso allora
> alle tacite offerte che sostengono
> le case dei viventi; al cuore che abdica
> perché rida un fanciullo inconsapevole;
> al taglio netto che recide, al rogo
> morente che s'avviva
> d'un arido paletto, e ferve trepido.

> . . . I think then
> of the silent offerings that sustain
> the houses of the living; of the heart that renounces
> so that a child might laugh unaware;
> of the clean cut that lops off, of the dying
> pyre that flares up once more
> with a dried-up stick, and blazes waveringly.

The final word of the poem—*trepido*—is emblematic of the continuing marginal hope of the speaker, an edginess not resolved within the confines of the poem, for *trepidazione* is defined as a state of mind "anxious, suspended, awaiting an event, between the opposing stresses of hope and of fear."[59] If we remember the poet's self-definition in the poem beginning, "Dissipa tu se lo vuoi" (cancel out if you wish), of "Mediterraneo" as a "favilla d'un tirso" (spark of a beacon) and his assertion there that *to burn* is his only meaning ("bruciare, / questo, non altro, è il mio significato"), we understand that this rekindled pyre describes the poetic consciousness itself, which has fought its way back to some hope, to some belief in the essentiality of continued expression.

The chrysalis of this poem is not fully developed into the butterfly of subsequent poems; nor is she a completely abortive creature, for her birth and flight depend on the ultimate resolution of tensions and doubts on the part of the poet that cannot occur until much later in his development.[60] It is in this sense that we might understand Montale's comment on "Riviere" (Coasts), the final poem of *Ossi de seppia*, a poem that he called "a synthesis and a cure both too premature."[61] The "undivided soul" (anima non più divisa) of that poem is, and will remain, only a hope within the confines of *Ossi di seppia*; and the desired "serene port of wisdom" (porto sereno di saggezza) is far from the agonizing and yet vitalizing uncertainties of the rites of passage that the young poet must first undergo. In "Crisalide" as well as in "Arsenio" and "In Limine" we experience the poetic self *in fieri*,[62] fully immersed in the dynamic process that I have designated as marginality.

In *Ossi di seppia*, then, the poet seeks to establish his position, his own unique space and time. The garden (orto) is identified with enclosure, past time, physical and spiritual limits; the wind and sea with openness, potentiality, boundlessness. In later collections other spatial and temporal images emerge. The house, the room—as in "La casa dei doganieri" (The Customs House) and the "Mottetti"—the mists and smoke of memory, especially in *Le occasioni*, are all signs of imprisonment; and the beloved's eyes, her flight, the rainstorm, magical moments of epiphany, amulets are all images of escape. The poet's voice typically situates itself dramatically between these oppositions in its own eternal present, a present to be understood in the purest Augustinian sense as what is neither past nor future but is defined only in relation to them.

In regard to this method of definition by negation or opposition that Montale employs almost obsessively, and its relationship to the marginal, Turner writes: "Liminality may perhaps be regarded as the Nay to all positive structural assertions, but as in some sense the source of them all, and more than that, as a realm of pure possibility whence novel configurations of ideas and relations may arise.[63] We see this borne out in many of the stylistic and thematic choices Montale makes: the well-known assertion of "Non chiederci la parola" (Don't ask of us the word), for example, where the poet writes of "ciò che *non* siamo, ciò che *non* vogliamo" (what we are *not*, what we do *not* want), as he insists on the as yet unfixed yet positive potential of the emerging poet, which presents itself as a nay to any traditional yeas. Furthermore there are the poet's many recourses to paradox (oxymoronic structures, contrary-to-fact constructions, the *forse*, or "perhaps," that proliferates throughout his poetry) and finally his constant unwillingness to clarify,

37
The
Marginal:
Readings
of the
First
Voice

his programmatic acceptance of what Avalle calls "the equivocal structure" in statements ostensibly presented as clarification.[64]

The speaker in the poems of *Ossi* is portrayed as separate and different from the other, unable or unwilling to seek the integration or salvation so enthusiastically urged for her. The entire "Mediterranean" suite is dominated by images of the sea as unattainable otherness—"vastità" (vastness), "vasto e diverso / e insieme fisso" (vast and diverse / and yet fixed)—opposed to the human limits of the poet. It is a source of completely natural musical speech—"salmastre parole / in cui natura ed arte si confondono" (salty words / in which nature and art merge)—far superior to the poet's "balbo parlare" (stuttering speech) or "lamentosa letteratura" (doleful literature). This separative impulse that presents the poetic speaker as apart from that which is socially the norm—"la gente nell'affollato corso" (the people in the crowded streets)—or from that which is thoroughly untamed by social structures and representative of the natural, eternal order (the sea) consistently results in the placement of the poetic voice in a sort of limbo, a marginal zone of neither-nor. Incapable of full identification either with tradition and normative social structures or with the unconscious life force represented by the sea, the poet must forge a residence that is marginal both spatially and spiritually, a place in which his poetry can be created and from which it can emerge to explain, enrich, and possibly even possess the zones to which it does not essentially belong. As I have sought to make clear, this space is one of creative potentiality in a positive sense, and it is also one of epistemological density (poetry as "more a means of knowledge than of representation").[65]

Montale's poetics is one of construction, of contemplative creation, which moves toward understanding rather than the representation of an already understood reality or self. What is most striking about this first collection is the way in which both thematic and stylistic elements are thoroughly imbued with a quality of struggle and process. Yet this is accomplished without relinquishing the understated control that characterizes all of Montale's poetry. There is no uncertainty or tentativeness in the poems' structure, even while they express a deeply tentative faith in the power available to poetic creation to break through to some "definitive *quid*." The key of the poetic voice is, from the beginning, a minor one that consistently avoids hyperbole and ostentation. This minor key is immediately evident in the title of the first collection: cuttlefish are unpoetic, even banal, creatures used more often as an ingredient in stews than in poems. Montale's selection of these trite creatures as emblems of his poetry clearly aligns him with the muted poetry of the crepuscular and Ligurian poets who preceded him. But his title also gives us a much more important interpretive clue. The bones of the cuttlefish are finely honed, whitened, and purified remains, products of the sea's cleansing action. Montale's *Ossi* are verbal skeletons stripped down to elemental stylistic precision through the poet's patient search for absolute expression. As Contini has aptly noted, the titles of Montale's collections are always "pregnant ... with autocritical intelligence."[66] So it is with this first collection as with the second, *Le occasioni*—"occasions" that are as marginal as the private spaces and times that allow them to come into being.

2
Style as Tension: Love and the *Avventura Stilistica*

I N Montale's "Imaginary Interview" the poet writes of "the Selvaggia or the Mandetta or the Delia ... of the *Motets*,"[1] and in a note to the poem "Iride" (Iris) in *La bufera e altro* he identifies this personage of *Le occasioni* with Clizia, the woman-angel of the later collection.[2] As is typical of Montale's explanatory notes, however, these clarifications do nothing to illuminate the true identity of the beloved. What is useful in the poet's references to the lady of the "Motets" are the stilnovistic and, more specifically, the Dantesque allusions that serve to orient the reader to the kind of experience of love being recreated in the poems. Two of the *senhals* (emblematic names) suggested for the lady by Montale himself in the comments quoted above are those of the beloveds of Cino da Pistoia and Guido Cavalcanti, poets who, along with Dante, are considered to be part of the *stil novo* school. The name Clizia, given to the beloved in the third collection, is itself explicitly connected by Montale to a Dantesque source in the epigraph of "La pri-

mavera hitleriana" (Hitler Spring)—"Né quella ch'a veder lo sol si
gira" (Nor that one who turns to see the sun)—a line generally attributed with some doubt to a poem by Dante to Giovanni Quirini, in
which Clizia is a mythic lady enamored of Apollo and who is transformed by the sun god into a sunflower. Be she Selvaggia or Mandetta
or Clizia, then, Montale's beloved is to be understood as partaking of
the stilnovistic tradition. Finally there is Montale's description of the
"Mottetti" as an "autobiographical novelette."[3] Given the ties to
Dante already indicated, this phrase would suggest, if somewhat
obliquely, that this *libello* ("little book," Dante's description of his autobiography) is Montale's *Vita nuova*. It is his most sustained love poetry at this point in his career, and retrospectively considered, it is a series that points to the emergence of the Clizia figure in *La bufera*, much
as Dante's "little book" prepares for the triumphant emergence of the
Commedia's Beatrice.[4] The title given collectively to these lyrics points
also to their Dantesque inspiration, for *motet* is defined as "a vocal
composition in polyphonic style, on a Biblical or similar prose text,"[5]
much as Dante's book is presented as a gloss on the book of memory,
itself but a chapter in God's "book," history. We might understand
Montale's lyrics as glosses on his own book of memory, his past experiences with the woman when she was present in his life. The "Mottetti"
are not in any traditional sense religious poems, but their force does in
part derive from the transcendent significance of the woman in the
poet's personal search for salvation.

It is futile to attempt to identify exactly Montale's source of inspiration. The woman's actual identity is of no importance, and as Montale
states concerning the reality of Beatrice and Pietra,

> Perhaps lady Pietra truly existed; but as far as she is a stylistic ad-
> venture she will never be able to coincide with a real woman. If
> Dante then [at the time of the *Vita nuova*] had a precocious in-
> tuition of what Beatrice's ultimate significance was going to have
> to be (and the *Vita nuova* leaves little doubt in that regard) I
> would say that lady Pietra as well as the "Donna gentile" would
> have had to have been invented wholly if they had never existed:
> because it is impossible to imagine a process of salvation without
> the opposing role of error and sin.[6]

These words are eminently applicable to Montale's own stylistic adventure in which Clizia and Volpe (Vixen) play roles loosely analogous to

41
Style as
Tension:
Love
and the
Avventura
Stilistica

those of Beatrice and Pietra in Dante's complex process of salvation. In her early appearance in the "Mottetti," when she is as yet unnamed, the beloved becomes in her absence the *fantasma* toward which the poet's words extend, the point of clarification and hope that might make of his life more than a series of occasions and of his writing more than a series of words. From the beginning she is linked to light and fire, which are placed in opposition to the darkness, both physical and spiritual, that hovers about the entire second collection.[7] In "Il balcone" (The Balcony), the dedicatory poem of the collection, the poet announces his dedication of himself to the woman whose "certo fuoco" (sure fire) is opposed to his "tedio malcerto" (unsure tedium), as he rejects the "nulla" (nothingness) in favor of a meaning to be derived from waiting for and serving (*attendere*) her image. The space in which this poetry will be generated is again marginal, as is clear both in the image of the balcony itself (a betwixt-and-between location) and in the dynamics set up between active life outside—"la vita che dà barlumi" (life which gives off glimmers)—toward which the beloved yearns and the dark, contemplative space inside of which the poet and his memories reside—questa finestra che non s'illumina" (this window which is not illuminated). There is an emphasis throughout the "Motets" on the paradox of presence-absence, on past as present, and on regained loss, for it is not the lady who is finally brought back but rather the lover's loss of her that is fully understood through the elaboration of that loss into poetry. As in Dante's process of salvation, so too in Montale's is there the first step of introspection and the search for self-knowledge. Only later will this search be supplanted by poetry that has as its primary goal the appropriate praise of the lady, recognized as a superior being and thus necessarily unattainable.

When asked in a recent interview (1975) if his reading of Dante began while he was still in school, Montale answered, "Yes and after . . . Dante had a full tank (as a motorist would say) and for the others gas was scarce." In another interview, when speaking of his poetic ladies Montale stated that "Clizia and Volpe are placed in contrast, one salvational, as would be said today, the other of the earth . . . (they are) Dantesque, Dantesque."[8] The importance of Dante to Montale's ideation of his poetic ladies is thus made clear, but how are we to pursue the significance of the ties between the two poets? Technically Montale learned much from the great poet about whom he wrote, "Compared

with Dante poets do not exist."[9] Many critics have investigated his stylistic indebtedness to the medieval poet.[10] In considering the development of Montale's poetry in this second collection, and specifically in
the "Mottetti," it is perhaps more useful to trace the less specific yet no
less significant points of contact between them that have contributed to
Montale's implicit and explicit poetics. To do so I should like first to
turn back to *Ossi* in order to consider the final poem of that collection,
"Riviere," written in 1920. In the poet's own words it is "among the oldest poems," and it is situated at the end of the collection for something
other than chronological reasons (an ordering principle that underlies
the arrangement of all the collections).[11] It can be read as indicative of
future developments, as both a conclusion to the first volume and an
introduction to the second. Looking back to it therefore helps us to look
forward to the new orientation of the lyrics of *Le occasioni*, much as a
remembered future is implicit in every step of the *Commedia's*
progress.

In "Riviere" the poet bids farewell to the poetic world of the *Ossi*.
He does so by giving up "i voti del fanciullo antico" (the desires of the
ancient child), which involved an escapist desire to "svanire a poco a
poco; / diventare / un albero rugoso od una pietra / levigata dal mare
. . ." (fade away bit by bit; / to become / a rough tree or a stone / polished by the sea) in favor of a "volontà nuova" (new will), a desire for
integration that is expressed as follows: "cangiare in inno l'elegia; rifarsi; / non mancar più" (to change the elegy into a hymn, to remake
oneself; / to be lacking no longer). The last lines of the poem contain
the words *riaffluir* (renewed flow) and *rifiorire* (reflowering); these,
along with *rifarsi*, emphasize that the new hope is based on a concept of
renewal. The *ri-* prefix of these words insists on the process of reclamation that originates in past experience, in "ricordi lieti—e atroci" (remembrances both happy—and horrible) but that will be used in the
service of future fulfillment:

Ed un giorno *sarà* ancora l'invito
di voci d'oro, di lusinghe audaci,
anima mia non più divisa . . . [italics mine]

And a day *will be* once more the invitation
of golden voices, of bold enticements,
oh my no longer divided soul . . .[12]

43
Style as
Tension:
Love
and the
Avventura
Stilistica

This transforming impulse, which depends on the blending of opposites, is at the center of his elaboration of the "Motets." It is already at work in this early poem, which also depends on the tension of oxymoronic structures ("ancient child," "remembrances both happy and horrible," "cold lights") that strive to reach future fulfillment through a relived past ("reliving an ancient game," "I recall"). The linking of past and future in order to create a livable present is the program outlined in this poem:

Triste anima *passata*
e tu volontà *nuova* che mi chiami,
tempo è forse d'unirvi
in un porto sereno di saggezza. [italics mine]

Sad past soul
and you new will that calls me,
it is time perhaps to be united
in a calm port of wisdom.

The final goal is wisdom, or understanding and acceptance of both past and future in order that one might live in the present; this desire is very much the same as that implicitly expressed in the "Motets."

The recovery of one's past in order to confront one's present and future is central to the second moment of Montale's development as elaborated throughout *Le occasioni*. It is the Dantesque experience par excellence: retrospective illumination that subsumes and reinterprets occasions or lived moments in order to provide the way for overall patterns of meaning to emerge. Montale called "Riviere" "a too-premature recovery or cure";[13] and indeed it does enunciate a synthesis that is premature, for the poet must first pass through the experience of creating the second voice before coming anywhere near the "calm port of wisdom" he sought in 1921. That youthful hopefulness and desire to maintain a new will are at least partially fulfilled in the location of the lyric center in the beloved and in her role as bearer of meaning. With the "Motets" Montale has, as he wrote of Dante's progress in the *Vita nuova*, "gotten onto the tiger," that is, he committed himself, "and will not be able to get off again. His destiny is at this point definitively indicated"[14]: his poetic destiny, that is. The sunflower of *Ossi di seppia* now becomes "the one who according to myth was transformed into a sunflower." The "ansietà del [suo] volto giallino" (yearning of [its] yellow face) of "Il girasole" (The Sunflower) will be transformed into the yearning of the poet, expressed in "The Balcony" as "l'ansia di attenderti vivo" (the yearning to serve and wait for you, alive).[15] The poet dedicates himself to her without whom "life would have had no sense, no direction."[16] In an exquisite reversal of the original metamorphosis, flower becomes lady, who in turn becomes the source of the light that might show the poet some way out of the darkness of his confusion and solitude.

Montale called the "Motets" "an autobiographical novelette [which is] anything but dark and gloomy (tenebroso)."[17] The adjective refers both to the tone and to the central light metaphor of the suite. The pretext for the poems, the woman's absence, might first appear to be a relentlessly negative one, but the poems deny any such unilateral response. The beloved is absent, and Montale makes her absence felt, yet that absence is necessary to the creation of the poems. A recent poem included in the fourth collection, *Satura*, speaks directly to this literary paradox; in it Montale supplies us with a witty description of his attitude toward the beloved's absence that is no less serious for its antilyrical tone:

> Non posso respirare se sei lontana.
> Così scriveva Keats a Fanny Brawne
> da lui tolta dall'ombra. È strano che il mio caso
> si parva licet sia diverso. Posso
> respirare assai meglio se ti allontani.

> I cannot breathe if you are far away.
> Thus wrote Keats to Fanny Brawne,
> saved from oblivion by him. It's strange that my case
> *si parva licet* is other. I can
> breathe much better if you go away.

The reason for this is that proximity brings back painful memories of shared hopes and dreams that are in terrible contrast to realities. But, as the poet concludes in "Dopo una fuga" (After a Flight), together or not,

> So che se mi leggi
> pensi che mi hai fornito il propellente

45
Style as
Tension:
Love
and the
Avventura
Stilistica

necessario e che il resto (purché *non sia* silenzio)
poco importa.

I know that if you read me
you think that you furnished me with the necessary
propellant and that the rest (as long as it's *not* silence)
scarcely matters.

Just as Beatrice's death is the pretext essential to the young Dante's
final comprehension of her significance in his life as "an actual miracle," so Clizia's disappearance from Montale's life is the necessary propellant for the elaboration of her new presence as a stylistic adventure,
an adventure beginning with the "Motets" and reaching its ultimate
completion in the "Silvae" of *La bufera.* In his essay on Dante Montale
emphasizes several times the importance of the miraculous nature of
Beatrice, a thesis that "cannot be combatted with rational arguments."
He further says that he has no proof against "the miraculous nature of
the poem [the *Comedy*], just as the miraculous nature attributed to
that historical Beatrice whom we thought we could do without has not
frightened [me]."[18]
    As I have noted, it is possible to make an equation between the
Montalian concept of miracle as ultimate escape and the concept of
perfected form. The beloved seen as a miracle can thus be understood
to provide the possible escape route for freeing the poet from the prison
of a purely rational existence. The flashes of insight she provides turned
into flashes of brief lyric might illuminate the darkness and lead the
poet into the clarity of full metaphoric understanding beyond the
blindness of the literal. It is in this commitment to the search for
meaning that goes far beyond a simply technical stylistic adventure that
can be located the most profound identification of the "Mottetti" with
the Dantesque vision. They are poems that shine all the more brightly
for having emerged from the haze of memory and the blackness of loss
and silence.
    This series of twenty short lyrics located at the very center of the col-
lection—bracketed on either side by sixteen poems—is not unequivocally positive, for there is an underlying paradox that threatens to erode
the tenuous core of hope. It is the central oxymoron upon which the
poems are based: the absence-presence of the beloved. There is the danger that the etymological definition of *oxymoron*—pointedly foolish—

will finally win out over what that figure seeks to do: "keep united that which would remain separate."[19] In plain language, the lady is gone; in poetic terms, she has never been more present. Her presence is glimpsed, intuited, wrestled from the harsh silence surrounding the poet and is given no more specific ontology than *segno, barbaglio, pegno* (sign, glimmer, vow). But as Almansi and Merry make clear in their analysis of the series, this presence is entirely predicated upon her real and dramatic absence, for she "acquires a dynamic presence in the texture of the poems where she is declared to be most absent."[20] The danger is clear: were Montale to lose his faith in the conjuring power of words, the game would be up, and the past would become once more irrevocably cut off from any present reevocation. The poet's faith in the significance of this kind of linguistic presence is what sustains these poems; it is the force that allows for the full transformation of the promising *crisalide* of *Ossi* into the soaring *farfalla* of *La bufera e altro*.

This faith is, however, fraught with hesitations and doubts that result in a tense style, reflecting in poetic structures the interplay of hope and despair that makes up Montale's attitude toward the potential of language as a means of understanding, or in the case of the "Mottetti" as an instrument for retrieving what in existential terms is irretrievably past. Throughout the series the tone captures the poet's vacillation between confidence in the efficacy of his stylistic adventure and his constant awareness of the fragility of a purely poetic reevocation of what was once lived experience. It is this "running intellectual oxymoron"[21] rather than the specific rhetorical figure of the same name that creates the fundamental ambiguity and tension that inform these lyrics.

One of the ways in which an absent person can be made to seem present is through letters that mimic dialogue, reinforce intimacy, and affirm the possibility of contact over distance. Montale described these "Mottetti" as just such a means of combatting separation; he called them "brief poems dedicated, even sent by air mail (but only on the wings of fantasy) to a Clizia who was living around three thousand miles away . . ."[22] This form of poems written as if part of an exchange of letters with another culminates in the series of "Botte e risposte" (Thrusts and Parries) of later collections. The conversational, epistolary tone is most evident in the first "Motet," which begins: "Lo sai: debbo riperderti e non posso" (You know: I must lose you again and I cannot). A shared past is evoked in the iterative form *riperderti*. The lover has

47
Style as
Tension:
Love
and the
*Avventura
Stilistica*

already lost his beloved once and although by his own admission he must do so again, he cannot. The implied tension in this opening line establishes with great power the conflicting forces of logical necessity (*dovere*) and irrational desire (*potere*) that assail the solitary lover. There is no resignation to loss here but rather an insistence on the violent intensity of hope experienced by the lover as he searches for some sign of the beloved's continued presence. The edginess resulting from such a taut state is perfectly rendered in the sharp *t*'s of the line "come un tiro aggiustato" (like a precisely aimed shot) and in the grating *z*'s of the words *ronzìo* (buzz) and *strazia* (harrows). The "paese di ferrame e alberature / a selva nella polvere del vespro" (country of iron and masts / like a forest in the haze of the evening) provides a strikingly appropriate physical context for the spiritual and emotional confusion of the lover who searches for the "segno / smarrito" (sign / lost). This adjective, *smarrito*, isolated by the enjambment from *segno* and thus given a primary position in the line, applies with equal force to the mislaid sign and to the lover himself, who is lost without his lady. The phrase from Dante's *Comedy* "because the right path was lost" (smarrita) comes to mind. Dante's voice rings too in the line of the "Motet" "E l'inferno è certo" (And hell is certain) and creates an implicit analogy between the medieval pilgrim's spiritual confusion and the modern-day lover's bewilderment.[23] Although the final line has the ring of inevitable closure, it seems less a logical conclusion to the taut psychological state depicted in the preceding lines than a forced finality that at least offers the unequivocality and resolution of complete pessimism.

This capitulation to unrelieved misery is belied immediately in the second "Motet." It is energetic, courtly, poignant, anything but representative of the resignation to loss suggested in the final line of the first. Already we hear the variety of tone that characterizes the series, as well as the recourse to a shared past put to the service of an assertion of continuing hope. Here the memory is of a return: "Poi scendesti dai monti a riportarmi / San Giorgio e il Drago" (Then you descended from the mountains to bring back to me / Saint George and the Dragon). The beloved's scarf, which she waved in the poem "Verso Capua" (Toward Capua) in the preceding section of *Le occasioni*, is now transformed into a banner that also waves, but now in the heart of the lover: "che s'agita alla frusta del grecale / in cuore" (which waves at the lash of the north wind / in the heart). The final phrase of this most chivalresque poem—"E per te scendere in un gorgo / di fedeltà, immortale" (And for you to descend into a whirlwind / of fidelity, immortal)—has the flourish of a heroic gesture, even if it is conditioned by the contrary-to-fact subjunctive form *potessi* (would that I could), which makes of it a defiant wish in the face of obdurate reality .

The verb *scendere* (descend) appears twice in this very short poem, first to describe the beloved's reappearance and then to indicate the desired action of the lover. It is a loaded term for Montale, as is already established in *Ossi*. There are multiple uses of this verb in "Arsenio" ("you descend," "descend," "descend in the midst of darkness"). In the poem "Incontro" (Meeting), added to the second edition of *Ossi di seppia* and, according to the poet himself, indicative of the new direction of the second collection, we read: "Prega per me / allora ch'io discenda altro cammino / che una via di città . . . / ch'io / scenda senza viltà" (Pray for me / then that I may descend another road / than a city street . . . / that I / may descend without cowardice). In later poems included in *Le occasioni* the verb comes to signify the movement of life itself: "E scende la cuna tra logge / ed erme" (And the cradle descends among loggias / and busts) in "Tempi di Bellosguardo" (Times of Bellosguardo); "Lo so, non s'apre il cerchio / e tutto scende o rapido s'inerpica . . ." (I know, the circle doesn't open / and everything descends or rapidly climbs) in "Costa San Giorgio." In *La bufera e altro* the descent is the movement of both good and evil. In "L'orto," where the angelic lady represents good, she descends as a messenger to lend her transcendental strength to the exhausted world. In "La primavera hitleriana," on the other hand, the world is threatened by "the monsters of evening" that join with the horrible "sound that, let loose from the sky, descends, conquers." Evil is also represented as descending on the world in "Piccolo testamento" (Little Testament), where "a shadowy Lucifer will descend on a prow / of the Thames, the Hudson, the Seine . . ."

The Montalian descent is always an essential movement, be it toward salvation or damnation. In the second "Motet" the descent of the woman results in the desire for a deeper descent on the part of the lover into a complete fidelity to her that would itself be immortal, rendering both her and the poet such. The placement of the final adjective in its detached position at the very end of the line allows for its possible assignment to *te* (you), *fedeltà* (fidelity), and / or by implication to the

49
Style as
Tension:
Love
and the
*Avventura
Stilistica*

poet himself, just as the adjective *smarrito* of the first "Motet" is applicable to more than one substantive. This is willed ambiguity, part of the strategy of the entire doubt-ridden series. Montale commented on his use of such equivocal constructions in a letter written to his friend Bobi Bazlen (May 10, 1939), in which he discussed certain stylistic choices in the poem "Elegia di Pico Farnese" (Elegy of Pico Farnese):

> It *often* happens (and often *willfully*) that I am equivocal . . . for example in the *Motet* of the woman who is about to emerge from the cloud:
> At a puff the lazy smoke . . . (?)
> persists in the point that enfolds you
> it is clear that *in the point* can have two meanings: *in the moment that* and *in the place that*, both of them legitimate. For Landolfi this doubt is horrible; for me it is a richness.[24]

Willful ambiguity is thus seen as a source of poetic richness by the poet himself, and we can rest assured that these and other instances of such constructions are a part of the stylistic adventure of *Le occasioni*.

The third "Motet" opens with an extended oxymoronic phrase that can be read as emblematic of the paradoxical relationship underlying the entire series:

Brina sui vetri; uniti
sempre e sempre in disparte
gl'infermi; e sopra i tavoli
i lunghi soliloqui sulle carte.

Hoarfrost on the windows; united
always and always disunited
the invalids; and over the tables
the long soliloquies on the cards.

The wonderfully expressive enjambment between the first and second lines is not completed with its subject until the third line, and so we first understand that the eternally united-separated are the lovers themselves. This is really not so wrong, for in fact the beloved is one of those invalids whose exile of illness is next juxtaposed to that of the lover-soldier. The movement of the poem is from remembered experience (her illness) to related memory (his war experience) to integration of the two in the "rough wing" (ala rude) that brushed the lady's hands. The angel of death hovered about them both in their separate but similar dangers, yet both were spared. It was for neither the moment when death is dealt out by the hand of Fate ("the long soliloquies on the cards"). The use of the present tense in the final phrase, "la tua carta non è questa" (your card is not this one), joins the two past experiences with the present moment. Finally the long soliloquies become the poet's solitary vigil over memories made words, resulting in his ultimate failure to bring the beloved back to him through poetry , carta (both "card" and "paper") having become the paper on which he now writes.

These first three "Motets," all written in 1934, form the opening chapter of the autobiographical novelette. In fact Montale later indicated that they were written with "a Peruvian woman [who] lived in Genoa" in mind,[25] a woman different from the one later called Clizia and who inspired the remaining "Motets." The next two poems, which begin, "Lontano, ero con te" (Far off, I was with you), and, "Addii, fischi nel buio" (Farewells, whistles in the dark), were both written later. The first is undated; the second is from 1939 and was added to the second edition of Le occasioni, as was the "Motet" that begins, "Ti libero la fronte" (I free your forehead). There is no radical shift from the first three to the next poems either in theme or in style, in spite of the different sources of inspiration. The fourth and fifth continue to depict the harshness of loss and the primacy of the woman to the meaning of past occurrences (her father's death, her departure by train). It is with the sixth "Motet," beginning, "La speranza di pure rivederti" (The hope of even seeing you again), written in 1937, that a new and essential semantic element comes into play: the woman as glimmer or flicker of light. The word barlumi (flickers) had already appeared in "The Balcony," but there it was life itself that gave off the gleam. Now the woman is the source of the glimmer—"un tuo barbaglio" (one of your flashes). The light images surrounding her multiply—"fólgore" (lightning flash); "brilla come te" (shines like you); "due / fasci di luce in croce" (two / crossed beams of light)—until in La bufera the true nature of her brilliance becomes manifest in poems such as "The Garden," "Hitler Spring," "The Eel" (L'anguilla), and "Little Testament." So with the sixth motet the implicit center becomes explicit; the lost sign emerges as the lady's glimmer of light, both physical and spiritual, in the darkness of separation.

The importance of the lady's eyes to the experience of love is at least

51
Style as
Tension:
Love
and the
*Avventura
Stilistica*

as old as the *stilnovisti;* what might now seem to us a tired cliché was in fact originally grounded in the physiology of love. *Duecento* and *trecento* poets believed that rays of light pour forth from the beloved's eyes, capturing the lover. The connection between light and beauty is also an ancient one. What is so new in Montale's use of this imagery is its believability for the modern reader; rather than seeming to be a borrowing from earlier love poets, the image appears to emerge naturally from the woman's function as bearer of hope and meaning to the doubting lover.[26]

Montale commented at length on the origin and elaboration of the sixth "Motet," which contains the first glimmer specifically connected with Clizia. It should be remembered that this poem was seen as hermetic and extremely elusive when it first appeared, and Montale's subsequent explanation of it seeks to tackle head-on the issue of his hermeticism. The perplexing part of the short poem was the parenthetical last stanza, placed typographically apart from the rest of the poem:

(a Modena, tra i portici,
un servo gallonato trascinava
due sciacalli al guinzaglio).

(in Modena, among the porticoes,
a liveried servant was dragging
two jackals on a leash).

The poet states in his explanatory essay that he saw two jackals on a leash one day in Modena and immediately thought: "Clizia loved droll animals . . . perhaps the two little beasts might have been sent by her, almost through an emanation? That they might have been an emblem, an occult citation, a *senhal?*" He goes on to describe how he wrote the poem on a tram ticket, first ending the poem with the last line of the second stanza ("un *tuo* barbaglio") and then completing it with "an example that might even be a conclusion," the parenthetical jackals.[27] I offer his own explanation here not in order to side either with the poet—who makes it all so clear, retrospectively—or with the early critics who, according to Montale's comments in the essay quoted above, were more guilty than he of obscurantism. What I do wish to emphasize is the almost magical and certainly instantaneous chemistry that caused Montale to link the rhyming *barbaglio-guinzaglio* so appropriately and, seen retrospectively, so fruitfully for his future elaborations of the poetic life of the beloved. For what was clearly a sort of happy *trouvaille* for the resolution of this poem served as the beginning point for a long and equally felicitous development of light and animal images in relation to the lady. Autobiography (the real incident in Modena) and literary tradition (the jackals understood as an occult, stilnovistic sign) thus merged to make possible the Montalian beloved's birth into fuller poetic reality.

Another example of this convergence of lived experience and succeeding stylistic adventure is found in the "Motet" that begins, "Infuria sale o grandine?" (Does salt or hail rage down?) dated 1938, in which the beloved's penchant for singing is evoked. (Another "Motet" of the same year also speaks of her voice, which "insists *do re la sol sol* . . . "). The last lines of "Infuria" read: "brilla come te / quando fingevi col tuo trillo d'aria / Lakmé nell'Aria delle Campanelle" (it shines like you / when you pretended to be, with your trill of air, / Lakmé in the Aria of the Bells). When asked many years later why the lady of this poem "indicates with her voice the 'Aria of the Bells' of Delibes' *Lakmé*? Is there perhaps some reference having to do with [its] content?" the poet replied: "I wanted to suggest an airy voice ('trillo d'aria'), a trilling one."[28] The result in the poem is that her vibrato is linked by rhyme to her brilliance (*brilla-trillo*) in much the same way that her love for strange animals (sciacalli al guinzaglio) was also tied to her glimmer of light (barbaglio), in both cases forming a unity of sound and sense. But in the case of *brilla-trillo* the sound-sense convergence does not end here, with this poem and this link; it extends in later poems to other double-*l* words having to do with the lady: *scintilla* (spark), *pupille* (pupils), and most significantly *anguilla* (eel). As early as 1938 Montale had called himself an "assorto / pescatore d'anguille" (an absorbed / fisherman of eels) in the "Motet" beginning, "La gondola che scivola" (The gondola that slides), establishing, if only obliquely, the connection between the eel and the beloved later exploited to its fullest power in the great poem "L'anguilla" of *La bufera*.

That these double-*l* words take on a special relationship to the poetic portrait of the beloved lady is made even clearer in Montale's comments on the writing of the poem "Elegy of Pico Farnese" (1939), in which the beloved is definitively angelicized in the lines "Ben altro / è l'Amore e fra gli alberi balena col tuo cruccio / e la tua frangia d'ali,

53
Style as
Tension:
Love
and the
*Avventura
Stilistica*

messaggera accigliata" (Far different / is Love and between the trees flash down with your torment / and your fringe of wings, frowning messenger). Referring to the choice of the word *prilla* in the phrase "nell'aria prilla il piattello" (in the air spins the little disk), the poet explained in a letter to Bobi Bazlen that it is there because of its tie to the preceding word, *brilla*, itself linked to Clizia's emblem, the sunflower, in the lines "parole / che il seme del girasole / se brilla disperde" (words / that the seed of the sunflower / if it shines scatters). The continued presence of the musical motif, also by now established as an integral part of the beloved's poetic physiognomy, is evident in Montale's gloss of the line "Il giorno non chiede più di una chiave" (The day needs no more than one key), which states that *key* "is used here to mean picklock . . . but perhaps (I just thought of it) also musical key would work (key of *fa*, of *sol*) in a kindred sense, and even diapason in the sense of a little instrument that allows for tuning etc."[29]

These glimpses into the process of writing and rewriting are invaluable, for we can begin to understand, if only partially, the complex operations of memory, feeling, and technical procedure that underlie the final result. What is clear in this instance is that certain words are chosen not only because they directly and unequivocally express a given meaning but also, and above all, because they evoke for the poet, and eventually for his readers, the truest and most abiding attributes of his beloved. It is almost as if the double-*l* words have become talismanic; they themselves are gradually being transformed into occult emblems of the lady's presence. It is not until we have reached the end of the elaboration of her myth that we can look back over these early *scintille* with a full sense of their total significance.

I am tracing here the emerging lineaments of the beloved as she is transformed into a poetic presence: she truly liked odd animals; she truly had lovely and brilliant eyes and a trilling vibrato. But all of these real attributes are metamorphosed according to the exigencies of poetic structure and rhyme into lexical leitmotifs that subsequently generate new poetic realities. In *La bufera e altro*, the double-*l* words are linked in terms of sound and semantics to the gems that are the beloved's most essential accoutrements: *cristalli* (crystals), *anelli* (rings), *gioielli* (jewels), *coralli* (corals). These, like her brilliance and her musical penchant, are real elements in her being; but now they take on metaphorical and eventually transcendental significance. The light of her eyes be-

comes the lover's point of spiritual clarification in the midst of the ob-
fuscations of his war-torn world; the jewels come to represent her superior strength and durability in a time of weakness and transience.[30]
These attributes of shimmering light and obdurate resistance come together ultimately in "The Eel," the great poem of the "Silvae" section
of *La bufera*, in which the woman is *sorella* (sister) of the eel, itself
scintilla (spark) and *gemella* (twin) of the iris that the beloved makes to
shine (*brillare*) among the children of man. And so perhaps from a simple *trillo* is finally born the beauty and power of the *anguilla*, the living
symbol of courage and endurance that summarizes Montale's long dedication to the beloved and to the good she represents.

I think that it is in the following manner that we might understand
Montale's comment that he "never invents anything."[31] His poetry
takes off from lived, direct experience, which is subsequently metamorphosed in the creation of poetry. The jackals are really seen, the
woman's voice really heard; yet it is equally true that they both become
elements in an "avventura stilistica" that has little to do with realism.
What woman would ever think or hope to be linked to jackals or to the
eel; and what woman would ever have foreseen how absolutely right
that union is? This is the alchemy of art that transforms *trillo* to *scintilla* to *sorella* to *anguilla*, generating meaning from insignificance.
What matter if Beatrice was not named Beatrice or Laura, Laura; the
poets make these names real, inevitable, and totally reflective of the essence of the women they represent. So it is with Montale's beloved.
Her eyes, her voice, her forehead and bangs, her taste for jewels, all real
according to the poet himself, are nonetheless only fully realized in the
poems that give them ultimate form and substance.

This poetic center, the beloved's absence-presence, which emerges in
the "Mottetti" and is completely developed in *La bufera*, depends on
the poet's tenuous faith in the efficacy of poetic forgery. I use the word
forgery both in the sense of that which is made and that which is fraudulent, an imitation of a reality. The final "Motet" emphasizes the artificial presence that these poems create out of the real absence of the beloved. It begins on a note of resigned acceptance, not untouched by
self-reflexive irony, of the limitations of both life and art: "but so be it."
We are then pulled back into the confines of the poet's room from
which these brief love letters are being sent "on the wings of fantasy"
and thus are brought full circle, for it was from a room that the voice of

55
Style as
Tension:
Love
and the
*Avventura
Stilistica*

the first "Motet" reached us. The objects on the poet's desk—*la valva* (the seashell), *la moneta incassata nella lava* (the coin encased in lava), *pochi fogli* (a few sheets of paper)—are, like the "Motets" themselves, reified bits of life, but they reflect a limited vitality. We realize that the few sheets of paper are the poems themselves, which have emerged out of the vastness of past experience, out of "la vita che sembrava / vasta" (life that seemed / immense). All is artificial and reduced, fixed in immutable form (the volcano painted on the shell, the shining coin encased in lava, the poems), but it is not a negative reductio ad absurdum; for if life is no longer immense, it is nonetheless representable in an intimate domestic object, the beloved's *fazzoletto* (handkerchief), which is small (breve) but no less precious for its smallness.

The "Motets" themselves are *brevi* (brief as well as small), as are the past moments they depend on, and as are the rare glimmers of meaning that the beloved provides. Her handkerchief can be understood as a sort of amulet, akin to the tiny white mouse that saves Dora Markus or to the iris of the eel, which is also called *breve* but which ultimately becomes the iris of "Little Testament," where Montale writes:

Solo quest'iride posso
lasciarti a testimonianza
d'una fede che fu combattuta,
d'una speranza che bruciò piú lenta
di un duro ceppo nel focolare.

Only this iris can I
leave you as testimony
of a faith that was attacked,
of a hope that burned more slowly
than a hard stump on the hearth.

In these brief poems, Montale shows that no detail either existential or stylistic is ever as insignificant as it might first appear; that little glimmers, subdued hopes, and small poems are no less essential a part of life and of art than their grander, more openly illuminating counterparts.

Read as a totality , the "Mottetti" are records of their own obsession with finality and clarity. They are final, fixed in their forms; but the presence from which they originate and toward which they aspire is ultimately mutable and ungraspable. These occasions do not add up to the Occasion; rather, much like Dante's *Vita nuova*, they point the way to a future poetic development that will have as its explicit center the beloved and the heightened significance of her myth in the poet's search for absolute expression. In this sense we are once again on the threshold of full poetic realization that will find completion in the great love poems of *La bufera*.

The Language of Doubt

Montale's beloved mediates not between the self and God but between the self and knowledge; in this sense the poet's search is epistemological rather than theological.[32] Throughout his poetry Montale is concerned with human knowledge—of the self, of the world, of the interrelationships between the two. There are implicit in his work the questions: What can be known? How does one come to possess knowledge? Where is knowledge to be found? His poetry is neither representational (describing how things are) nor transcendental (describing how they ought to be) but investigative: it is the record of a process toward understanding. The poet does not offer up knowledge—which would imply a resolution of doubts and contradictions—but rather presents us with his struggle with contradictions in the face of experience. Critics have tended to use terms such as *negativity, pessimism,* and *desolation* to describe the poet's *Weltanschauung*, yet throughout the poetry there is also evident a strain of subdued optimism and unironic hopefulness that has been equally noted and described.[33] This fundamental oxymoron, which might be called hopeful despair or despairing hope, finds expression on many levels—thematic, philosophic, stylistic—and the overwhelming sense that one is left with is that of a poetic voice that chooses not to choose but rather to portray the synergistic interrelationship of seeming opposites. In a different context Montale himself has referred to the "permanent oxymoron" of both human and literary experience.[34]

This is not to say that the poet does not value sure knowledge, clear vision, or decisive choice; it is obvious to anyone acquainted with his work that Montale deeply values both *conoscenza* and *coscienza*, with all the meanings ascribable to these words: "knowledge," "awareness," "conscience." The contemplative struggle as presented in the poetry

57
Style as
Tension:
Love
and the
*Avventura
Stilistica*

can be understood as preparatory, as a search that seeks ultimately for liberation from sterile solipsism and fixity of both the philosophic and existential sort. The poet searches for his definitive *quid* through the process of writing; as we follow that process through the six collections of poetry it becomes clear that, for Montale, to know is to possess oneself and the world: "*sapere*, ecco ciò che conta" (*To know*, here is what counts), as he writes in "Visit to Fadin" in *La bufera e altro*.

Hölderlin, a poet greatly admired by Montale, wrote that "man, he too, as a force for knowledge, must distinguish among different worlds, because only the opposition of contraries makes knowledge possible."[35] It is the opposition of contraries that Montale's poetry most typically addresses; and it is in the irresolution of opposites or contradictory propositions that what is most essentially Montalian emerges to sustain the vitality of his poetic enterprise. Within the context of these considerations, the term *marginality* once again proves to be a useful tool for the excavation of the poet's meaning, for it is in the space between the two opposing elements of any proposition, and in the poet's consciousness as it straddles that metaphoric space, that it is possible to locate the *point de départ* for what is elaborated into a conclusive form: poetry. The poems are, of course, necessarily fixed in their final forms, but within that formal fixedness is captured the dynamic fluidity that language both embodies and denies. Montale is a poet of such technical control that his poetry often seems to be the expression of absolutely assertive and unhesitant images, thoughts, or concepts. Seems, I say, because that surface control often conceals an uncertainty of stance, a mind in process, a refusal to finalize. Montale does not trumpet forth either certainties or doubts. His understated voice demands attention to minimal elements, and this is especially true when we consider stylistic issues.

There are certain lexical and syntactical recurrences in Montale's poetry, small bits in the overall mosaic, that nevertheless shed some light on the otherwise obscure tangle that is a total human life, both as it is lived and as it is expressed in poetry. They are: (1) the presence of the adverb *forse* (perhaps) in numerous phrases of otherwise absolute positive or negative assertive value; (2) the use of *se* (if) constructions, most often governed by the words *io non so* (I do not know) or some other form of the verbs *non sapere* (not to know) or *ignorare* (to be unaware of); (3) the employment of verbs in the subjunctive mood, especially

the imperfect subjunctive of hypothetical or contrary-to-fact propositions. In a more or less inversely proportional relationship to these
usages there is the relative infrequency of constructions that assert positively and unequivocally: the rarity of the adverb *certo* (certainly), for
example, or of some positive form of the verb *sapere* (to know) in an affirmative construction (although the increased use of such positive assertive forms in the recent collections, *Satura, Diario,* and *Quaderno,*
marks one of the more significant shifts from the early triptych to the
new Montale). To give some idea of the frequency of the *forse* and of
verbs expressing doubt or ignorance, I have found that there are approx-
imately one hundred sixty uses of these words in the first five collections. The adverb *certo* and some affirmative form of *sapere* appear only
forty times in the same collections.[36] The interest lies, of course, not in
numbers but in the ways in which these structural elements contribute
to the meaning of Montale's poetry. In considering these elements one
soon sees that what might appear to be simply a number of stylistic tics
is in fact a leitmotif as typically and importantly a part of the Montalian
vision as are the *tu* and the imperative. I seek ultimately to show that
the questioning mind revealed in these stylistic choices accepts doubt
and ambivalence as necessary and inevitable and that such an attitude is
tied to fundamental issues concerning poetic ambiguity, metaphorical
expression, and the etiology of the act of writing poetry as an instrument for seeking and attaining knowledge.

Before returning to such issues in more depth, however, it is first necessary to see the specific ways in which Montale employs the elements
outlined above. As in everyday speech, *forse* is most often used by
Montale to modify statements that would otherwise express unequivocal positivity or negativity. It functions, therefore, as a mediating element between two opposite possibilities, one stated, one implied. It also
serves as a rein or check on the overt expression of great emotion and
can in this sense be read as a verbal shrug that absolves the speaker from
any absolute commitment to the viability of his assertions. There are
discernible two directions in Montale's use of *forse.* In the first he veers
away from what would otherwise be a positive or hopeful statement
through the presence of the doubtful adverb, which implies its negative
or despairing counterpart. For example in "In Limine" the speaker
urges action that is to be undertaken by the unnamed other, presumably

59
Style as
Tension:
Love
and the
*Avventura
Stilistica*

a beloved woman. In a series of imperatives—"jump out," "flee," "go"—he encourages her escape; but the outcome of her hoped-for action—salvation—is finally presented as doubtful. The precarious contingency of such a goal is emphasized in the phrase, "Se procedi t'imbatti / tu *forse* nel fantasma che ti salva" (If you proceed you will bump into / perhaps the phantasm that will save you). (All italics throughout this discussion are mine, unless otherwise indicated.) The *forse*, linked alliteratively to the *fantasma* following it as well as to the *se* construction governing the entire proposition, underlines the doubt that infuses the speaker's seemingly positive and altruistic imperatives.

Another instance of a similar construction is found, again in *Ossi*, in the poem "Arsenio." The *tu* is exhorted to action ("follow it," "descend"), but once again such action is depicted not as positively conclusive but rather as conditioned by essential doubt: ". . . quell'istante / è *forse*, molto atteso, che ti scampi / dal finire il tuo viaggio" (that instant / is perhaps, long awaited, when you will escape / from the completion of your voyage). In the last lines of the poem *forse* reappears, again within an *if* construction:

e se un gesto ti sfiora, una parola
ti cade accanto, quello è *forse*, Arsenio,
nell'ora che si scioglie, il cenno d'una
vita strozzata per te sorta . . .

and if a gesture grazes you, a word
falls near you, that is perhaps, Arsenio,
in the hour that is dissolving, the sign of a
strangled life arisen for you . . .

The similarity of emotive and philosophic attitudes manifested in these two poems is deducible not only from these same usages (urge to action conditioned by *if* and *perhaps*) but also from the dramatic settings of both, in which wind and storm act as catalysts on the poet's hesitant hopes ("the wind that enters into the garden" and "the whirlwind" in the first; "the eddies" and the "salty whirling rain cloud" of the second). Both poems rise toward excited climaxes of potentially positive breakthroughs, but the opposite, negative pull evident in the syntactical and lexical choices results in a mitigation of that positivity, in a reiningin of absolute hope. At the same time that the poet suggests a positive outcome for his characters, he undercuts that possibility. The effect is related to the conversational use of *maybe*. "Maybe not" is more or less automatically heard as a negative echo of the apparently positive assertion. This locution is also particularly revealing of the speaker's attitude not only toward his interlocutor but also toward the very words he speaks, for he is free to utter what is essentially neither fully committed nor fully disinterested. In a similar way the examples cited above are essentially positive or hopeful utterances that are nonetheless presented with full awareness of their negative counterparts. Other poems in *Ossi* that contain such an effect include: "Incontro" ("perhaps I shall once more have an aspect"); "Riviere" ("it is perhaps time to be united / in a calm port of wisdom"); and "Casa sul mare" ("perhaps only he who wishes it can become infinite"). Read these lines without the adverb *perhaps* and my point becomes clear.

The other, and opposite, effect is found in those lines in which negative and despairing propositions are attenuated by the presence of *forse*. In these instances the poet conditions his negativity in such a way that the positive echo denies the absolute status of despair and creates a sense of the value of continued hope. There is an excellent example of this effect in the short untitled poem beginning, "Forse un mattino" (Perhaps one morning), included in the "Ossi" proper. Here is painted a hallucinatory scene of existential terror; the speaker is haunted by a sense of the nullity of the world and the precariousness of his grasp on reality. He fears that nothingness will clutch at his shoulders, the void will open up behind him: "Forse un mattino andando in un'aria di vetro, / arida, rivolgendomi, vedrò compirsi il miracolo: / il nulla alle mie spalle, il vuoto dietro / di me, con un terrore di ubriaco" (Perhaps one morning going along in an air of glass, / and dry, turning around, I shall see the miracle accomplished: / the nothingness at my shoulders, the void / behind me, with a drunkard's terror). Yet because of the first word of the poem—*perhaps*—the scene is presented as conditional, and the entire experience is kept at bay. Although it might be argued that the miracle would be a sort of positive breakthrough to the essentially provisory nature of the seen world, the words "nothingness," "void," and "terror" all point to the basically negative essence of such a transport. The initial *perhaps*, therefore, allows the poet to entertain what would otherwise be an intolerable possibility if stated unconditionally.

61
Style as
Tension:
Love
and the
*Avventura
Stilistica*

Another striking example of the use of *forse* as a stay against fearful, despairing, or negative propositions is to be found in the poem "Crisalide," in which the poet struggles against the anguish of entrapment in a fixed and inescapable fate. There are many similarities between this poem and the introductory "In Limine." In both the speaker is desirous of escape for an unnamed other; here he states explicitly that he would like to make a pact with destiny in order to "atone for / the [beloved's] joy with [his] punishment." Unlike the hope expressed in "In Limine," however, in this instance the unlikelihood of success is insisted on from the beginning. The other, who is identified with reflowering nature, is seen as weak ("they are yours these meager / plants"), her rebirth "a sterile secret," "a failed miracle." The vacillation between hope and resignation comes to a climax in the penultimate stanza. What hopefulness is contained in that one *perhaps* ("perhaps all is fixed, all is written"), embedded in so many images of fatal determinism! The entire spiritual battle being waged throughout the poem is encapsulated in that word, for it expresses the tenuous hope on which the bittersweet dream of ephemeral salvation is based.[37]

Other examples of this use of *forse* include the lines "E questa che in me cresce / è forse la rancura / che ogni figliuolo, mare, ha per il padre" (And this that in me grows / is perhaps the rancor / that every son, oh sea, has for his father) from "Giunge a volte" in "Mediterraneo," and "Così / forse anche ai morti è tolto ogni riposo" (Perhaps / thus even from the dead is taken all rest) from "I morti" (The Dead). In the poem of the "Mediterranean" suite that begins, "We do not know," the poet's doubts are expressed in a series of phrases that incorporate both uses of *forse:*

forse il nostro cammino
a non tócche radure ci addurrà
dove mormori eterna l'acqua di giovinezza;
o sarà forse un discendere
fino al vallo estremo . . .
Ancora terre straniere
forse ci accoglieranno . . .

perhaps our road
to untouched glades will lead us
where murmurs eternal the water of youth;

or it will be perhaps a descent
to the last valley . . .
Once more foreign lands
perhaps will greet us . . .

In this poem the marginal position of the speaker is explicit, for he is poised between the opposing propositions, and no decisive choice of one or the other resolves the tension of doubt in which he finds himself.

It is evident from these and other moments in the first collection that the basic dichotomy that is played upon through the presence of the modifier *forse* is that which is also thematically present throughout *Ossi:* entrapment and escape. At any moment at which one is suggested the other is implied, so that we gradually come to see that in both of its functions, either as a rein on completely positive or negative visions of experience, the *forse* calls into question the absolute status of one or the other. In this context, it is useful to consider the etymology of the word. *Forse* is derived from the Latin phrase *fors sit,* from Fors, the goddess of fortune, signifying, "It might occur . . . hence, with the accessory notion of casualty."[38] Without pressing the point too heavily, I would nonetheless like to suggest that the ties with fortune, chance, and contingency as represented by the etymological background of *forse* may be considered as indirect, even subconscious substantiation of the deep personal significance such a lexical choice represents for the poet. Montale is struggling against the stifling and frightening possibility of a fatalistically predetermined existence; the repeated use of *forse* in this first collection, where the struggle is most evident, might be seen as an indication of the poet's dependence on the concept of chance. He seeks to avoid the utterance of final and unequivocal pronouncements (determined or predetermined truths) and instead transfers the responsibility to a modern Fors, whose clarity of vision is beyond the insight available to mere mortals, and antivatic poets. *Forse* is an adverb that indicates doubt, probability, approximation, attenuation.[39] In all of its functions, then, it is word that works against absolute affirmation and that tends toward understatement of an opinion, a belief, a hope. Montale's desire, as expressed in his "Imaginary Interview," to wring the neck of traditional poetic rhetoric and eloquence, understood as the language of persuasion, can be seen as at least partially fulfilled through this lexical

63
Style as
Tension:
Love
and the
Avventura
Stilistica

choice, which refuses to accommodate certainties and, therefore, the confident tone of the poet who knows.

This lexical leitmotif is not limited to the first collection of poetry. It appears numerous times throughout *Le occasioni* also; however, there is a discernible shift in the context in which it most typically appears. In this second collection the adverb is often used in conjunction with a statement having to do with a feminine figure, the memory of whom is of particular significance to the poet. Although diverse, the multiple feminine presences in this collection (Gerti, Liuba, Dora Markus, the unnamed woman of the "Mottetti" and of the poem "La casa dei doganieri") are all united by their capacity for survival and meaningful action, and the speaker is both impressed and confounded by their strength. In "Carnevale di Gerti" (Carnival of Gerti) the woman is presented as a modern-day witch or seer who believes in readable signs that clarify the future. The speaker is tempted to believe in her attempts at fortunetelling, but his skepticism is evident in the phrases: "hai ritrovato / forse la strada che tentò un istante / il piombo fuso . . ." (you have found again / perhaps the road that was suggested for an instant / by the molten lead) and "nulla torna se non forse in questi / disguidi del possibile" (nothing comes back except perhaps in these / misleadings of the possible). Dora Markus is another *tu* who confounds the poet; she is exhausted (stremata), and her heart is a "lake of indifference." Yet she endures and even exists, perhaps only because of an amulet, a tiny white ivory mouse kept in her purse: "forse / ti salva un amuleto che tu tieni / vicino alla matita delle labbra . . ." (perhaps / an amulet saves you that you keep / near your lipstick). Both of these women are in possession of some knowledge or instinct that leads to hope and possible salvation; yet Montale does not assert their superiority in an absolute manner but rather qualifies it with the small word that throws all into doubt.

The negativity of some assertions is also softened in this second collection, as it was in the first, by the use of *forse*. In the fifth "Motet," beginning, "Addii, fischi nel buio" (Farewells, whistles in the dark), for example, Montale deftly paints a scene of desolation and loss in seven short lines. Everything seems horribly automated and inhuman as the beloved departs by train, and the lover states, "Forse / gli automi hanno ragione" (Perhaps / the automatons are right). There is of course the chance that they are not right, that there is some feeling left in the world, as the doubting adverb indicates. In the poem "Stanze" (Stanzas) the poet writes of a woman who is *ignara* (unaware); she did not realize her significance in his life. Now that she is gone he attempts to describe her. But she is finally unattainable, even through description, and all that remains is darkness: "La dannazione / è forse questa vaneggiante amara / oscurità che scende su chi resta" (damnation / is perhaps this raving bitter / obscurity that descends on the one remaining). There is a similar effort at reclamation in "Nuove stanze" (New Stanzas), a poem that can be read as a companion piece to "Stanzas." There is however a certain progression toward understanding here, since the "doubt of before" (il dubbio d'un tempo) is in the last stanza replaced by an assertion of comprehension: "Today I know what you want" ("Oggi so ciò che vuoi"). The earlier doubt was the fear that perhaps even the privileged lady did not understand the meaning of events: "Il mio dubbio d'un tempo era se forse / tu stessa ignori il giuoco che si svolge / sul quadrato" (My doubt of before was that perhaps / you yourself are not aware of the game being carried out / on the square). In these lines we read three words expressing doubt—*dubbio*, *forse*, and *ignori*—and that *forse* both attenuates and yet subtly intensifies the poet's fears.

There are many more examples of usages of *forse* in this and the four remaining collections, but I shall not attempt to examine them here.[40] There are certain generalizations, however, that are applicable to the typical use of the adverb: it usually appears in a primary position, either at the end of a line, thus forming an enjambment,[41] or at the beginning of a sentence, thus modifying the entire thought that follows. It is also used most commonly in connection with the beloved woman or with some figure or occasion of great importance to the poet; almost all the poems in which it appears are of an extremely intense emotional timbre. The function as rein or check is thus in direct relationship to the intensity of the experience being recreated in verse. It is as if Montale cannot allow himself to express any absolute or unqualified exaltation or grief but must instead contemplate it as merely probable or dubious. This lexical feature contributes greatly to the understated quality of much of Montale's verse and reveals much about his contemplative bent, reinforcing as apt his self-definition in "Mediterraneo" as "uomo intento che riguarda / in sé, in altrui, il bollore / della vita fugace—uomo che

65
Style as
Tension:
Love
and the
*Avventura
Stilistica*

tarda / all'atto" (an intent man who watches / in himself, in others, the fervour / of fleeting life—a man who is slow / to act). Doubt is a particularly human experience; nature, as represented in Montale by the sea and the wind, does not, cannot embody hesitation, skepticism, self-conscious balancing between one reality and another. The pure and simple existence of the Mediterranean, which the poet would so like to emulate in the early poetry, is simply not within the grasp of the human mind, held sway by conflicting and contradictory forces. The communicative thrust in all of Montale's poetry as evidenced in the repeated use of the imperative, a direct call to the reader's involvement, and of the *tu*, the imagined or invented interlocutor, is balanced and tempered by the reticence of the poet in the face of fully confident assertion. He is no more privileged than the nonpoet in the search for sure knowledge, and we are called to listen not to certainties but rather to a voice that echoes our own consternation.

It is striking to find such a consistent attitude toward experience and knowledge throughout the six collections of poetry; even more striking is the presence of the *forse* in very early and generally unread poems, one contained in the series "Accordi" (Chords), published in the journal *Primo Tempo* in 1922 and entitled "Violini" (Violins); another unpublished until it appeared in Silvio Ramat's *Omaggio a Montale* (1966) and in an appendix to his book *Montale* (Vallecchi, 1965): "Elegia" (Elegy), dated January 26, 1918. In the latter poem, the world is seen as "a great fragile bubble of crystal" that threatens to burst if there is any movement. The last stanza reads:

Non muoverti.
Come un'immensa bolla
tutto gonfia, si leva.
E tutta questa finta realtà
scoppierà
forse.
Noi forse resteremo
Noi forse.
Non muoverti.
Se ti muovi lo infrangi.

Piangi?

Eugenio
Montale:
Poet
on
the
Edge

Don't move.
Like an immense bubble
everything is swelling, rising.
And all of this fake reality
will burst
perhaps.
We perhaps shall remain
we perhaps.
Don't move.
If you move you'll break it.

Are you crying?

Without arguing the merits or weaknesses of this early attempt by the young Montale, I would suggest that the repetition of the adverb *forse* can be read here as evidence of the poet's orientation that blossoms fully in later poems (note also the use of the negative imperative and of the implied *tu*). The poet's preference for incertitude and for the linking of opposites is even more evident in the poem "Violins," which begins: "Gioventù troppe strade / distende innanzi alle pupille / mie smarrite" (Youth too many roads / stretches forth before my eyes / [that are] confused) and continues several lines into the poem: "tutto vaneggia e nella luce nuova / volere non so più né disvolere" (everything raves and in the early light / I no longer know how to wish or to unwish). Here the young man is caught in the dilemma represented by choice; he is at the crossroads and situates himself on the ambivalent bridge between two or more possible resolutions, but no resolution is forthcoming, either then or in poems written in Montale's full maturity and old age. The poet's attitude toward this all-pervading doubt is most revealingly expressed in the final lines of "Elegy": "Forse è in questa incertezza . . . la più vera ricchezza . . ." (Perhaps in this uncertainty is the most true richness).

The second stylistic element I should like to consider is the use of *if* constructions governed by or involving the verbs *sapere* and *non sapere* (to know, not to know) and *ignorare* (to be unaware). Much the same effect is achieved through this syntactical usage as is created through the repeated *forse*, for the poet does not state that he is ignorant of something but rather that he does not know if something is as he conceives it to be. Thus a similar avoidance of positive assertion is

67
Style as
Tension:
Love
and the
*Avventura
Stilistica*

achieved, and the poet maintains his preferred position on the edge between implied resolutions of uncertain propositions. Perhaps one way of stating this preference for the assertion of nonassertive attitudes is to say that Montale typically does not even know what he does not know; thus even unequivocal negative knowledge is denied. Examples are to be found in all of the collections, but perhaps the most striking are in the third, *La bufera e altro*. In the poem "Due nel crepuscolo" (Two in the Twilight) the poet presents two people in a place surrounded by hills and infused with a soft, watery light (un chiarore subacqueo). In the third stanza we understand that the scene is a twilight one: "nel punto che resiste all'ultima / consunzione del giorno" (at the point that resists the last / consumption of the day). This twilight atmosphere is especially appropriate as a frame for the emotional and spiritual atmosphere, for a vague sense of bewilderment fills the speaker. The adjectives that describe the landscape, objects, and actions in the poem are equally applicable to the speaker himself (a process typical of Montalian objective correlation): *sfuggevole* (fleeting), *ignota* (unknown), *impallidita* (wan), *attonito* (amazed), *spenta* (spent), *molle* (soft), *tardo* (late). Although the poem is quite descriptive, it in fact paints an indescribable state that might best be called *trasognato*, a walking dream state in which nothing is clear or seizable, nothing is knowable. The *tu* to whom the poet directs his words is like a dream character: different, unrecognizable, alien. When he writes "Non so / se ti conosco" (I do not know / if I recognize you) we are at the heart of the poem; this unknowability is beautifully emphasized by the enjambment, which lengthens to infinity the not knowing, making of it the central image of the entire poem.

In "Argyll Tour" all is description—of sights and of sounds—yet the core of the experience recreated here is to be found in one phrase, placed this time within dashes: a parenthetical phrase that, as is so often true in poetry, and particularly in Montale's understated verse, is basic to our understanding of the poem.[42] In the midst of the description we read: "catene che s'allentano / —ma le tue le ignoravo—" (chains that slacken / —but yours I was unaware of —). What these chains refer to is less important than the fact that the poet expresses his ignorance of their significance, an ignorance that is not relieved by the senses, by that which is seizable, describable, knowable: "i bimbi" (the children), "il puledrino" (the pony); "odor di sego / e di datteri" (odor of tallow / and of dates); "oscene risa" (obscene laughs).

The poem "Il sogno del prigioniero" (The Prisoner's Dream), which concludes the third collection, also makes use of the verb *ignorare*, this time in a bitterly self-parodic manner. The metaphoric prison described in the poem is finally a prison of existential uncertainty alleviated only by dreams ("sleeping I believe myself to be at your feet"; "my dream of you is not ended"). The prisoner performs a series of actions ("I sniffed," "I looked around me," "I got up," "I fell down again"), but they are ultimately futile gestures that do nothing to relieve his basic uncertainty concerning how it will all turn out in the end: "e ancora ignoro se sarò al festino / farcitore o farcito" (and still I am unaware if I shall be at the feast / the stuffer or the stuffed). In this grotesque image is contained the full force of Montale's total existential doubt.

The poet's inability to know is most often connected with his pursuit of the beloved. She is the essential object of his mnemonic search, and it is in the poem "L'orto" (The Garden) that Montale's inability to seize her is expressed more insistently, and perhaps more beautifully, than in all the other love lyrics.[43] The phrase *io non so* (I do not know) is repeated five times in "The Garden" in an anaphoric construction that controls the extended sentence of which the first two stanzas (twenty-six lines) are made up. The phrase is repeated four times before what is not known is expressed; between the first and the second *I do not know* the scene itself is described: "nel chiuso / dei meli lazzeruoli" (in the enclosure / of the crab-trees). Between the second and the third the locale is specified as a garden: "nell'orto / dove le ghiande piovono" (in the garden / where the acorns rain down). Between the third and the fourth the lady's footsteps and their significance to the poet are mentioned. Finally, after the fourth *I do not know*, the sentence is grammatically and semantically completed—"io non so se il tuo passo che fa pulsar le vene / . . . / è quello che mi colse un'altra estate" (I do not know if your steps which make my veins pulse / . . . / are those that struck me another summer)—and again after the fifth—"io non so se la mano che mi sfiora la spalla / è la stessa" (I do not know if the hand that grazes my shoulder / is the same). This repetitive construction thus builds climactically toward the resolution of the long sentence: an admission of ignorance that in this case serves to point out the lady's transcendental and overwhelming otherness as a messenger from another realm. In other words the unknowability of the beloved is now her

69
Style as
Tension:
Love
and the
*Avventura
Stilistica*

most knowable quality: she who can read time like a book, she who is God's favorite, she who has a "hard crystal glance" and an "amethyst heart" that allow her to see "straight to the core" of events where the poet's limited understanding can never reach.

The fervor of this poem culminates in an affirmation in the final stanza, in an indubious statement of certainty expressed in the word *certo* (certainly). It is a statement that strikes us as being that much more powerful, following as it does the long repetition of negative and hesitant doubt of the preceding stanzas. The word *certo* leaps out at the reader as an anomaly and, as such, a victory of great proportions. But sadly, and appropriately to Montale, it is a certainty couched in a conditional contrary-to-fact construction that negates the possibility of its realization:

> . . . Se la forza
> che guida il disco *di gid inciso* fosse
> un'altra, certo il tuo destino al mio
> congiunto mostrerebbe un solco solo.

> . . . If the force
> that guides the *already cut* record were
> another, certainly your destiny to mine
> joined would show one single groove.

The poetics of doubt as expressed in assertions such as "I do not know" and "perhaps" becomes defensible and indeed inevitable in the face of a destiny understood as a cut record of temporal and spatial constrictions, a destiny that cannot be modified except through dreams and through the alternative life that poetry alone can create.

In *Ossi di seppia* there are several instances in which the poet gives a kind of essential weight or assertive value to his not knowing, as in the "Osso" that begins "Ciò che di me sapeste" (That which you knew of me). In the fourth stanza of that poem Montale writes: "Restò così questa scorza / la vera mia sostanza; / il fuoco che non si smorza / per me si chiamò: l'ignoranza" (Thus remained this rind / [as] my true substance; / the fire that does not die out / for me was called: ignorance). And again in the poem that begins, "Tentava la vostra mano la tastiera" (Your hand played over the keyboard) the lover assumes the lady's inability to sight-read some unknown piece as a sign of his own

inability to find words to express himself: "Nessuna cosa prossima tro-
vava le sue parole, / ed era mia, era *nostra*, la vostra dolce ignoranza"
(No proximate thing could find its words, / and it was mine, was *ours*,
your sweet ignorance). What is perhaps the most famous of Montale's
expressions of ignorance is to be found in the poem in *Le occasioni* entitled "La casa dei doganieri" (The Customs House), justly considered
to be one of his greatest. The last line of this haunting poem is the simple yet powerful "Ed io non so chi va e chi resta" (And I do not know
who goes and who remains behind).

There are instances, especially in the recent collections *Satura,
Diario del '71 e del '72*, and *Quaderno di quattro anni* (Notebook of
Four Years) in which knowledge is positively asserted. That knowledge,
however, as in "L'orto," is most often painful: it does not lead to the
breakthrough or escape from solipsism and predestination that the poet
seeks but rather confirms his belief that he—unlike Gerti, Dora
Markus, or Clizia—is doomed to a prison of self-conscious entrapment
in contradiction. In the first poem of *Diario del '71 e del '72*, "A Leone
Traverso" (To Leone Traverso), Montale writes: "Mai fu gaio / né
savio né celeste il mio sapere" (Never was it gay / or wise or celestial,
my knowledge). It is true that whatever the poet asserts positively as
knowledge is usually not gay or celestial but rather sad and profoundly
of this world. Usually the knowledge is given to others, as in "Botta e
risposta I" (Thrust and Parry I), a prefatory poem to *Satura*, in which
the poet writes a poetic autobiography in response to the beloved's letter. He writes of a life spent in the Augean stables, of a divinity that
never appeared, of his attempts at liberation from existential horror and
his failure. The final line of the poem sums up what may be known
from all this: "ora sai che non può nascere l'aquila / dal topo (now
you know that the eagle cannot be born / of the mouse). Sad knowledge indeed. In the lovely thirteenth poem of "Xenia I" Montale writes
of his late wife's brother, who "died young," and who "wrote unpublished, unheard music." The poet loves this boy whom he has never
known and says to Mosca: "Ma è possibile, / lo sai, amare un'ombra,
ombre noi stessi" (But it is possible, / you know, to love a ghost, ghosts
that we ourselves are). In poem 5 of "Xenia II" Montale again writes to
his late wife, stating that their journey together is over and that he always walked next to her and gave her his arm as they descended stair-
cases because "[sapevo] che di noi due / le sole vere pupille, sebbene

71
Style as
Tension:
Love
and the
*Avventura
Stilistica*

tanto offuscate, / erano le tue" ([I knew] that of us two / the only real
eyes, even though so cloudy, / were yours). And in poem 14 of "Xenia
I" the poet asserts the sameness of opposites, a sameness that his wife
alone understood: "You alone knew [sapevi] that motion / is not different from stasis, / that the empty is the full and the serene / is the most
diffuse of clouds." This merging helps him to understand her death;
and yet even this knowledge is finally useless: "Eppure non mi dà riposo / sapere che in uno o in due noi siamo una sola cosa" (And yet it
gives me no rest / to know that in one or in two we are one sole thing).
Knowledge gives no repose, provides no comfort, when it is knowledge
come too late.

Satura's "Il primo gennaio" (The First of January) is a counterpoint
melody to the earlier poem "L'orto"; in the former, the repeated *so* [I
know] is a reverse echo of the *non so*'s of the latter. The more recent
poem is again written to a beloved woman whose laughter "explodes,"
and who is an "innocent / unaware animal." The poem is also structured around the anaphoric repetition of a word—this time *so*. Again
what is known is neither gay nor celestial but is rather a series of quan-
daries created by the insouciant woman: "So che non c'è magia / di fil-
tro o d'infusione / che possano spiegare come di te s'azzuffino / dita e
capelli" (I know that there is no magic / of potion or infusion / that
might explain how they fight, / your fingers and hair); "So che quello
che afferri, / . . . / brucia e non se n'accorge" (I know that that which
you grasp, / . . . / burns and is unaware of it). All the knowledge of the
woman that the poet possesses is of a profoundly private and even contradictory nature. Montale knows only that knowledge of this sort does
not serve to describe and thus to possess the absent beloved any more
than did the lack of it in the poem of many years before.

The shift away from a struggle with contradiction, as seen in the
three earlier collections, to an acceptance of the inevitability of unresolved paradox, seen in the latest three, is apparent in the increased emphasis on summary statements that distill the essence of what Montale
has come to know through his long life and career as poet. Yet, as is
evident in the above examples, that knowledge tends to be expressed in
terms of unresolvable paradoxes. The cumulative effect is similar to
Montaigne's "que sais-je?" rather than a clear knowing that leads to
comfort, absolute clarity, or unquestioned engagement in life. What
was once seen as choice, between imprisonment and escape or stasis

and action, is now stated as a necessary resignation to the impossibility of resolving conflict through unilateral choice, or what might be understood as a shift from *forse* to *fosse* (were it so), from potentiality to the unattainable contrary-to-fact in which so many of Montale's expressions of desired certainty are couched.

The subjunctive in Italian is a powerful and subtle resource; its usage, although formally dictated in great part by established rules, is nonetheless open to the expressive whims of the speaker. There is, for example, a great difference in meaning and effect between the phrases "penso che Dio esiste" (I think God exists) and "penso che Dio esista" (I think God may exist) or between a wish stated in the indicative— "voglio andarci" (I want to go there)— and in the subjunctive—"magari fossi lì!" (If only I were there!). With some important exceptions the subjunctive is conspicuous in Montale's three early collections for its rare appearances, except in those turns of phrase in which it is required grammatically. In the three recent collections it appears much more frequently, and in more diverse usages, indicating one of the significant stylistic innovations of the new Montale. An insistence on the dubitative force of this mood is to be found in *Satura, Diario,* and *Quaderno* that is not present in the early poems, where instead the subjunctive of hypothesis and volition most commonly appears.

In the "Ossi" proper the program poem that begins, "Non chiederci la parola" (Do not ask of us the word), includes the first truly noticeable use of the subjunctive, a use that recalls its single appearance in the preceding poem, "I limoni" (The Lemon Trees): "il filo da disbrogliare che finalmente ci *metta* / nel mezzo di una verità" (the thread to untangle that finally *might put* us / in the midst of a truth). In this line (my italics), and in the first and last stanzas of "Non chiederci," we read the subjunctive of hypothetical existence, which also has strong volitional force. This is a usage that expresses lack: the speaker is looking for something or someone he does not possess but the existence of which is willed or desired. The first and last stanzas of "Non chiederci" are constructed entirely around negatives and this particular brand of subjunctive: "Non chiederci la parola che squadri" (Don't ask of us the word that might square); "lo dichiari" (might declare it); "risplenda" (might shine); "Non domandarci la formula che mondi possa aprirti" (Do not demand of us the formula that might open worlds to you); ciò che *non* siamo, ciò che *non* vogliamo" (that which we are *not,* that which we do

73
Style as
Tension:
Love
and the
*Avventura
Stilistica*

not want). The middle stanza, bracketed as it is by these subjunctive and negative verb forms that emphasize their hypothetical quality, illustrates grammatically what it portrays in its image of the self-assured man: the assurance projected by the indicative of factual assertion—"se ne va sicuro" (goes along sure of himself); "non cura" (does not care); "stampa" (stamps)—to which the man is firmly anchored. In this poem the subjunctive in and of itself makes clear the nonexistence of the word and the formula and seconds the appropriateness of the poet's refusal to entertain demands for their coming into being through poetry. Yet there is a fundamental paradox created by the negatives and antifactual subjunctives upon which the poem is built. The poet does not simply state that the word does not exist; he summons it out of its basic non-existence, even while simultaneously banishing it from the realm of the real, by tying it to the subjunctive form that follows it. The construction has almost a conjuring power, much like the imperative (*fiat lux* is perhaps the prime example). This is clearly not logical discourse; the subjunctive employed in this way both posits the existence of its subject and at the same time places it in a space that can only be called antiindicative, where it lacks factual or even subjective concreteness.

Susanne Langer, discussing Freud's principle of ambivalence, writes: "In literature, the words 'no,' 'not,' 'never,' etc., occur freely; but what they deny is thereby created. In poetry there is no negation, but only contrast." She gives as an example Swinburne's "The Garden of Proserpine," in which a series of denials leads up to the "final assurance": "Only the sleep eternal / In an eternal night." Langer asserts that this poem ends with only "one positively stated reality, Sleep."[44] I think that the process of negation to be found in Montale's poem also implies contrast (most obviously with vatic poetry). But it finally goes one step farther along the road of ultimately unresolved ambivalence, for the negatives culminate not in a contrasting positivity, as in the Swinburne poem, but in a final negative ("ciò che *non* siamo, ciò che *non* vogliamo"), which is not a resolution or a filling up of the lack created by the preceding lines but rather an intensification of that lack. We are not told what it is that poets are not or what they do not want; we are given no final assurance except that of continued nonpositivity. The only positively stated aspect of the poet's art—"sì qualche storta sillaba e secca come un ramo" (if only some twisted syllable and dry like a branch)—is of an entirely formalistic, even purely auditory nature. It avoids altogether the epistemological and existential implications of the hypothetical "word" of the first stanza, which might, if it existed, provide form not only for poetry but also for the human soul: "l'animo nostro informe" (our formless soul). The final paradox of this poem, then, is that it *is* a poem, in spite of its essential denial of its own ontological status. It is a sort of double negative that adds up to a positive, but only because its negative charge—its message and its formally negative structural components—finds expression in the undeniable presence, or positivity, of words on a page. The result is akin to the oxymoronic presence-absence by which the "Mottetti" are animated and also to the ambivalence expressed by *forse* and the dubitative verb forms. In all these instances the question is not one of simple contrast or the merging of opposites; rather there is a concentration on lacks—of knowledge, of existential certainties, of a beloved person—that become the fullness of created expression: poetry.

As can be seen in this early poem, language itself is at the center of Montale's uncertainty. His interest in and perplexed relationship to human utterance in the form of poetry are evident from the very first, not only in this explicitly metapoetic text but also in the "Mediterraneo" suite. In it Montale is obviously preoccupied with the musical potential of poetry, and he greatly exploits the lyrical possibilities of the Italian language. In writing later of his goals during the composition of the poems that would make up *Ossi di seppia*, Montale stated that his "desire for adherence remained musical, instinctive, nonprogrammatic." The poet also insisted on the importance of the sea, asserting that "in the *Ossi di seppia* everything was attracted and absorbed by the tumultuous sea . . ."[45] The focus would seem to have been primarily on sound rather than sense. This is borne out in the poet's descriptions of the sea, which are concerned overwhelmingly with its sonorities rather than its colors, emphasizing its auditory rather than its visual pull on the young man. As we read through the nine poems of the "Mediterranean" suite we begin to hear the sea more than to see it through such phrases as: "un suono d'agri lazzi" (sound of harsh play); "più sordo o meno il ribollio dell'acque" (more muffled or less the seething of the waters); "voce / che esce dalle tue bocche quando si schiudono / come verdi campane" (voice / that comes forth from your mouths when they open / like green bells); "la tua musica" (your music); "la tua pagina rombante" (your seething page). It is as if we were sharing in a blind

75
Style as
Tension:
Love
and the
*Avventura
Stilistica*

man's reponse to the sea, felt and internalized as pure sound. The poet's relationship to this sound is one based on admiration and, more importantly, envy, which becomes in one of the poems the rancor of the son toward his superior father.

For poets language is very much sound as well as sense: one might even say sound over sense. For Montale, who had nourished early hopes for a career as a singer and who has insisted throughout his career as a poet on the importance of music to his verse, I think the attraction of pure sound cannot be minimized. (Think too of his early suite *Chords*, in which he sought to imitate the sounds of musical instruments in his verse.) Montale has continuously expressed his belief in the identification of poetry with music: "poetry, [which] in itself is already music, a music of second rank worthy, or unworthy, of the first"[46]; "I know that the art of the word is also music, although it has little to do with the laws of acoustics."[47] Speaking of his last three collections and the changes in them from the first three Montale stated that "there is the fact of ear, of musical ear (the critics do not pay enough attention to it): I wanted to play the piano in another way, a more silent, more discreet way."[48] And in his Nobel Prize speech the poet wrote that poetry originally was born from "the necessity of joining a vocal sound (the word) to the beat of the first tribal music. Only much later could word and music be written in some way and thus differentiated. Written poetry appears, but the common parentage with music makes itself felt . . . slowly poetry becomes visual because it paints images, but it is also musical; it joins two arts in one."[49]

The poems of "Mediterranean" are both an embodiment and at the same time a denial of the lyrical, auditory enchantments of poetry. From their initial appearance critics have spoken of their great lyricism: Sergio Solmi wrote of their "high, very musical rhetoric"; Alfredo Gargiulo found them to be the most important poems of the collection because of their great music; Silvio Ramat wrote of "stylistic inventions (and here often musical ones)"; Marco Forti stated that they are "the most richly orchestrated and most sonorous series of the book . . ."[50] Interestingly though, Montale himself called the suite a "disintegration."[51] Many years later when asked his opinion of the "so very contrasting judgments which critics have made of ["Mediterranean"]"— such as Contini's rejection of Gargiulo's positive opinion, instead calling the "Ossi" the most important series in the collection—the poet gave a characteristically noncommittal response: "There was no preliminary idea, I continued to write until I exhausted the subject. Frankly I couldn't say which of the critics might be right; and then critics, if they live a long time, often change their minds."[52] The myth of the sea and its significance to Montale's later poetry that are here initiated cannot be minimized; but I do not think that only the subject was exhausted in these nine poems. The ambition to write a musically inspired and nurtured poetry is also exorcised here, as the symphonic wholeness of the sea's great voice is understood to be beyond the grasp of human language if it is to be more than auditively seductive. Not that music will become completely extraneous to Montale's poetry, for this is clearly not possible and certainly not desirable, but that the nonverbal art form—music—will become a subsidiary of the chosen verbal one—poetry. What might be understood as the hierarchy in the young poet's mind will finally be reversed, with words accepted in both their positive and negative potential and melody made of pure sound understood as unavailable to speech.

The early primary attachment to music is clear throughout Montale's "Intervista immaginaria," in which he writes of his beginnings as a poet. The pages spill over with references to music, metaphorical and analogous images of poetry as music, poet as musician: "I wrote my first verses as a boy . . . But I did not publish and I was not convinced of myself. More concrete and stranger ambitions occupied me. I was then studying in order to make my début in the part of Valentino, in Gounod's Faust"; "A poet must not ruin his voice 'sol-faing' [solfeggiando] too much . . ."; "I obeyed a need of musical expression"; "Le occasioni were an orange, or better, a lemon lacking a slice: not exactly that of pure poetry in the sense I indicated above, but in that of pedale, of deep music . . ."[53] Voce (voice) is also a word the poet uses repeatedly in referring to the art of poetry. The connection between the two arts that he felt from the first years of his writing career was reasserted fifty years later in the Nobel Prize speech. Montale told me in a conversation a few years ago that music is much more important to his poetry than critics had ever thought or investigated. Montale's love for the musical, sonorous, purely auditory aspects of poetry is nowhere more explicitly revealed than in the "Mediterranean" poems, and nowhere more decidedly rejected as an impossible love. The sea, padre (father), possesses this music "in which nature and art are mingled" naturally

77
Style as
Tension:
Love
and the
Avventura
Stilistica

and irrevocably, just as a human father possesses the mother, who is thus forever forbidden union with the son. Rather than *rancor* Montale might well have written *hate*, more precisely *love-hate* when attempting to define his relationship to this paternal source of inspiration and emulation.

If, then, this essential music is not within the reach of the poet's art, that art must be viewed as partial, lacking, marginal. Montale's fundamental sense of inferiority is clearly expressed in the descriptive phrases ascribed to the sea and to the poet; the former possesses a "solenne ammonimento" (solemn warning) in contrast to the "piccino fermento" (teeny ferment)[54] in the poet's heart ("Antico, sono ubriacato" [Ancient One, I am drunk]). The sea is "vastness"; its "delirium" transcends time and space to reach the stars; while the poet's life and art are inescapably tied to the limits of individual consciousness. The last two poems of the suite express the poet's resigned acceptance of this difference. In the penultimate all of the force of the ambivalent love-hate explodes in the first word, *potessi* (if I could only). This is a subjunctive verb form, the contrary-to-fact imperfect subjunctive that Montale uses sparingly and always at especially crucial points. More than this, it is the verb *potere* (to be able) that carries the heavy semantic weight of this form of impossible longing.[55] By using this verb in the subjunctive form Montale makes clear his complete inability to accomplish what he would so wish to: to bring his own "balbo parlare" (stammering speech) up to the level of the sea's perfect and limitless eloquence.

In many other instances throughout Montale's poetry his use of the verb *potere* is revealing of his sense of inadequacy, both existential and artistic. The first subjunctive contrary-to-fact form of it appears in the "Osso" that begins, "Ciò che di me sapeste" (That which you knew of me), a poem that emphasizes the muted partiality of the poet's existence. In an implied oxymoron the poet's surface or rind (scorza) *is* his core or essence (vera . . . sostanza). In the last two lines of the poem Montale writes to his beloved of an impossible desire, that he might "detach" this "shadow self" and give it to her as a gift: "Potessi spiccarla da me, / offrirvela in dono." The verb form emphasizes the absolute impossibility of the fulfillment of such a desire. In the "Motet" that begins, "Molti anni" (Many years), the form again appears at a moment of great emotion, when the lover wishes he could fix the beloved's return as printed words on a banner and then descend into a whirlpool of eternal fidelity to her:

> Imprimerli potessi sul palvese
> che s'agita alla frusta del grecale
> in cuore . . . E per te scendere in un gorgo
> di fedeltà, immortale.

> If I only could imprint them on the banner
> that waves at the lash of the North Wind
> in my heart . . . And for you descend into a whirlwind
> of fidelity, immortal.

When the verb *potere* is used in the indicative it is typically in a negative, conditional, or limited construction and thus similarly captures the poet's sense of impotence, as in "Non chiederci la parola" (Do not ask of us the word): "Codesto solo oggi possiamo dirti" (This alone today are we able to say to you).[56] Other examples are "potrei prestarti un volto" (could I but lend you a face) in "Serenata Indiana" of *La bufera*; and "Lo sai: debbo riperderti e non posso" (You know: I must lose you again and I cannot) in the first "Motet." The impotence contained in these lines is linked most explicitly to language itself in the penultimate poem of "Mediterranean," for there we read that the poet has only "le lettere fruste / dei dizionari" (worn-out words / of dictionaries) and "frasi stancate" (exhausted sentences), in direct contrast to the powerful words of the sea.

The ephemeral quality of words is perfectly captured in an image of the last poem of the sea suite, when Montale writes: "Dissipa tu se lo vuoi / questa debole vita che si lagna, / come la spugna il frego / effimero di una lavagna" (Cancel if you wish / this weak life that complains, / like the sponge the fleeting / line on a blackboard). Poetry is mere traces, labile signs that can at will be expunged by the "salty words / in which nature and art mingle" of the sea. Montale's recognition of this fundamental inferiority and his decision to continue writing in spite of it are manifest in these lines from the final poem:

> Presa la mia lezione
> più che dalla tua gloria
> aperta, dall'ansare

79
Style as
Tension:
Love
and the
*Avventura
Stilistica*

che quasi non dà suono
di qualche tuo meriggio desolato,
a te mi rendo in umiltà . . .

Having taken my lesson
more than from your open
glory, from the panting
that almost gives forth no sound
of one of your desolate noons,
to you I give myself over in humility . . .

"That almost gives forth no sound": this is not complete capitulation to silence, from the beginning a tempting solution for this poet, but rather a resigned and yet resolute embrace of a poetics of muted expression that cannot equal the open glory of pure music. If the sea, the element of water, with all its symbolic weight of purity, life-giving power, and fluidity, is outside the grasp of the human instrument, language, then the poet must turn to another element. This he does, with great implications for the future elaboration of his poetry, in the final lines of the last poem of "Mediterraneo," where he writes: "Non sono / che favilla d'un tirso. Bene lo so: bruciare, / questo, non altro, è il mio significato" (I am / only a spark of a beacon. Well I know it: to burn, / this, nothing else, is my meaning). Thus fire is substituted for water—fire, which is perhaps superior to water as a symbol of potential creativity but also inferior in that water can extinguish its force, destroy its being. Nonetheless Montale embraces it as his element and finally as the element most intimately connected to the beloved woman who is "scintilla" (spark) as he also is "favilla" (spark).

As I have said, the subjunctive mood appears rarely in the first collections, but never is it of small import. A brief suite of poems entitled "Notizie dall'Amiata" (News from Amiata) concludes the second collection, *Le occasioni*. In the second poem of this suite there is to be found another instance of a significant subjunctive. In these poems the longing to seize the beloved and to achieve immortality with or through her, expressed so chivalrously, even lightly, in the "Motet" that begins, "Many years," is now transformed into despairing awareness of the utter impossibility of fulfilling such a desire. The privacy of the poet's love as represented in the image of the room, hermetic and void of contact with the outside world except in those signs that penetrate through, bearing to him something of the woman's continued reality, is now invaded by the realization of the broader implications of a personal suffering.

The first poem of "Notizie" harkens back to the solipsistic exclusivity of love as expressed in the "Motets"; the lover is once again in his room, from which he writes to the lady, waiting for her "icon" to be revealed to him. But this attempt to keep her all to himself is clearly a failed one, as the second poem in the suite makes clear. It begins "E tu seguissi" (Would that you were following), in a locution that at first appears to echo the simple desire for her presence that informs many of the earlier love poems. But the desire for her now extends far beyond repossession, for that which the poet wishes she too were following are "le fragili architetture / annerite dal tempo" (the fragile architecture / blackened by time) and "l'alluccioĺio / della Galassia, la fascia d'ogni tormento" (the glittering / of the Galaxy, the wrapper around every torment). Time and the galaxy are inclusive images that take over the suite's development until, in the last poem, the torment is no longer private but rather the universal desolation of all living things in which the solitary lover shares. Now the contrary-to-fact form is truly contrary to fact: the lady is not with him, the dribble of time cannot be stopped ("il gocciolìo . . . ; il tempo fatto acqua") and all that is left is the "trickle of pity" (filo di pietà) at which the porcupines drink. The finality sought throughout the "Motets" is attained here, for the purely private, hermetic experience of love of that season must end if not in reunion with the beloved in real time and space then in a realization of the impossibility of such a reunion. Life itself is basically hostile toward the fragile inner life of the poet. As Almansi and Merry conclude, "Emotion and experience are contradictory."[57] Here, as in the poem that begins, "Would that I could force," of "Mediterranean," in "Would that you were following," of "News from Amiata," the adversative conjunction ma (but) establishes once and for all the opposition of desire and reality: "but it is not so." (In the poem from "Mediterranean" the conjunction is even more strongly adversative: invece, or "instead.") As with the use of forse, in these structures we find (desired) thesis and (lived) antithesis, with no possibility of a reconciling synthesis of the two.

I believe that the most powerful and heart rending of all the contrary-to-fact subjunctives in Montale's poetry is to be found in the stu-

81
Style as
Tension:
Love
and the
*Avventura
Stilistica*

pendous poem "L'orto." As I have discussed, the anaphoric construction of the poem builds on the repeated "I don't know's" of its extended syntactical sweep (four stanzas, three sentences) and inevitably carries the reader headlong into the climax of the unforgettable last stanza, which begins: "O labbri muti, aridi dal lungo / viaggio per il sentiero fatto d'aria ..." (Oh lips mute, dry from the long / voyage along the path made of air). Inevitable also is the final image of the complete separation of lover and beloved, for by now the lady is no longer a woman but a "messenger / who come[s] down," far beyond the privately shared past intimacy evoked in the first two stanzas. The final lines of the poem are the expression of the only certainty available to the lover: that were it possible, he and the beloved would be united in their destinies. It is not possible, however; like identical parallel lines they are fated to be forever apart in their sameness, perhaps to meet only at infinity. The musical motif so often associated with the woman in the "Motets" and in other earlier poems is again present in these final lines, but it is now the mechanical registering of music, the record, rather than a harmonious melody that serves as the basis for the metaphor of inexorably divided fates. It is in this final image that we find the contrary-to-fact verb form that captures so perfectly the poet's longing as well as his awareness of its impossibility: "Se la forza / ... *fosse* / un'altra ..."(If the force / ... were / another). The enjambments in these final lines bring out the full meaning of the phrase: if the force were another (total alterity is, of course, an ontological impossibility) and not merely more accommodating of human needs than it is, then the lover's destiny and the lady's would show a single groove ("certainly your destiny to mine / joined would show one single groove"), joined forever—precisely what the enjambment between *mine* and *joined* shows is not possible. This is a great image that, in spite of the separation that the very words and construction assert, speaks of a profound union, a certainty that cannot be diminished even by the poet's own eroding doubts.

In all the stylistic elements discussed in this chapter—the oxymoronic basis of the "Mottetti," the frequent appearance of the adverb *forse* and of verbs of ignorance, and the rare but essential contrary-to-fact subjunctive as it is woven into the fabric of the first three collections—it is possible to discern the essence of the poetic universe of this Montale, or, to appropriate one of the poet's own metaphors for these early collections, to read the *recto* with a sense of its continuity and development. As with a human life, however, the extractable essence is not the life itself but only one way of understanding that life. It is clear that Montale is doubt-ridden, yet he sustains his belief in poetry as "one of the very many possible positivities of life" in spite of its necessary reliance on the imperfect means of expression available to man in linguistic structures. That belief is in turn sustained by the beloved, whose presence-absence provides the fuel for some of the most memorable and perfect of Montale's poems.

That Montale is assailed by doubt—concerning himself, experience, the world, language itself—is a fact that has been generally recognized by critics since the appearance of *Ossi di seppia*. In this way he partakes of and exemplifies the sensibility that permeates the art of the last fifty years or more, an art that has tended increasingly toward a self-questioning, an emphasis on its own limitations, and an acceptance of the essential marginality of the artist in confident, industrial, consumer-oriented societies. In addition to his constitutional sense of reality as an ultimately unseizable concept, the poet also expresses in his art an awareness of this general marginality of poetic production; his response is to embrace it and to state that poetry is "an absolutely useless product, but almost never harmful."[58] Useless, harmless, it is therefore outside the structures of utility and power upon which modern societies are built and sustain themselves. But to be useless and harmless is not to be nonexistent. It is inevitable that Montale should adopt this attitude toward his own writing of poetry, given the political and cultural milieu into which he was born, and given his personal preference for privacy and his horror of the commingling of political, sociological, and economic considerations with artistic ones. He is in this sense a hermetic poet and has always been open to attacks on his ivory towerism, his noninvolvement characterized as a flight from an engaged stance.[59] Critics who admire his poetry have often tried to defend him from these attacks by politicizing his art or by searching for and finding messages of humanitarian or historical content that I do not believe are present.[60] What Montale has written about from the very beginning—his landscapes, his desire to escape from the prison of his own existential and intellectual limits, love, the potentialities of poetic expression—are all issues of great pertinence to a modern public. But the poet does not

83
Style as
Tension:
Love
and the
Avventura
Stilistica

choose them as such; rather he is chosen by them. His doubt-ridden poetry exists not in the service of message but of form, not of timeliness but of the timelessness of fully realized art.

Montale's poetry begins on the edges—that uncertain space in which it seeks to define its own being. The poet conceives of his poetry as nonrepresentational, as "more a means of knowledge than of representation." But he also rejects the definition of his verse as philosophical poetry, as that which "spreads ideas." Rather than the diffusion of ideas or truths it is "the search for a specific truth, not for a general truth" that he believes is the primary activity of the poet.[61] His specific truth is centered on the experience of love; but as in Dante and Petrarch his beloved is absolutely unattainable in any but linguistic terms. His faith in the lady becomes, therefore, faith in the poetry by and through which the poet's search for his truth is carried out. Any human activity—and the writing of poetry is certainly such—must have human motivations and antecedents; a sort of bloodless, utterly pure dedication of self to Art is as alien to Montale as it was to poets as philosophically oriented as the *stilnovisti* or as technically obsessed as Petrarch. That is, there can be no simplistic distinction between Montale's formal aspirations to absolute expression and his need, both personal and widely shared, to find some existential and emotional anchor in love. Indeed the poet himself has commented, concerning his shift in tone and theme from the early collections to the recent poetry: "Perhaps I realized that I could not go on singing the praises of Clizia, and of the Vixen and Iris, who after all no longer existed in my life."[62] The existence or nonexistence of these women as such is not the issue, of course. Rather the fuel that they provided and that fired Montale's poetic activity for so long has been used up, the stylistic adventure is over, and other motivations must be found if Montale is not to adopt the solution of Mallarmé, "who in the last ten years of his life no longer wrote poetry."

Montale did not adopt this solution, of course. We have three collections of poetry to show that he indeed found and exploited other fuel. This is not to say that the beloved have been entirely abandoned but rather that these poetic ladies are no longer centers of the new poetry. Instead the subjects of poetry itself, language, and Montale's deep skepticism concerning the epistemological potential of poetry come to the fore as the primary raw materials of his second season. Love is no longer represented as providing a possible escape route from the prison of life.

Fire and Ashes

The motif of fire, introduced obliquely in *Ossi di seppia* and subsequently developed in *Le occasioni* (especially in the link between the light or flash of hope and the beloved established in the "Motets"), reaches its climax in the fire of Clizia-Iris, the poetic figure of *La bufera e altro*, who is in the poet's words "the sphinx [who] returns" in order to lend her transcendental strength to the poet, the modern-day "Nestorian."[63]

In *Ossi di seppia* fire is not yet directly connected to the lady; rather it is relative to or evocative of the dry, hot summer season that establishes the atmosphere of these early poems. In "Falsetto" the young girl Esterina "burn[s] her limbs in the sun"; in "Minstrels" the poet's heart is spoken to as that which "burn[s] / . . . among the slates of summer." In the "Ossi" proper several poems include naturalistic images of fire and heat: the "scorching wall" of "Nooning"; the "scorching heat" of the poem that begins, "Glory of the extended midday"; "the parched garden" and the "sultry weather" of "The Canebrake." In the "Mediterranean" suite such images also abound: "the sultry weather" (poem 1); "in the land where the sun cooks" (poem 2); "the earth that sends forth sparks" (poem 5). In the poem "Scirocco" there is the "burnt countryside" and in "Eclogue" "these saturnalia of heat"; "Chrysalis" speaks of the "sultry noon" and "Moire" of "the sun that flames." Further examples can be found in "Delta," "Meeting," and "Coasts." In all of these instances the heat is the real heat of the sun and summer air that serves to create the merciless, penetrating aridity of this poetic landscape. Yet already in the *Ossi* there is established a connection between the naturalistic and the metaphysical, and as Maggi Rombi notes: "To light, to burning are in fact continually connected life, time, existence . . ."[64] One of the most obvious of these ties is that of the heat and sun of midday with the existential momentousness of that hour. This interpenetration of the naturalistic and the symbolic is deepened in the next two collections through the development of the feminine figure whose "sure fire" becomes the emblem of positive life, in contrast to the dark,

85
Style as
Tension:
Love
and the
*Avventura
Stilistica*

unilluminated death of the spirit, which threatens to overwhelm her faithful admirer. There is, then, a significant shift from the images of fire and light in *Ossi* to those of *Le occasioni* and *La bufera*. In the first they typically emphasize what is negative and static in human existence, in contrast to the positive force of the sea and the wind, while in the next two collections they suggest the positivity of hope and dedication to an illuminated and illuminating ideal.[65]

As I have already discussed, the woman becomes explicitly connected with images of light and brightness in the "Mottetti"; yet in poems that appeared before the "Mottetti" the motif of fire and its deep spiritual significance for the poet had already begun to emerge. For example Gerti in the poem "Carnevale di Gerti" is forever linked in our minds with the "piombo fuso," the molten metal with which she seeks to divine her and the poet's future. Liuba carries with her "il gatto / del focolare" (the cat / of the hearth), a homey image of the life-giving and sustaining fireplace. The image of possible salvation in "The Customs House" is a fiery one as well: the "light of the tanker," which "is lit up / rarely." In the companion pieces "Stanzas" and "New Stanzas" the woman is described in terms having to do with fire. In the first the poet discerns "a last corolla / of light ash that does not endure / but, scattered, precipitates." In the second the smoke of her cigarette forms arabesques the sense of which she, like a seer or a transcendentalized Gerti, is able to read. The poem is filled with images evoking a tenuous, semiextinguished fire and a smokiness that is cut through only by the "eyes of steel" of the beloved. In "News from Amiata" the woman's icon will break through the quotidian setting of the poet's room through "the fireplace / where the chestnuts explode." These and many other images in the second collection create a background of smoldering, blazing, or steadily burning fire that perpetuates the flame of the poet's anxious wait for and dedication to (*attesa*) the lady. The motif of fire plays with the cliché of the fire of love yet avoids its stereotypical modes of expression. The poet himself does not burn; rather everything around him, including his memory of the woman, burns with her absence-presence, with her flash, with the sparks of insight that she provides and that the poet then elaborates into poetry.

The natural flame of the sun toward which the sunflower extends in the early poem, gradually transmuted into the ambivalent fires of the second collection,[66] becomes in *La bufera e altro* a more public image of impending destruction and, at the same time, the emblem of Montale's continuing belief in the value of personal fulfillment in and through love. This positive-negative charge to the image of fire runs throughout the third collection, where, true as always to ambivalence, the poet does not opt for one or the other. The impending conflagration of the world (most immediately because of the war but certainly not exclusively because of it) threatens the entire texture of these poems; yet at the same time the beloved's flame, which also threatens the lover, is welcomed, if at times in what might be called an ecstasy of anticipated self-annihilation. Examples of the negative images appear in "Ballata scritta in una clinica" (Ballad Written in a Clinic), "L'orto," and "Il sogno del prigioniero" (The Prisoner's Dream). In these and other poems fire, smoke, and similar images represent a world in violent dissolution; rather than purifying or transforming, the flames are destructive in their frightening intensity. Yet positive images abound also. In "Per un omaggio a Rimbaud" (For a Homage to Rimbaud), "Iride," "Nella serra" (In the Greenhouse), and "Piccolo testamento" (Little Testament), for example, the poet insists on a private, intensely unshared trial by fire, which centers around his love for the lady or ladies who continue to provide some meaning to his search for personal salvation.[67] There can be no doubt that a more historically pertinent dimension comes into play in *La bufera e altro*. Montale weaves his most hermetic emotional responses to the by now angelicized lady into a web of external contingencies that evoke most immediately the disaster of the war and the broad social and cultural, not to say human, threats that it poses to the world at large. The very fact that Clizia becomes a transcendental figure in this collection means that the poet is aware of, is indeed basing his portrait of her on the realities from which she in her privileged status escapes.

Angelo Jacomuzzi has most convincingly argued that the beloved becomes representative of a more general religious impulse in *La bufera e altro*.[68] His and other critics' readings of the third collection have shown the deep ties with a Dantesque vision, a more inclusive concern with the fate not only of the solitary lover but of mankind at large, for which the *donna angelicata* (angelicized lady) functions as a bearer of transcendental hope beyond the limits of immediate historical realities. Montale himself made clear the Christian symbolism to which the be-

87
Style as
Tension:
Love
and the
*Avventura
Stilistica*

loved is explicitly tied in *La bufera*: she "returns to us as a continuation and symbol of the eternal Christian sacrifice. She pays for everyone, atones for everyone."[69]

There is evidence as well of a similarly Dantesque culmination of a slowly evolving *avventura stilistica* that begins in the "Mottetti" and reaches its final and complete realization in *La bufera*. In his comments on Dante Montale insists on the organic, evolutionary aspect of the figure of Beatrice from her first appearance in the *Vita nuova* to her final significance in the process of salvation. Similarly in his commentary on his own poetry Montale writes of the beloved as an evolving presence. The stilnovistic lady (as the poet comments, "call her what you will") of the "Mottetti" is developed in the poems of "Finisterre," where she becomes "woman or cloud, angel or stormy petrel," and she is ultimately the "cristofora" (Christlike figure) of "Iride."[70] One stylistic indication of this slow emergence is the development of auditively similar double-*l* words in relation to the beloved (*scintilla, gioielli, sorella, anguilla*). Later we recognize her in the *coralli* of "Gli orecchini" (The Earrings) and thus in all the gems associated with her: the jades of "La frangia dei capelli" (The Bangs); the gems of "Il tuo volo" (Your Flight); the "amethyst heart" of "L'orto." The fire and light motifs associated with her from her first appearance as *scintilla* and *barbaglio* are similarly continuous through *La bufera* and are linked to the secondary motif of her eyes as source of that light. "L'anguilla" (The Eel), the last poem of the "Silvae" series, is the final, climactic poem to the beloved, the one in which her linguistic reality is most explicitly asserted. All her attributes are brought together to form the essence of the poem: the double-*l* words—*scintilla* (spark), *gemella* (twin), *brillare* (to shine), *sorella* (sister), and of course *l'anguilla* (eel); the light and fire images— *una luce scoccata* (a darting light), *il guizzo* (flash), *scintilla* (spark); and the identification of the persistent beloved-eel with Love itself—"torcia, frusta, / freccia d'Amore in terra" (torch, whip, / arrow of Love on earth). All of the fuel is thrown onto this final fire; even in its structure as one continuous sentence, the poem expresses its inevitable push toward finality. The beloved blazes forth in all her splendor in this unforgettable poem.

With this poem the fire burns out. The next series of poems is called "Madrigali privati" (Private Madrigals), and in them Montale depends on a different experience of love (he tells us in a note to "Iride" that this figure is not to be identified with Clizia),[71] which results in poems "tend[ing] toward unscaled heights of privacy."[72] They are almost a slap in the face of those who seek some sort of binding poetic faithfulness to Clizia, as if the same rules governing romantic involvement applied to the elaboration of poetry. Although the poet has added two poems at the beginning of the series in the latest edition of the volume (*Tutte le poesie*), thus pushing "Se t'hanno assomigliato" (If They Have Compared You) out of its initial spot, the striking contrapuntal relationship of this poem to "L'anguilla' is still evident. They are both made up of one continuous question and are both thirty lines long. They both depend on an analogy between woman and creature—eel and fox. The fox (Volpe) even shares in some of the angelic attributes of Clizia ("wings"; "the presage / of your incandescent forehead"). But the poet now insists on the absolutely private and unsharable quality of love, as if to deny the preceding, more universal, emphasis.[73] This insistence is the result of a belief in poetry rather than in any realities, immediate or transcendental, that it might evoke. Montale's only sure reality is primarily poetic creation itself rather than the events, large or small, universal or personal, that it may express. The poet, therefore, continues to construct his art in that marginal zone that mediates between history and self-referentiality, between the symbolic fire of the war-weary, hope-bearing lady and the ashes of completely self-enclosed poetry, whose essential raison d'être is simply itself.

The last two poems of *La bufera* illustrate this persistent marginality that characterizes even the most apparently autobiographical, declamatory, and historical of Montale's poems. The final section of *La bufera* is entitled "Conclusioni provvisorie" (Provisional Conclusions), the first poem of which is "Piccolo testamento." In both cases the adjectives are reductive and self-effacing, thereby serving to counter the weightiness of the nouns they modify. Even at this final point Montale is still shying away from any true finalizations. The lack of permanency that characterizes any literary statement is in fact the essential message of "Little Testament." The poet makes use of the fire motif in order to express this fragility: the poem is built around images of light, fire, and ashes, the ultimate extinction of the sparks that sustained the poetry of this great season. Like the earlier metapoetic text that states, "Do not ask of us the word," this poem too finds its form in negatives. Even its

89
Style as
Tension:
Love
and the
Avventura
Stilistica

own status as graspable relic is radically undermined: "Questo che a notte balugina / nella calotta del mio pensiero, / ... / non è lume di chiesa o d'officina / che alimenti / chierico rosso, o nero" (This that at night flickers / in the skull of my thought, / ... / is *not* light of church or factory / that might sustain / red cleric, or black); "*Non* è un'eredità, un portafortuna ..." (It is *not* an inheritance, a good-luck charm); "... l'orgoglio / *non* era fuga, l'umiltà *non* era / vile, il tenue bagliore strofinato / laggiù *non* era quello di un fiammifero" (pride / was *not* flight, humility was *not* / vile, the tenuous spark struck / down there was *not* that of a match). The positive assertions are, typically, limited syntactically and semantically: "*Solo* quest'iride posso / lasciarti ..." (*Only* this iris can I / leave to you); "ma una storia *non* dura *che* nella cenere / e persistenza è *solo* l'estinzione" (but a story endures *only* in ashes / and persistence is *only* extinction).[74] So what is offered as testimony is ephemeral and inevitably disappearing: ashes, an iris, the tenuous spark. Words, in fact, words are offered that cannot stand up to the extinguishing power of events to come:

quando spenta ogni lampada
la sardana si farà infernale
e un ombroso Lucifero scenderà su una prora
del Tamigi, del Hudson, della Senna
scuotendo l'ali di bitume semi-
mozze dalla fatica, a dirti: è l'ora.

when turned off all lamps
the sardana will become infernal
and a shadowy Lucifer will descend on a prow
of the Thames, the Hudson, the Seine
waving sooty wings half-
severed from the effort, to say to you: it is time.

The shift to the future tense so rarely used by Montale cannot be ignored; it has the solidity of unavoidable fact. Lucifer will descend, and his infernal fires will replace the fire of hope that is described in the past remote tense—"una speranza che bruciò," (a hope that burned)—as irretrievably past, thus relegating it to a time forever gone.

Two opposing emotions merge in the final lines of this poem to establish the oxymoronic foundations of this poetic season: pride and humility. They both sustained the fire that is now being snuffed out as a new angel replaces the angelicized lady of *Le occasioni* and *La bufera*. The lady's "penne lacerate" (lacerated feathers) in the "Motet" that begins, "Ti libero la fronte" (I free your forehead), are now the "sooty wings" of the new bearer of light. This figure is not unequivocally negative, for this "shadowy Lucifer" will prove to have much in common with *Satura*'s "L'angelo nero" (The Black Angel), a poem that many critics have recognized as a poetics in miniature of the new season. "Little Testament" can be read as both a conclusion to one mode of poetry and an indication of the new mode to come. It remains, therefore, within the realm of the provisional, and its final open-endedness must be seen as its most essential message.

In his study entitled "Religiosity of *La bufera*" Angelo Jacomuzzi points out the central importance of Montale's slow-burning hope, which the critic calls "a gnoseological dimension" that reflects "one of the fundamental constants of the poet's attitude toward the world." He further asserts that this hope is conditioned by the equally constant ignorance that makes of Montale's poetry an expression equal to a "vigilant watch" or "wait" (attesa) for some breakthrough to understanding.[75] These two basic elements, ignorance and vigilant watch or wait, that Jacomuzzi delineates within the context of the issue of religiosity are also the keystones of my critical structure as elaborated around the concept of marginality. It is not surprising that there should occur such a similar emphasis, for the marginal as I have been describing it is a metaphysical space that involves religious, philosophical, and poetic issues fundamental to any serious investigation of the limits and potentialities of human knowledge, such as is in Montale's poetry. I would not, however, limit the essential aspect of the crisis expressed in *La bufera* to that which is religious, as do Sergio Antonielli and others.[76] Rather, I would see this crisis as subsumed under the more inclusive heading metaphysical, or in strictly literary terms metapoetical, in which religious, social, and historical issues play an important but neither a unique nor even a primary role. The beloved, the visiting angel, the Beatrice of this stylistic adventure cannot function any longer as mediatrix between this order and another, transcendental one; nor can she provide the fire that sustains the creation of poetry. There has to be an underlying faith in the reality of truth or truths so that knowledge of her may lead to further clarifications. But as Jacomuzzi points out

91
Style as
Tension:
Love
and the
Avventura
Stilistica

Montale's is a poetry "without faith in itself,"[77] an uncertainty far more pertinent to future developments in his verse than even his existential and religious uncertainties. Without the tenuous presence of the beloved the poems fall back on their own inadequacies, on their own dependence on the creating consciousness assailed by ambivalence, distrust, and doubt.

In the final poem of *La bufera*, "Il sogno del prigioniero" (The Prisoner's Dream), Clizia has truly disappeared, and the signs of her presence that once sustained the poet's hopes for a lay miracle have become recognized openly for what they are: linguistic signs—words. Montale called this prisoner one "of the existential condition"; but he is also one of the literary condition. The prisoner, like the poet, is utterly alone; there are no visitations from the winged lady, only "il zigzag degli storni . . . / mie sole ali" (the zigzag of the starlings . . . / my only wings). He is enclosed in an entirely inward, hermetic dream made up of self-generated illusions. The verb used to describe the creation of these final irises is *suscitare*, "to conjure up," as in "ho suscitato / iridi su orizzonti di ragnateli" (I have conjured up / irises on horizons of spider webs); it is a word that emphasizes the absolutely subjective, internally generated status of the entire enterprise of dreaming and of elaborating poetic myths.[78] Yet the tone of this poem is far from a despairing one. The final lines make explicit the poet's desire to go on waiting and dreaming in spite of the admittedly illusory nature of this activity: ". . . L'attesa è lunga, / il mio sogno di te non è finito" (The wait is long, / my dream of you is not yet ended). Thus, in the final poem of the volume, under the heading of "Provisional Conclusions," at a moment of apparent summary and closure, Montale places one of the most open-ended of any of his lines: words that explicitly contradict the sense of an ending and instead point to the new elaboration in poems to come of the unfinished dream. "The Prisoner's Dream" is a demystifying poem; yet in spite of the lady's avowed disappearance Montale will go on writing. We can clearly see that it is neither content nor emotions that ultimately provides the fuel for Montale's future poetry but rather the "real [standard] of language and of style."[79] If there is only one certainty, it is Montale's continued dedication to his art.

The first phase of the stylistic adventure ends with the closing poems of *La bufera e altro*. Although they are animated by many diverse thematic and stylistic preoccupations, the first three collections can all be seen retrospectively as positive steps toward the poet's goal of absolute expression. They reflect to be sure a profound core of ambiguity and existential uncertainty, but they express as well a strong faith in the possibility of attaining knowledge through poetic creation. If Montale had stopped with *La bufera* we would still have a unified and even progressive poetic statement that carries certain basic presuppositions concerning experience and language to a satisfying poetic conclusion. But he did not stop there. The three collections that follow not only comment significantly on the first three but also offer a radically new approach to poetry that demands serious critical attention in and of itself.

3

The *Retrobottega*: Readings of the Last Voice

$\mathbf{I}_{\text{T}}$ is correct to see the last three volumes of Montale's poetry as discontinuous from the first three, as new, different, even alien to the established themes and styles of the earlier verse. And as with any difference there is initially the curiosity to know it and thus in some way to make it familiar and safe. There is also a stronger disposition to criticize negatively, to seek out the frailties and flaws in this difficult newness or—another tactic—to show the ways in which these poems really are not so different after all from the Montale of "Meriggiare," "La casa dei doganieri," or "L'anguilla." In a recent interview Montale typically emphasized both the affinities with and the departures from his earlier poetry, thus effectively opening the way to and condoning either reaction:

> Some poems of *Satura* (like "The Arno at Rovezzano") could also figure in *La bufera*; then there is the intermezzo of *Xenia*, then a part that is newer, more aphoristic . . . The first three books are written in "tails," the others in pajamas, or let's say in afternoon

clothes . . . In the last collections there are recoveries from the
first ones, just as there are themes, motifs, and characters from the
Butterfly of Dinard. The accent, voice, and intonation are
changed.[1]

Montale describes the difference in terms of voice more than of themes
or even overall stylistic choices; he further says that he is now "playing
the piano in another, more discreet, more silent manner."[2] His comments consistently underline the attenuation of the poetic voice in
words such as *rovescio della medaglia* (other side of the coin) and *retrobottega* (back of the shop).[3] Critics have recognized this shift in tone,
characterizing it above all as more prosaic, closer than ever before to
everyday speech, open to slang, dialect, foreign terms, and all the other
elements that constantly mold a spoken idiom. Others have emphasized
the thematic realness of these poems written to and of Montale's late
wife, friends, and enemies or revolving as many of them do around
diaristic detail: a strike, a stray bird, a day at the beach, and so on.[4]
These critical reactions are appropriate and helpful in defining Montale's new season, and I would not deny that a vein of the prosaic and
quotidian runs through all these collections. Yet it is also in these
poems, more so even than in the first three collections, that Montale
concentrates on a decidedly unprosaic, unquotidian issue: poetry itself—what it is, where it comes from, what it does, how it is born and
sustained. Although primarily writing of his own poetry, Montale faces
the problematic issue of poetry in a much wider sense. This interest in
writing poetry about poetry is clearly evident in poems that announce
themselves as such: "La poesia" (Poetry), "Le rime" (Rhymes), and
"Le parole" (Words) in *Satura*; "La mia Musa" (My Muse), "Il poeta"
(The Poet), and "Le Figure" (Figures) in *Diario*; "Un poeta" (A Poet),
and "I poeti defunti dormono tranquilli" (The Dead Poets Sleep
Quietly) in *Quaderno*. There is also, however, a less evident yet nonetheless constant subtext in many other less obviously metapoetic
poems, which, like white noise, provides an unheeded hum under the
seemingly primary message. Montale may have decided to soft-pedal his
music at this point in his career, but the complexity, ambiguity, and intellectual rigor that characterize his earlier poetry are still at work in
these apparently easier poems.

There is a basic paradox created by the nature of these new poems.

95
The
Retrobottega:
Readings
of the
Last
Voice

On the one hand Montale deemphasizes the estranging qualities of poetry by using more prosaic language and more accessible themes.[5] On the other hand he subtly emphasizes the fact that by its very nature poetry is thoroughly imbued with its own estrangement from the reality of life and from the language of quotidian exchange. The poems are slices of life, yet they are isolated on the page, surrounded by blank margins that remind us how separate from the flow of life they really are.[6] How then can the terms *prosaic* and *quotidian* be reconciled to the apparently antithetical substantive they modify: *poetry?*

This question can be answered by considering first the stage directions given by the poet in the titles of these collections. *Satura*, like *Ossi*, *Le occasioni*, and *La bufera*, is "pregnant . . . with auto-critical intelligence."[7] The word *Satura* indicates a mixed style and hints at the satirical element at play.[8] In restoring the word to its Latin form the poet is separating his poetry from the Anglo-American tradition of *satire* (a word based on the false etymology from the Greek term for satyr play) and emphasizing its true Roman origins. This is not to say that Montale limits his poetry in *Satura* to anything that can be called formal verse satire; rather he makes use of the lower-key and often darkly comic voice made available by the satiric form. *Satura* may also be read as an adjective modifying the understood substantive *poesia* and meaning "raggiunta il più alto valore possibile di certe sue caratteristiche" (in scientific terms, "having reached saturation point").[9] In this sense it is both a positive and a negative term indicating fulfillment and, conversely, exhaustion of potential.[10] In other words, this poetry seeks to contain all that poetry can contain, including linguistic, thematic, and stylistic elements that are traditionally thought of as unpoetic. Under this title, then, Montale presents a radicalized poetry that demands that the question of the interrelationship of the quotidian and the literary, of everyday speech and poetic language, be confronted not only as a symptom but indeed as the very etiology of this new season.

Diario (Diary) and *Quaderno di quattro anni* (Notebook of Four Years), the fifth and sixth collections, respectively, even more openly call attention to their quotidian and prosaic nature in the neutral titles the poet gives to them. They are a diary, a notebook, the poet's jottings in the margin of his lived life, or at least they are ostensibly such. Montale has, however, assiduously noted the date of composition of each poem, and we see from these dates that in fact he has ordered the poems not according to a strict chronology but rather with some other more self-conscious principle of presentation in mind. Theme is obviously one of the aspects of that ordering; yet there seems to be a stylistic and even purely aural linkage at work too. The poet himself commented concerning *Satura*, in a gloss that I believe to be pertinent to the last two collections as well, that "it would be an error to read one poem only and to seek to dissect it, because there is always a cross-reference from one sound to another, and not only this, but even from one poem to another."[11] To use Montale's words concerning the *Commedia*, what we have in these recent collections, even more so than in the first three books, is "un'immensa ragnatela di correspondenze" (a huge web of correspondences), which is spun, grows, and ultimately forms the pattern of the whole.[12]

We are indeed "depistati" (off the track)[13] if we equate more prosaic verse with more ingenuous verse, just as we are mistaken to listen to this new voice as if it were Montale the man chatting with us over tea, although even that form of apparent sincerity is extremely deceptive. Montale says of *Satura* that "there was a necessity for realism . . . a language that would detach itself from traditional language, let's say."[14] This necessity has its origins in the demands of poetry and not in the service of some sort of nonliterary confession or direct appeal, concepts that are thoroughly alien to Montale the poet. It might appear that I am overstressing the literary essence of these collections; after all, they are made up of poems and therefore we read them as poems. Yet now there is the problem of being drawn into a confused critical stance regarding these poems precisely because they speak in a conversational tone of real people and events that were or are part not only of the poet's life outside of poetry but also of our shared context of the directly experienced world. The tendency is to respond to them more as statements of fact than of fancy, which indeed in part they are, and to focus attention on Montale as a propounder of personal, political, and ethical visions that he merely happens to communicate to us in verse form. Montale has shown in his journalism and in his critical prose pieces that he is perfectly capable of writing directly, from the position of commentator or judge of society, culture, or history. In his poetry his goals are different; if he has something to say, it is something inextricably tied up with the poetic form by which it is given life. His new poetry is still a stylistic adventure, but it is now based on a new set of motives that are

97
The
Retrobottega:
Readings
of the
Last
Voice

no longer contained in the early triad of *paesaggio, amore, evasione.* There is a deeply nonquotidian and unrealistic core within these recent poems, no matter how closely they are linked to daily reality in themes and language. Commenting on the linguistic realism of *Satura,* the critic Maria Corti writes, "In effect the new language, in its results, not only is never denotative, but it has no realistic aspect; there is no 'miniepisode' that holds from this point of view. We are before a great writer who cannot not produce violent shifts in the very act in which he seems to accede and incline to linguistic codification . . ." She goes on to call Montale's "recourse to today's language . . . subversive" and the "words" of today's society "monstrous" in their estranged poetic context.[15] The prosaic and quotidian aspects of these new collections are undeniable, but their real function is understood only if we keep firmly in mind the poetic goals they serve.

Before we turn our attention to the poems themselves, there is another question that presents itself. Simply put: Why did Montale decide to change direction, to alter his voice so drastically at this late stage of his career? As Maria Corti rightly notes, this new poetry was an "unexpected event" quite surprising to readers and critics of Montale's first three collections.[16] What might have seemed to be a brief interlude, a casual flirtation with a new style in the little privately printed volume entitled *Satura,* suddenly emerged as a much more serious commitment with the publication of the volume *Satura,* followed shortly by *Diario* and *Quaderno.* Montale himself asserted many years ago that "the great seedbed of every poetic invention is in the field of prose."[17] He had talked about the interrelationship of prose and poetry in many interviews and critical essays, so it did not come as a complete shock that he should begin to write poetry in a lower-keyed, less hermetic tone. Conscious, however, of the necessity of explaining his decision, Montale provided some very revealing comments after the appearance of *Satura:* "If the poet M. had died no one would have spoken of an untimely demise. But he did not die and when he began again to write verse, after many years of prose-prose, the need to show the 'envers du décor' inexorably prevailed upon him."[18] The reason presented here is directly tied to Montale's years as journalist, writer of "prose-prose," a reason that Maria Corti, among others, accepts as the most direct cause of the shift in style and tone. I would certainly not deny the relevance of what the poet himself sees as one of the reasons for his about-face, but I would also emphasize the significance of the phrase "but he did not die." It is clear from this and other statements in recent years that Montale is perfectly aware of the dangers of being buried alive by his own reputation. To be anthologized is a sort of "embalming of the classic,"[19] and to have attained the status of a living classic is a dubious distinction for the individual who is thus honored. The poet has with a touch of black humor called himself a "mummy" in discussions with me. His recourse to the *passato remoto*, a past verb tense usually applied to events or people long gone, when speaking of himself in many poems in the latest collections shows how directly Montale confronts the issue of his own continuing life as a kind of *embarras de richesse* as far as some critics are concerned. The statement "but he did not die" is almost one of defiance, therefore, an assertion of a new offensive against the rigor mortis of fame and canonization. From this point of view Montale cannot fail to do something unexpected, something un-Montalian, precisely in order to avoid becoming simply an echo of himself.

Jacomuzzi and others read the new language as representative of a more general crisis of language as it is deformed, misused, and trivialized in the consumer society of today.[20] According to this reading Montale's long-standing distrust of the power of language to express reality or to act as a tool for knowledge is now developed to its fullest, as Montale openly asserts what before was more implicit than explicit: only a "partial language," a stuttering speech, can capture the poet's consternation in a world in which words are mirrors of ultimate chaos, ambiguity, and ignorance. Andrea Zanzotto points out, however, that the strategy is not so simple; he writes of a " 'speaking on the edge' that denies the by now banalized and publicized destruction of language, *and* fully expressive language, as well as the 'partial language' to which the poet says he is resigned, while in fact he eludes it by imitating it and thwarting it."[21] Montale is not unequivocally giving himself over to a total linguistic pessimism; he is rather going as far as possible with a basic oxymoronic impulse that includes apparent opposites within a unity made up of "the most congested polysemy."[22] Montale speaks of a distribution of "harmonics" through *Satura*; this musical analogy holds both aurally and semantically, for the unity of the frequency and the variable components that make up that unity function at a level of both sound and sense.

99
The
Retrobottega:
Readings
of the
Last
Voice

There is, however, a reading of the recent verse that distinguishes itself from the rest because it is decidedly negative, even damning, in striking contrast to the positive, laudatory responses of most critics. According to this reading, by Almansi and Merry, "Montale has allowed himself to become vulnerable. The poet is much more easily identified: the way back to the author is publicly signposted for the reader."[23] Montale has become the servant of his intentionally new style rather than having that style serve him and his goals. Thus, for these critics, the word play is too obvious, the structural ambiguity too transparent; the poetry finally becomes "occasional verse, written with a racy vocabulary under casual stimulus." The poems of *Satura* do not, therefore, "survive the trial of isolation." The unforgettable individual poems of the first three collections are superseded by a generally forgettable new group that does not crystallize into any especially striking single poems or even lines from poems. This criticism provides a useful and necessary counterperspective on the new poetry. It is difficult to separate the accomplishment of the recent collections from the reputation established in the first three; but it is a disservice to both the poet and his poems to read them with one eye closed, so to speak, seeing only the positive aspects of their newness and shutting out any weaknesses that such newness might represent. My own critical judgment is that the new richness finally outweighs the impoverishment suggested by Almansi and Merry, although I too must struggle against the great weight of Montale's previous achievement, much as the poet himself has done, in order to judge his recent contribution.

The Retrospective Glance

There is one decidedly new stylistic element in *Satura* that can serve as an example of the enriching aspect of the search for a different voice. It is the repeated use of *-ibile* or *-abile* adjectival forms.[24] In the first poem of *Satura,* "Il tu" (The You) Montale builds the rhyme of the poem around three past-participial adjectives: *depistati, moltiplicati,* and *duplicati* (derailed, multiplied, duplicated). These are impoverished adjectives, pseudoadjectives, in that they derive directly from a verb and do not describe quality or quantity in the way in which most adjectives do. They are in brief prosaic adjectives.

In the second poem of the collection, "Botta e risposta I" (Thrust

100

Eugenio
Montale:
Poet
on
the
Edge

and Parry I), the usage appears once more in the words *asolante* (loung-ing in Asolo), *voluta* (desired), and *risvegliato* (reawakened). The parry introduces the first *-ibile* adjective forms, first in "invisibili spiragli" (in-visible fissures) and then in the isolated, climactic line, "Ed infine fu il tonfo: l'incredibile" (And finally there was the thud: the incredible). In "Xenia I and II," there are eleven *-ibile* adjectives. As in the case of the summarizing "incredible" of "Thrust and Parry I," the majority of these eleven encapsulate the essential emotion that underlies the poem in which they appear. In poem 5 of "Xenia I," for example, it is Mosca's "senso infallibile" (infallible sense) that is the subject of the poem. In poem 8, although it is the smoke of the poet's cigars that is "volubile" (erratic), in fact the word describes perfectly the elusive and shifting manner in which the late Mosca communicates with the poet; thus it really can be attributed to her. Poem 1 of "Xenia II" speaks of the "punto . . . incomprensibile" (incomprehensible point), that if dis-covered would describe the essence of Mosca's life. Poem 4 concerns the "incredibili agnizioni" (incredible insights) of Mosca; poem 12 speaks of the pleasure she took in disjointed events that make life break out of its "insopportabile / ordito" (unbearable warp); and in the final poem of the series Montale joins together the *-ibile* and past-participial adjective forms in the phrase "una realtà incredibile e mai creduta" (a reality not to be believed and never believed). *Volubile, incomprensi-bile, insopportabile, incredibile:* all these adjectives express the ultimate unbelievability of Mosca's death, which is of course the central theme of "Xenia." By using these *parole sdrucciole* (words accented on the third from the last syllable rather than, as is far more common, the penultimate syllable) Montale draws attention to their exceptional au-ditory appeal. It is this phonic or musical aspect that first makes them stand out; but it is ultimately their collective semantic weight that links them together into a melody made of diverse harmonics, all of which, however, return to the fundamental note of the unbelievability of Mosca's death.

On a thematic level the poems are all basically monotonal; all speak of and to the "caro piccolo insetto" (dear little insect), Mosca. The ad-jectives are but one small element in the diversity in unity of the series. Yet I believe them to be an important element in the understated qual-ity of these poems, which while expressing a great loss never fall into a pathetic or self-pitying tone. The loss is not to be believed and is thus

101
The
Retrobottega:
Readings
of the
Last
Voice

bearable and expressible. This reading may also help account for the conversational tone of the poems: the poet is able to write to his late wife as if she were present precisely because in some very basic and emphatically nonmystical sense she *is* present. This paradoxical unity of opposites is expressed in poem 14 of "Xenia I," where Montale asserts that "il moto / non è diverso dalla stasi, / [che] il vuoto è il pieno e il sereno / è la più diffusa delle nubi" (motion / is not different from stasis, / [that] the empty is the full and the serene / is the most diffused cloud). Paradox provides comfort, then, and the incomprehensibility of Mosca's death becomes its only comprehensible aspect, just as many years before the woman-angel's unknowability was her most knowable attribute. The oxymoronic impulse that informs the "Mottetti" is still at work; indeed it has become the primary figure, both implicitly and explicitly, in these recent poems. Following Montale's admonition in our reading of "Xenia," "above all I insist that it would be an error to read one poem alone and to seek to dissect it, because there is always a cross-reference from one sound to another,"[25] we see that indeed the poet has given good advice and that it is only in such comprehensive readings that the full significance of individual stylistic innovations such as the *-ibile* forms can be grasped.

In "Gerarchie" (Hierarchies), the first poem of "Satura I"—that is, the section immediately following "Xenia"—Montale shows how conscious he is of his use of verbal adjective forms. The poet had stated concerning the elaboration of these new poems that "the new voice . . . is greatly enriched by harmonics, which it distributes throughout the body of the composition. This was done unconsciously in great part; then, when I had some examples, of myself, let's say, then it could be that I followed the teachings that I had given to myself."[26] In "Hierarchies" the play on formal elements is the very message of the poem. The *-ante* adjectives echo one another: *importante* (important), *predicante* (one who preaches), *arrestante* (one who arrests), *totalizzante* (totalizer), *pulsante* (throbbing). The words *predicato* and *l'arrestato* are coupled with the gerundial forms of the same verbs. And in the final two lines there is a cascade of *-ibile* and *-abile* words: *l'improbabile* (the improbable), *l'avvenibile* (the occurrable), and *pulsabile* (throbbable). The combination of all these sounds that bounce off one another and the absurd alliteration of the final line, "il pulsante una pulce nel pulsabile" (the throbbing a flea in the throbbable) conspire to undermine the

102
Eugenio
Montale:
Poet
on
the
Edge

pomposity of the hierarchical vision that is seemingly being pro-pounded.

Maria Corti rightly insists that ethical-political satire is at the heart of these rhetorical extravagances, especially in poems such as "Hierar-chies" and "Fanfara" (Fanfare), which have as their theme the meaning of history.[27] "Fanfare" closes the section "Satura I," endowing the chapter with a symmetry of sorts, since it too is a satiric attack on the view of history as system, classification, and progress. This poem also fairly explodes with rhetorical devices. There are again the many -ibile and -abile words— irreversibile (irreversible), fallibile (fallible), credibili (credible), tascabile (pocketable)—as well as short, hammerlike lines filled with figures such as zeugma, anaphora, and alliteration, which combine to create a highly effective parody of the confident voices of propaganda that assail modern political man. In these poems the repeti-tion of -ibile adjectives is put to very different use from that in "Xenia." Nonetheless the same disbelieving stance underlies both uses, although in the case of "Xenia" the disbelief is sorrowful while in the others it is disdainful and darkly humorous.

Continuing to follow the thread of -ibile words through Satura we encounter these adjectives in several poems with diverse themes. "Götterdämmerung," "Divinità in incognito" (Incognito Divinities), "L'angelo nero" (The Black Angel), "Laggiù" (Down There), and "L'altro" (The Other) are all poems concerning the divine; in them, re-spectively, we find the words inconoscibili (unknowable), invisibili (in-visible), tangibili (tangible), incomprensibile (incomprehensible), ine-spungibili (inexpungible), and non responsabili (not responsible), adjectives that sum up very effectively Montale's conception of the di-vine.

In those poems in which Montale writes explicitly of poetry rhetori-cal devices also proliferate. In "Poetry" words are personified: "Appena fuori / si guardano d'attorno e hanno l'aria di dirsi: / che sto a farci?" (Scarcely out / they look around and seem to say to themselves: / what am I doing here?). In the second part of the poem a pointed rhyme en-circles the intervening lines: "con orrore—l'autore" (with horror—the author). In "Rhymes" an outrageous rhyme made up of an elided form of of and the and the feminine form of the pronoun those (delle, quelle) shows just how true it is that the poet cannot repel them (respingerle). And again we hear the echo of -ibile words in impossibile of the lat-

103
The
Retrobottega:
Readings
of the
Last
Voice

ter poem. The remaining poems of *Satura*, which take as their themes
time, autobiography, and the course of present and future events, continue to play with words. Time and again we hear the new music of
-ibile in such words as *inesplicabile* (unexplainable), *commestibile* (edi-
ble), *inabitabile* (uninhabitable), *illegibile* (illegible), *ineccipibile* (un-
exceptionable), and so on.[28] In *Diario del '71 e del '72* and *Quaderno di
quattro anni*, along with the by-now recognizable adjectives *impossibile,
incredibile, invisibile, inesplicabile*, there appear several rare terms such
as *infiocchettabile* (adornable) in "L'arte povera" (The Poor Art), *af-
fittabile* (rentable) in "Trascolorando" (Changing Color), and *impoti-
posizzabile* (describable in vivid terms) in "Diamantina" (Adaman-
tine), all from *Diario*, and *inoccultabili* (unconcealable) in "Lagunare"
(Lagoonal) and *esistibile* (existable) in "La vita l'infinita" (Life the Infinite), from *Quaderno*. Thus Montale's attachment to the form is such
that he seeks out or even creates *-ibile* words not even existing in current
usage.

The definition of *-ibile* and *-abile* adjectives states that they indicate
the possibility of a passive quality.[29] Certainly the passivity of these adjectival forms is of some significance; the poet ascribes some passive
quality to the words thus modified rather than asserting in a more direct
verbal form that he or anyone else is responsible for the activity implied
in the verb on which the adjectives are built. In other words an event or
a thing that is incomprehensible contains that quality in itself; the quality does not necessarily reside in the beholder. The great majority of
these adjectives used by Montale are negative forms, and thus the quality inherent in the words they modify is negative: impossibility, incomprehensibility, inexpressibility, invisibility. Yet even these negative qualities have not been activated, completed, fixed once and for all, as they
would be if the past participial form were used. The collective impact is
that of a world rampant with potentially positive but more often negative inherent qualities, a world that is beyond the control of the poet,
describable perhaps but ultimately unseizable. The poet, or more exactly
his words, are not able to do more than point to the abilities or inabili-
ties of entities, people, events, and objects that are self-sustaining and
are beyond the transforming, deforming, informing, performing power
traditionally assigned to poetry. I believe that Montale is expressing this
same sense of the limits of poetry and of life in *Diario*, in the poem
"Asor," addressed to the socially-minded critic Asor Rosa, where he

104

Eugenio
Montale:
Poet
on
the
Edge

writes: that poetry "*sta* come una pietra / o un granello di sabbia" (it *exists* like a rock / or a grain of sand). The decision to use these adjectival forms, with all their implicit philosophical weight, while perhaps at first unconscious is, I think, soon seized upon as one of those lessons Montale consciously elaborates and distributes throughout the new poems. It is also perfectly possible that he liked the sound of these words, which have a pleasant liquidity and musicality in their proparoxytonality. Whatever the poet's motive might have been in choosing to use these words, the result is nonetheless clear: collectively they add a new tonality to the poems and draw attention to the auditory level that creates the different music of this season.

Maria Corti writes of "new threads," such as the *-ibile* adjectives, that have been introduced into the "usual Montalian language."[30] The new poetry is not, however, so new as to be unrecognizable as Montale's; both thematically and stylistically there are many Montalianisms. This harkening back to the earlier verse is accomplished in many ways and to many ends.

In response to a question concerning the homogeneity and/or evolution of his poetry throughout the new collections, Montale said that the last two books, *Satura* and *Diario*, are "decisively diaristic [and] are understood better knowing the preceding ones."[31] As with the work of any poet, Montale's latest poems are most deeply understood when read in the context of his prior achievement in order to trace the continuities, discontinuities, constants, and radical innovations. As I have already pointed out, these latest collections reflect a high level of self-consciousness not only of their newness but also of the "Montale classico" from which they deviate. *Satura* opens with two prefatory poems that explicitly point backward: "Il *tu*" and "Botta e risposta I." In the first Montale takes on the subject of one of his best-known stylistic constants: the second-person singular *you*, most often present in the imperative form. The poet offers a corrective to the critical view that has spoken of the *tu* as an institution, as Montale himself has done, blaming himself for the misunderstanding.[32] Yet as Almansi and Merry have so rightly insisted, the poem, palinodic as it might first appear, does little to establish the nature of the *tu*. If instead the poem "stands for an intellectual operation which admits of radical reversals of meaning,"[33] as it ultimately seems to do (the images of multiple mirror distortions and of the bird who does not know who he is point to this reading),

105
The
Retrobottega:
Readings
of the
Last
Voice

then this new stance is no more final than the earlier one. What is certain, however, is that the Montale of now is engaged in a reconsideration of the Montale of then, and that this retrospective vision is fundamental to the present poetry.

"Botta e risposta I" is a poem that has aroused many complex critical responses. Jacomuzzi reads it in an allegorical key and insists on the theological component that, although ironical and thus distanced, is nonetheless fundamental to the vision of experience it propounds.[34] Mario Martelli uses it as the basis of a book-length study, *Il rovescio della poesia* (The Reverse Side of Poetry), in which he reexamines many fundamental myths of Montale's poetry through it, especially that of the beloved, whom he ultimately associates with poetry itself.[35] Andrea Zanzotto, himself a poet, states in the opening lines of his article "Da 'Botta e risposta I' a *Satura*" that the poem "sums up the past and delineates fairly explicitly the future of a poetic evolution."[36] If these and other critics do not always agree in their interpretations of the poem, there is a basic consensus in seeing it as a great synthesis involving both past and future poetic goals and motifs. The poem is dated 1961 and is the oldest of the new poems of *Satura*, all the rest of which date from 1964 onward. But in addition to the moment of its composition, which aligns it with the summary poems "Little Testament" and "The Prisoner's Dream" of the *Bufera*, there are also its many explicit references to all of the preceding poetry, as far back as the *Ossi*, carrying us through the *Occasioni*, *La bufera*, and even the prose of the *Farfalla di Dinard*.

The "Botta" opens with an address to Arsenio, a poetic character who had not appeared since the poem of the same name, written in 1927. In the "Risposta" names surge up like spirits out of the haze of times long past: Gerti, Liuba, Clizia, "la serva zoppa" (the lame servant).[37] The multiple animal and bird references—the turtledoves, cattle, a cricket, ants, the eagle, the mouse—remind us of the many such significant creatures in Montale's other poetry and prose, from the lizard who is so like Esterina in the early poem "Falsetto" of *Ossi di seppia* to the felled horse and the falcon of the "Osso" that begins, "Il male di vivere" (The evil of living), the moth of "Vecchi versi" (Old Lines), the buffalo of the poem of the same name, the polyp of "Indian Serenade," the eel, the spider of Clizia's dream,[38] and so many others, all part of the haunting "Montalian bestiary."[39]

106
Eugenio
Montale:
Poet
on
the
Edge

In a poem as consciously weighted with poetic memories as is "Botta e risposta I" even single words and phrases resonate with past echoes: the *inganno mondano* (worldy deception) harkens back to the *inganno consueto* (usual deception) of the "Osso" beginning, "Forse un mattino" (Perhaps one morning); the *tremule ali* (tremulous wings) and *ghiaccio* (ice) to past images of the storm-blown Clizia; the capitalized *Lui* (He) to the divinity of the "Silvae" series in *La bufera*; and so on.[40] All these past elements, however, are now incorporated into a radically new poetic context that looks forward; the change is signaled by means of an ancient figure, that of the poetic enterprise as voyage. The interlocutor in "Botta" states "che sia tempo / di spiegare le vele" (that it be time / to set sail), bringing to mind, among other such moments, the first two lines of the *Purgatorio*, "per correr migliori acque alza le vele / omai la navicella del mio ingegno" (in order to travel on better waters the little boat of my wits now sets sail), in which the poet is making the shift from the hellish landscape of the first Canticle to the higher spiritual and artistic challenge of the mountain of purgation. The scatological imagery of "Botte e risposta I"—"corridoi, sempre più folti / di letame" (corridors, more and more full of dung), "i bastioni d'ebano, fecali" (the ebony, fecal bastions), "il vorticare sopra zattere / di sterco" (the swirling about on rafts of excrement)—also indicate a violent shift that will later be explicitly glossed by Montale's new conception of poetry as expressed in "Dopo una fuga" (After a Flight) in *Satura*. There he writes: "La poesia e la fogna, due problemi / mai disgiunti . . ." (Poetry and sewers, two problems / never disjoined). The vehement self-deprecation of this poem—"ora sai che non può nascere l'aquila / dal topo" (now you know that the eagle cannot be born / of the mouse)—also continues throughout the new poems, in which are emphasized the inadequacies, both artistic and existential, of the poet himself.

In spite of these new and radical elements the pointedly clear references to Montale's past poetry continue throughout *Satura*. The "rete a strascico" (trawl net) of the poem "La storia" (History) recalls the net of "In Limine," the first poem of *Ossi di seppia*. The train station setting of "Nel fumo" (In the Smoke) brings to mind the same setting of the stupendous "Motet" that begins, "Addii, fischi nel buio" (Farewells, whistles in the dark). The gerundial "tossicchiando" (coughing) of the more recent poem is a subtle echo of the coughs of the earlier

107
The
Retrobottega:
Readings
of the
Last
Voice

"Motet." Other obvious echoes include the "ossi di seppia" of "Piove" (It's Raining) and the "amazing face" of the lady of "La belle dame sans merci," which harks back to "that face" of the "Motet" beginning, "Non recidere, forbice" (Don't chop off, scissors).

The poem "Proda di Versilia" (Shore of Versilia) of the "Silvae" section of *La bufera* is resurrected piecemeal in many poems of *Satura*. The first line of the earlier poem, "I miei morti che prego perché preghino / per me" (My dead to whom I pray that they might pray / for me) is heard in poem 10 of "Xenia I," where the poet writes: "Pregava? . . . Anche per i suoi morti / e per me." (Did she pray? . . . Also for her dead / and for me). The line from "Proda," "quella vita ch'ebbero / inesplicata e inesplicabile" (that life which they had / unexplained and unexplainable), which refers to Montale's beloved dead, is obliquely echoed in the line "realtà incredibile e mai creduta" (reality not to be believed and never believed) of poem 14 in "Xenia II," which also finds its inspiration in the death of precious things and people. The "alberi sacri alla mia infanzia, il pino / selvatico, il fico e l'eucalipto" (trees sacred to my youth, the wild / pine, the fig and the eucalyptus) are brought back to life in *Satura*'s "Botta e risposta III" in the lines "Di quel mio primo rifugio / io non ricordo che le ombre / degli eucalipti" (Of that my first refuge / I remember only the shadows / of the eucalyptus trees). The "dear ghosts" of "Proda" are hovering about "Xenia I," poem 13, in the lines "Ma è possibile, / lo sai, amare un'ombra, ombre noi stessi" (But it is possible / you know, to love a ghost, ghosts that we ourselves are). Even the mosquitoes in spite of which the young poet dozes "in the corner room" reappear in "Botta e risposta II," where Montale writes: "spire di zampironi tentano di salvarmi / dalle zanzare che pinzano, tanto più sveglie di me" (the coils of mosquito repellant try to save me / from the mosquitoes that bite, so much more awake than I am).

Other echoes of earlier poems include "a wall to climb" in the poem that begins, "Che mastice tiene insieme" (That putty holds together), a sure echo of the many walls of *Ossi di seppia*; "Scoprimmo che al porcospino / piaceva la pasta al ragù" (We discovered that the porcupine / liked pasta with meat sauce) in "A pianterreno" (On the First Floor), which brings to mind the porcupines that "drink from a trickle of pity" in the last poem of *Le occasioni*, "News from Amiata." The gods who protect "il tuo lontano focolare" (your far-off hearth) in "Ex

108
Eugenio
Montale:
Poet
on
the
Edge

voto" make us remember "the cat of the hearth," Liuba's pet in "A Liuba che parte" (To Liuba Who Is Leaving). The "light muffled step" of the recent "After a Flight" softly echoes the "passo che proviene / dalla serra sì lieve" (step that comes / from the greenhouse so lightly) but that is not "felpato dalla neve" (muffled by the snow) in the "Motet" beginning, "Ecco il segno" (Here is the sign). Finally there is "la costa San Giorgio" of the recent poem "Senza salvacondotto" (Without Safe Conduct), which also takes us back to the *Occasioni*, this time to the poem "Costa San Giorgio."

These explicit echoes of earlier poems make us aware of the presence of implicit ones, or what Montale calls in "Botta e risposta III" "le ombre che si nascondono / tra le parole, imprendibili, / mai palesate, mai scritte, / mai dette per intero" (the shadows that are hidden / among the words, unseizable, / never manifest, never written, / never entirely said) and that "hanno una forma di sopravvivenza / che non interessa la storia, / una presenza scaltra, un'asfissia che non è / solo dolore e penitenza" (have a form of survival that does not interest history, / a wily presence, an asphyxia that is not / only grief and penitence). These shadows haunt the new poems of *Satura* and are the cumulative weight of all of the great and unique themes, characters, and unforgettable images and lines of the first three collections, which are now asphyxiated by the alien atmosphere in which they almost imperceptibly float. But the retrospective glance is not motivated only by grief and penitence, is not simply nostalgia for the youthful season of the *Ossi*, the intensity of the "Mottetti," the vigor and virility of *La bufera*. Nor do I believe that Montale is completely ironic in recalling his previous achievement, although irony, self-parody, and even bitterness all play a role in these poems. Rather what Montale succeeds in doing is to maintain a sort of double image of the then and the now, totally choosing neither, privileging neither as more true, more fundamentally Montalian. To use a personifying analogy, his poetry has aged; and just as aging in a person means both growth and loss, so do these poems represent both necessary newness and equally necessary erosion of the still present earlier poetry. When we look at a photograph of a person taken fifty years ago we are both moved and disbelieving; that youthful image is no longer to be seen in the old face before us. And yet paradoxically it is there, hidden perhaps but discernible to the knowing and loving eye. If we know only the aged person the doubling is not possible; but if we knew the younger, an added dimension is

109
The
Retrobottega:
Readings
of the
Last
Voice

gained. These poems are understood better knowing the preceding ones not because they derive directly from them but because they are part of the organic whole that is Montale's total opus. The new thematic and stylistic elements, the new prosaic tone carry us into the at first disturbingly un-Montalian space; the direct and indirect use of well-known materials on the other hand provides a comfortable sense of intimacy even with these markedly different poems. In spite of the fact that much of the earlier poetry is being satirized and even bitterly rejected, we still remember what all the characters, places, and myths meant to us, and to the poet, and find pleasure and even solace in their continuing lives.

Montale writes in "Il *tu*" that "in me the so many are one even if they appear / multiplied by mirrors." The poet makes great use of the fun-house mirrors of rhetorical play: multiple harmonics, self-reflexive irony, and all the rest of the many highly polished surfaces available to the great stylist as he elaborates a new voice. But I do not believe that we are being asked to stop at the surface. Nor would I insist that there is some essential and totalizing *unum* that can be paraphrased and mined from the latest poetry to be carried away by readers of Montale as his last true message. If in fact there is a message in his poetry, early and late, it appears to be that of the folly of asking for any essence not profoundly imbued with ambiguity, doubt, self-questioning, and ultimate irresolvability. In these latest poems we find ourselves forced back to the poet's refusal to see poetry as "the word that might square off from every side / our formless soul" ("Non chiederci la parola" in *Ossi di seppia*). Montale continues to situate his poetry between such ideal plenitudes and the emptiness of silence, in the intermediate space of which he writes in the poem "Pasquetta" (Easter Monday) of *Quaderno,* "There was perhaps a third road / and it chose me."

The concept of marginality is also to be found in the last three collections. One poem of *Satura,* "L'angelo nero," is an example of the betwixt-and-between poetics of this new season, as it is both an expression of the innovations that mark Montale's recent poetry and a continuation of some of the most constant elements in all of his work. Thus the poem can be seen to fall somewhere between the historically and culturally determined shifts to which all art is subjected and the aesthetically rather than historically determined self-referentiality of Montale's poetry as it has developed over the last fifty years.

"L'angelo nero" invites overreadings such as that contained in Oreste

110

Eugenio
Montale:
Poet
on
the
Edge

Macrì's study entitled "Demonism in Montale's Poetry."[41] The poem is such a masterpiece of muted, restrained, and yet wholly lyrical expression that I am tempted to put aside exegesis in favor of the pure pleasure of a simple and uncritical enjoyment of it, perhaps to counter at least in part the sort of dissection to which it has been subjected. To be fair, however, it must be admitted that the poem strongly attracts extensive and even excessive critical response, because it is so clearly great, so obviously a return to the powerful voice of the Montale of the high season, especially *La bufera*. This poem too is wholly unforgettable, from its opening lines—"O grande angelo nero / fuligginoso riparami / sotto le tue ali" (Oh great angel black and / sooty shelter me / under your wings)—to what is felt to be its inevitable and perfectly right closing—"grande angelo / di cenere e di fumo, miniangelo / spazzacamino" (great angel / of ashes and of smoke, miniangel / chimney sweep). It also appeals to critics because of its apparently theological-allegorical thrust and its implied ties with the other angel in Montale's poetry, the central angelicized woman of the earlier poems. Though I shall leave such sweeping themes as demonism to Macrì, I shall succumb to the critical urge so far as to suggest some more modest and less synthesizing views of the poem's greatness and importance within both the immediate context of *Satura* and the much wider context of all of Montale's poetry.

The most obvious figure through which the poem is elaborated is the oxymoron. The angel is both "great" and "little," "constant" and "inconstant," "dark" and "white," both sooty and burnt out (fuligginoso) and yet blazing forth with a death-dealing radiance (fulgore). This construction of linked contradictions is, of course, tied to earlier moments such as in the "Motets," in which Montale bases his poetry on the unity of opposites, but here the context is the less lofty, more accessible world of *Satura* rather than the admittedly more rhetorical, artificial one of *Le occasioni*. The oxymoronic language is felt to be different here because it is more natural, more inevitable, given the object of description—the angel—who is "non celestiale né umano" (neither celestial nor human). The poem immediately preceding "L'angelo nero," entitled "Divinità in incognito," explicitly prepares the way for this minidivinity in such lines as "numinose fantasime non irreali, tangibili, / toccate mai" (numinous phantasms not unreal, tangible / never touched) and "una divinità, anche d'infimo grado" (a divinity, even of inferior

111
The
Retrobottega:
Readings
of the
Last
Voice

rank). In addition many of Montale's references to the divine throughout his poetry and prose have established the poet's personal God as partaking of human as well as of transcendental qualities. The equivocal status of the angel is therefore entirely consonant with Montale's conception of the divine as expressed in such poems in *Satura* as "Che mastice tiene insieme," "Ex voto," "Laggiù," and "L'altro" and also in the earlier collections, in which Montale consistently emphasizes the importance of the incarnated God, most clearly in the figure of the beloved: a living, breathing, vulnerable woman who nonetheless possesses transcendental strength and vision.[42]

Montale's angel is slightly the worse for wear: its wings are worn down to "a few fringes"; it is sooty and made of "ashes and smoke"; it hides under the shawl of the chestnut vendor and is finally reduced to a "miniangel / chimney sweep." Thinking back to the importance of fire and light to Montale's most positive lyrics, especially those centered around the beloved Clizia but also used to define his poetic enterprise in general, we are struck by this chimney sweep, whose function it is to tend to the fire-giving hearth in the most humble of positions. This divinity is thus still associated with fire, but the fire is now entirely domesticated in the guardian chestnut vendor and in the timid, soot-covered angel. The angel is linked to dust, grime, smoke, embers, and soot rather than to the blaze of a fully kindled and raging fire, yet it can flash forth "in swift lightning." It is soon clear to us that Montale is using the angel as an analogy to his poetry itself. The most obvious clue that the poet is writing about the creation of poetry (which, as Montale would no doubt insist, is an additional and not an exclusive level of significance[43] is in the phrase "incomprensibile fabulazione" (incomprehensible fabulation). This paradoxical angel can exist only in the words that conjure it up. Akin to the *lupus in fabula*[44] that appears only by being talked about, the divinity is given a provisional life that is finally neither real nor fictional. This provisional life—poetry—is only a residue of some classical or romantic notion of full discourse, revelation, or self-expression, the ashes of the fire of inspiration here entrusted to the angel–chimney sweep and earlier tended by the war-weary Clizia. Yet, as the poet insisted in "Little Testament," "a story only lasts in ashes."

That poetic inspiration is a flash essentially out of reach of the poet is a concept subtly played upon by Montale in many other recent poems in which images of light and fire are satirized. In "La belle dame sans

112
Eugenio
Montale:
Poet
on
the
Edge

merci" the poet is unable to recapture the departed woman's image because his fire is "suffocated" and is nothing more than the spark of a
pocket lighter. In *Quaderno* in the poem "Il fuoco e il buio" (Fire and
Darkness) Montale explicitly connects "L'Ispirazione" (Inspiration)
with a fire that now needs nothing more than "il tascabile briquet / se
ci fosse una goccia di benzina" (the pocket lighter / if there were only
a drop of fuel). "I ripostigli" (The Storerooms) of the same collection
returns to the image of the lighter, now directly equated with the
poet himself: "Ero un accendino / a corto di benzina" (I was a
lighter / short on fuel). Here the beloved's innocent eyes, "which contained everything / and even more," are unknowable by "us men furnished with pocket lighters, / with lamps no." This is the same self-
deprecating stance expressed in "L'angelo nero," yet unlike the other
poems just cited it succeeds in being what it implicitly states the poet is
incapable of writing: an inspired, wholly convincing piece of lyricism.
This is in a way the poem's essential oxymoron. The weakest poems of
this late season are precisely those in which Montale resists his great poetic gifts in order to declaim their disappearance from his life; when he
weaves his self-parody, cynicism, and hopeless hope into poetic structures that transcend them, then the resultant tension creates a deeply
moving lyricism that is all the more effective as it defies its own open
recognition of the fundamental inadequacies of poetry.

In what sense are Montale's conceptions of the divine and of poetry
mutually dependent? If we accept that "L'angelo nero" is as much
about poetry as it is about the divine, it would seem to follow that the
two are linked; yet this would appear to contradict Montale's lifelong
insistence on the purely human limits of poetry understood as necessarily partial and flawed discourse. Yet we remember the "definitive *quid*,"
the "lay miracle," the poet's equally sustained insistence on the search
for a *varco*, a way through to understanding and escape from the limits
of human consciousness and experience that poetry might provide. For
Montale the divine is not separable from the immanent; he is as much
an incarnational poet as was his great master, Dante. By this I mean
that both poetry and the divine must be incorporated or expressed concretely in order to be accessible to human consciousness. Poetry understood as the inexpressible, that which can exist somewhere other than in
words on a page, is as alien a notion to Montale as that of a divinity who

113
The
Retrobottega:
Readings
of the
Last
Voice

is by nature beyond the realm of the tangible or the humanly know-able.[45] Both, however, are ultimately irrational and therefore reachable not through reason but through what can be thought of as gnosis, or to use Montale's word, *l'agnizione*, the recognition of relationships, meanings, and presences on both a perceptual and a conceptual level.[46] To know in this way is, however, finally not to know, for *agnizione* is from the Latin *agnosco*, the root of *agnostic* and *agnosticism*, both terms associated with the unknowability of reality. The definition of *agnosticism* given by Devoto and Oli in the *Dizionario della lingua italiana* (p. 61) uses a particularly Montalian turn of phrase: "dottrina filosofica che afferma l'incapacità della mente umana a conoscere la realtà in se stessa, che resta appunto inconoscibile" (a philosophic doctrine that affirms the incapacity of the human mind of knowing reality in itself, which remains, precisely, unknowable). Montale's black angel is knowable in its ties to real, tangible, and particularly humble human aspects and activities, but it is not truly known in its essence through or by them. Rather it remains out of reach, between the true and the false, in that realm of neither-nor in which both gods and poetry reside.

In his reading of the poem "Sul lago d'Orta" (On the Lake of Orta) in *Quaderno* the critic Stefano Agosti seeks to show the play on the word *tra* (between) that informs the poem. This critic's tools are for the most part Derridian; I would not go so far as to agree with his assertion that "poetic creation, without either generic or chronological distinctions, is by definition a practice of textuality" and as such remains always on the level of *signifiants* rather than any clearly perceivable *signifiés*.[47] Yet Agosti's insistence on the importance of the concept of betwixt and between in this poem is entirely consonant with my own use of the term *marginality*, as when, for example, he writes: "The place of Poetry . . . is the zone of the undecidable, the *interstices*, the *between*. Situated on the margins, on the rims, on the edges [lembi] (and in the limbo) of semantic and classificating fields in opposition, poetry is precisely the working of these margins and edges, the weaving of this *between*, with as its goal the neutralization of the oppositions that make up systems of meanings . . ."[48] The *angelo nero* resides entirely in this zone between oppositions; it and the poetry it represents seek to neutralize opposites, insisting on the paradoxical nature of both the divine and the poetic. The poem also makes clear the great results available to

114
Eugenio
Montale:
Poet
on
the
Edge

poetry that is humbler in theme and tone while at the same time implicitly insisting on the presence of more traditionally poetic themes (the beloved, poetry itself) and language as the basis for its newness.

There is a vitality to this new poetic enterprise, and we can sense the pleasure that underlies the word play, the thematic diversity, even the self-parody of which the poems of *Satura* are in large part made. There is, however, a sinister side to the poetry of this season that threatens the very possibility of continued production, thus creating an implicit tension between the activity of poetic creation and its opposite: silence. Silence, or the capitulation to the impossibility of poetry, has long beckoned to Montale. Certainly from as early on as the "Mediterraneo" suite of *Ossi di seppia*, in which the poet writes of the inadequacies of poetic expression in such phrases as "doleful literature" and "stuttering speech," the precariousness of Montale's dedication to writing in spite of the limits of literature has been clear. But that dedication does not in any sense hide his profound distrust of language or his respect for the integrity and meaning of emotions and experiences that cannot be expressed in words. To cite but a few instances, in "Ballad Written in a Clinic" (Ballata scritta in una clinica) in *La bufera* there is the "ululo / . . . muto" (silent howl) of both Mosca's wooden dog and the poet himself, in contrast to the "voce / che irrompe nell'alba" (voice / that erupts in the dawn), a voice of chaos. In "Visit to Fadin" (Visita a Fadin) in the same collection Montale writes of his friend Fadin, whose lesson of "daily decency" has not been fixed in words because the young man's words "were perhaps not the sort that are written." The first example emphasizes the inadequacy of language to express intense emotion, the second its inability to capture the ethical significance of a man's life that is, simply for having been lived, an *exemplum* for others.[49] Distrust gradually modulates into discouragement and disgust. By the end of *La bufera*, and clearly by the poems of *Satura*, there is discernible a bitterly negative attitude toward the expressive powers of language.

The disgust that Montale feels for the inadequacies of human language is explicitly stated in the sixth poem of the suite "After a Flight," where he writes: "Poetry and sewers, two problems / never disjoined." This phrase indicates not simply an isolated moment of disheartenment but rather a deeply felt belief that determines the tone of many of the recent poems. If life is understood as the indiscriminate consumption of

115
The
Retrobottega:
Readings
of the
Last
Voice

ultimately meaningless or at least incomprehensible and disparate occasions, as a giant mouth into which all is stuffed without any individual or transcendental control or plan, then the reexpression, the processing of a life through poetry makes of that expression the conduit for nothing more than the waste products that inevitably result from consumption: in short a sewer. Sewers deal with the unspeakable, with the once vital and essential sustaining elements of life that have necessarily deteriorated into unwanted, useless relics that must be disposed of somehow and yet that ultimately return to become part of the life-sustaining cycle from which they emerged. Montale's antiprogressive historical stance has been well documented, especially since the appearance of these last poems. I believe that his disgust with words is directly tied to his disgust with events, with what is commonly called history, which he sees as an unreadable, completely random, and essentially negative process of repetition, consumption, and degradation: a cesspool. Given such a view of history and language, Montale's reliance on the lay miracle is the only recourse open to him.

Montale's overall pessimism regarding history is tempered by his firm belief in the value of individual life. This belief sustained his early poetry, made possible the myth of a salvation-bearing woman, and continues to provide some positive glimmers in the poems directed to his dead wife. The "Xenia" poems are manifestations of his belief in the irrepeatability of one unique existence. That point that is beyond the grasp of the poet and that is the essence of Mosca's meaning is the anchor to which Montale clings as the events of a "reality not to be believed and never believed" threaten to overwhelm him, to bury him under "an atrocious erosion / of oil and dung," with the utterly negative result of a loss of individual identity ("Xenia II," poem 14). This strong belief in the value of the unique individual has very deep roots in the earliest poetry and in the origins of that poetry. We remember Montale's assertion in his "Intervista immaginaria" that he is not seeking "a philosophical poetry that spreads ideas . . . The poet's need is the search for a precise truth, not for a general truth. A truth of the poet-subject that might not deny that of the empirical man-subject. That might sing of that which unites man to other men but not deny that which disunites him and renders him unique and unrepeatable."[50] The "precise truth" is pursued throughout the first three collections; the search for this truth provides both the thematic direction of and the

116
Eugenio
Montale:
Poet
on
the
Edge

forms of expression with which the poetry is modulated and sustained. Montale has always distrusted the efficacy of language and history; the new poetry adds a disturbing doubt concerning the reality of precise truth that erodes even further the poet's tenuous faith in poetry's potential.

The title of *Satura* indicates that it is a miscellany; yet it is also a consciously organized book that moves from its opening poems toward an end understood in both senses of the term. *Satura* begins with two prefatory poems ("Botta e risposta I" and "Il *tu*") that look backward as well as forward. They are followed by the "Xenia" series, poems that are also backward looking. They speak of a person no longer present and quite literally summon her back from the realm of the dead, not only in order to recreate her and Montale's past life together but also in order to consider the possible meaning of such a shared past in the present moment. Thus we are in the realm of history, but it is individual, unique history—or to put it more directly, memory. The many echoes of earlier poetry also belong to the realm of memory, but memory that is literary and therefore shared, public, violable. The collection can be read in its totality as the movement toward relinquishing these personal and public memories, the gradual process of letting go, the clearing of ground for the truly new, the fundamentally transformed vision of Montale, which finds full expression in the succeeding volumes, *Diario* and *Quaderno*. In this sense the fourth collection is transitional, belonging completely neither to the earlier season, as represented by *Ossi*, *Occasioni*, and *Bufera*, nor to the post-Montalian Montale of the last two.

Hermeticism is practically synonymous with *solipsism:* the so-called hermetic poets are turned inward, involved in creating a language accessible to an élite: those who are equally involved in poetry and its goals. This adjective has been applied to the early Montale, especially as represented in *Le occasioni*, but also generally to his pre-*Satura* production. The application of such a term is quite appropriate, especially in view of Montale's ahistorical stance, insistence on highly private themes, and often difficult style. *La bufera* opens out onto the immediate realities of a shared, lived experience—the war—but is still a collection most intimately tied to a personal search for salvation and meaning. Stylistically Montale was still involved in what can be thought of as a highly literary pursuit, as he struggled with inherited forms, most no-

117
The
Retrobottega:
Readings
of the
Last
Voice

tably the sonnet, in the pursuit of his own definitive *quid*. The shift to more prosaic poetry in *Satura* is a clear indication of the poet's desire to create a much more accessible public voice that might break down the barriers between literary or privileged discourse and the speech of everyday life, used and understood by all. Relinquishing a high style in favor of a *tono prosaico* goes hand in hand with the movement toward the positive communicative potential of such language. This change in direction makes *Satura* an exciting experiment with serious stakes not only for Montale the individual poet but also for the future of poetry in a wider sense. Yet in becoming less hermetic Montale also reveals his doubt concerning the reality of private truth, a doubt that weakens even further his long-standing yet hesitant hope that poetry might lead to some sure knowledge or revelation. The same fundamental and unavoidable inadequacies that lay at the heart of the earlier enterprise still underlie the new one. These are the inadequacies of any literary discourse: not only to translate experience into words but more importantly to modify or explain that experience in such a way as to overcome its ultimately precarious, fleeting, and insignificant nature. The poems of *Satura* put up a good fight, so to speak; but Montale's final conclusion is that both life and poetry, public or private, are futile, unknowable in their essence, transitory, touched here and there by brief sparks of the divine, but ultimately unilluminated and unilluminating.

Satura closes with two poems that express Montale's tenuous hope, his final recourse in the face of such devastatingly negative conclusions. In "Luci e colori" (Lights and Colors) Mosca reappears in one of her *visite mute* (silent visits), which is called, in a wonderfully colloquial Milanese term, "gibigianna che tagli la foschia" (a flash that might cut through the haze). She is associated with "a little worm / that was wobbling by with difficulty," which the poet picks up on a piece of paper and throws out into the courtyard. He adds: "You yourself must not weigh more." The worm is discarded on a piece of paper; Mosca is also let go on a piece of paper—the poem itself. In the final poem of the collection, "L'altro" (The Other), Montale calls our dealings with the Other or God "un lungo inghippo" (a long swindle), making use this time of a *romanesco* slang word. He ends the poem with an image of the flamingo, which "astute . . . hides / its head under its wing and believes that the hunter / doesn't see it." Both poems, although on different subjects, are about necessary self-deception. The little worm is not,

118
Eugenio
Montale:
Poet
on
the
Edge

of course, a sign from Mosca or Mosca herself; but the care with which it is made to crawl onto a piece of paper in order that it be thrown out alive into the courtyard, and the connection made between its infinitesimal weight and Mosca's, are poignant indications of the poet's desire to go on believing that minute gestures matter. In the final poem the self-deception is even more ironically expressed in the figure of the bird that, in hiding its own head, believes itself to be invisible to the hunter. This is a transparently ridiculous ploy, but it is called "astute" by Montale, for what alternative is there? Self-protective gestures are all that are left—futile perhaps, but evidence of the poet's continued ties to a life and poetry that have reached the truly marginal state neither of hope nor of despair but of endurance.

Diario and *Quaderno:* A Survivor's Journal

Diario del '71 e del '72 has time as its ordering principle; the title tells us that this is a collection of poetry written day by day and extending over a specific two-year period. In the index each poem is dated to emphasize this diaristic format. This is a rather puzzling emphasis for a poet who has made it clear that he does not believe in the value of documentation—in history—and yet the insistence does not end there. In the poet's brief notes to the collection he writes that the reader "will note that in *Diario del '72* four months did not produce any poetry. Reasons of sickness were the cause of this lamentable (or praiseworthy?) lacuna." This note makes it obvious that Montale expects his readers to pay attention to dates, but to what end? Perhaps poetry is to be read as a parallel to life: a day = a poem. It is as if the writing of poetry has become a sort of automatic reflex impeded only by sickness, just as the normal activities of everyday life are so impeded. The passing days are being measured out not in coffee spoons but in poems that prove both to the poet and to us that he is still alive. This approach goes a step beyond the miscellaneous, apparently eclectic scheme of *Satura,* which does in fact come together to form a distinguishable whole made up of specific preoccupations, both thematic and stylistic. *Quaderno di quattro anni* is another diaristic collection, continuing the day-by-day, year-by-year structure of *Diario* and including poems from 1973 to 1977. Montale has, of course, been selective; unlike Petrarch, who emphasized the autobiographical, organic nature of his *Canzoniere* by includ-

119
The
Retrobottega:
Readings
of the
Last
Voice

ing poems that number 365 plus one, Montale has chosen a less obviously symbolic number of poems. The note provided by the poet
turns out to be a typically paradoxical explanation, as there are just as
many unrepresented months in *Diario '71* as in *'72*. The point, however, is made: poetry and life unfold simultaneously, and both are expressions of endurance that has as its only real obstacle sickness and its
possible fearsome outcome, death.

Montale's ironic attitude toward his age and eminent reputation
quite clearly figured in the making of *Satura*. In an interview conducted
in 1962, before the publication of *Satura*, the poet was asked to discuss
the reasons for his long silence. He answered: "First of all I had the impression that having already published three books that are, after all,
three parts of the same autobiography, I could also be quiet, because I
had already said all of the essential . . . In the end I hope that I am still
able to do something. Not exactly a book, but an appendix, that yes."
He then added: "In a practical sense I should have already died. The
great poets die young. It's clear that I am a very small [minor] poet, because I don't die."[51] In another interview published in 1971, after the
appearance of *Satura*, Montale commented on the long intervals between his first four books:

> You have noticed that every thirteen, fourteen years one of my
> books of poetry comes out. It is not a question of planned inter-
> vals. I publish when a certain accumulation has been produced in
> me, that is, when I realize that a certain number of poems "make"
> a possible book. I do not believe that it is possible that a fifth book
> of mine will appear. That should occur in 1985. This is not to be
> hoped for, either for me or for others.[52]

Instead the fifth collection appeared in 1973, only two short years after
Satura, followed in 1977 by the sixth, *Quaderno*. Gianfranco Contini
calls *Diario* "the diagram of a survival."[53] The accumulation that implies a gradual process over time is now supplanted by a prolificacy as
unexpected as anything ever before in Montale's fifty-year career.

It would seem that the Muse has returned with a vengeance, yet this
is precisely what the poet denies in the opening poems of *Diario*. The
first two poems of the collection, given under the title "A Leone Traverso" (To Leone Traverso), a translator of Rilke and old friend of
Montale's, are explicit meditations on poetry, specifically on Montale's

120
Eugenio
Montale:
Poet
on
the
Edge

own recent poetry. Poetry is imagined as a "bedeviled" woman playing hide and seek; she is hard to catch by the toupee, flighty and somewhat ridiculous figure that she is. The poet is equally discouraged by the possibility of simply letting himself go "sulla corrente" (on the current trends), experimenting as did "il neoterista Goethe" (the innovator Goethe). The unusual noun takes us back to "Xenia I," poem 6, where the poet wrote to Mosca: "Fu pure il mio terrore: di esser poi / ricacciato da te nel gracidante / limo dei neòteroi" (It was my very worst fear: that I might then be / thrown back by you into the croaking / slime of the neoterists). In the second poem Montale uses what is to become the essential tense of this collection: the past remote. He writes "Sognai anch'io di essere un giorno mestre / de gay saber; e fu speranza vana" (I too dreamed of one day being a master / of the gay science, and it was a vain hope). Both the dream and the hope are thus relegated to the irretrievable past; what makes up the present is "a dried up laurel" and "music" that "recedes," the only things left after all the other possibilities are discounted.

The image of poetry as receding music is picked up in another poem of *Diario* entitled "La mia musa" (My Muse). It too is an apologia pro arte sua, which begins: "My muse is far away." The celesta and the vibraphone are abandoned now in favor of a "quartet / of straws"; the music of the spheres is no longer sought, but rather a humble melody is "the only music [I] can bear." The grotesque image of poetry decked out in a toupee is also in this poem, for the Muse is said to have left behind her "storeroom / of theatrical dress"; she now has only "one sleeve" with which to direct the motley quartet.

The next poem of *Diario*, appropriately entitled "L'arte povera" (Poor Art), speaks of Montale's penchant for painting his little watercolors on wrapping paper using wine, coffee, and toothpaste to produce his tints. The identification of this humble art with the poet's survival mentality is made clear in the final lines of the poem, where he writes of these paintings: "È la parte di me che riesce a sopravvivere / del nulla ch'era in me . . ." (It is the part of me that succeeds in surviving / of the nothing that was in me).

These poems are not, then, evidence of a renewed vitality, a surge of strong, youthful inspiration, but are instead the dilapidated, worn-out remains of a poet whose Muse is dressed in "scarecrow's rags" ("My Muse") and who will time and time again use the past-remote tense in

121
The
Retrobottega:
Readings
of the
Last
Voice

referring to himself. They are, to use a perfectly suited French idiom, *de trop*, or as Montale translates that saying, *un sovrappiù*.[54] This is self-deflation carried to its most extreme limits; yet the programmatic humiliation is directed not only at the poet himself but more importantly at poetry in its present context. All these comments of the poet's concerning his art have mainly to do with style rather than content or message. His music is muted, his tints brought into being through the use of the most inartistic of materials; the Muse is dressed in the rags of a scarecrow. It is not so much the essence of his poetry as the form that is systematically humiliated throughout these last two collections. As is made collectively clear in the many poems of the collections, this emphasis on form is tied to Montale's basic uncertainty concerning the reality of any content, be it existential or literary. Montale presents himself as a survivor and his poetry as survival in humble form of what is experientially and philosophically formless: life itself. His tattered Muse reflects, therefore, his view of contemporary poetry as necessarily debased, given the fundamentally unillumined reality from which it emerges.

It might seem a mistake to extend Montale's attitude toward his recent poetry to the possibilities open to poetry in general. This is, after all, the final offering of an old, disillusioned man who, in reconsidering his own past life and work, has reached the conclusion that it adds up to very little. Yet I believe that this reading of the significance of *Diario* and *Quaderno* is reductive and does not take into account the awareness with which Montale takes this stance or the seriousness with which he assumes the explicit role of what might be called a poet's poet: one who cares deeply about the state of the art, not only his own but that which is being born or will be born long after his own voice has become silent. The question asked in his Nobel acceptance speech, "Is Poetry Still Possible?" is at the heart of these recent poems that strain against the many negative elements toward which the poet has always tended. Uncertainties, inadequacies, cynicism, bitterness, silence: all of these erode Montale's, and all artists', dedication to art. Add to these Montale's age, his conservative and contemplative bent, and it becomes evident that a poetics of survival is not only understandable but inevitable, and not for this poet alone. Much of modern art can be seen as the struggle against representation or imitation of reality; artists tend more and more to reject the idea that reality is graspable, expressible, or even

122
Eugenio
Montale:
Poet
on
the
Edge

real. Montale has always held this view, and the emphasis on form in these recent collections is entirely consonant with earlier, more thematically oriented poetry in which certain motifs had an important role. We might think of *Diario* and *Quaderno* as simply pushing further into the land of themelessness; both collections are finally, exquisitely, and consciously themeless.

Most critics of *Diario* have recognized the primacy of style in these poems and have concentrated their critical efforts on formal issues. Almansi and Merry seek to point out the weaknesses in the rhetorical strategies employed by Montale in this collection. They write that "everything can be smuggled into the territory of great revelations through rhetoric and style" but conclude that this is not the case here, where more often than not "the verbal pyrotechnics misfire."[55] More positive critical reactions also center on the formal aspects of the collection. For example Giuliano Gramigna writes of a "new enunciation" manifested "in a sort of reduction that is not so much conceptual as purely linguistic." This newness is effected by means of a constant recourse to "the anonymous blabla" of everyday speech, which creates "a 'pedal' giving the uninterrupted bass note." For Gramigna, this newly reduced, radically lowered tone is accomplished "with amazing vitality," and the result is poetry that renews itself "not 'from outside' but 'from inside.' "[56] Gianfranco Contini calls the prosaic tendencies of *Diario* "a countermelody" that depends in great part on "words now in fashion."[57] Continuing along these lines Claudio Scarpati insists on the Montalian "method of description / assertion, already put into practice in *Ossi di seppia* and now bent to the ends of a moral comprehension of the present moment and of an estrangement from its banality by means of the banal itself." Thus the banalization of poetry is carried out in order to wake us up "from our acritical torpor" and to force us to make a "thoughtful, meditative leap" from that torpor to an awareness of the significance of our trite language, and, through it, of our conceptions of reality that it reflects.[58] Marco Forti uses Montale's own phrase "the permanent oxymoron" as the essential defining and shaping figure of this last season, showing the ways in which the constant linking of opposites forms both the stylistic and philosophical background of the poems.[59]

All these readings recognize and cogently detail the deeply prosaic core of *Diario*, which has its most immediate origins in *Satura* but

123
The
Retrobottega:
Readings
of the
Last
Voice

which goes back much farther to implicate Montale's basic desire from the very beginning of his career to create a "countereloquence." I cannot but agree with these conclusions, given my own reading of Montale as always eager to give vent to his essential distrust of the possibilities of lyric to sing or to express anything other than a partial, self-consciously ambivalent truth. But I believe that these readings of *Diario* do not go far enough in determining where lie both the strengths and the weaknesses of such an explicit concentration on the inadequacies of language, self, and art. Is there not the danger of self-indulgence and of a retreat into banality that is not primarily a positive tactic but also a cover for the poet's own weakening expressive powers? Is there not also an abyss yawning beneath such willfully banalized poetry that threatens poetry's very raison d'être? In his most recent poetry Montale is making seminal proposals concerning directions for future poetry, but he is doing so at the risk of destroying some of the most fundamental strengths of his earlier verse.

Angelo Jacomuzzi speaks of Montale's "phenomenology of language" and quite correctly points out Montale's identification of poetry on the one hand with the "orphic condition of the word," primarily in "Mediterraneo," and on the other with the demystifying properties of language. These contrasting views put him squarely in the midst of "an entire tradition" of modern poetry that has tried one or the other solution to the problem of what poetry is. But as Jacomuzzi also correctly points out, Montale's first three collections are based not on a *primum formale,* or "formal primum," as Contini puts it, but rather on "that crisis of the concept of reality . . . that Montale translates into that absence of certainty concerning the real, which is his first true declaration, then developed, confirmed, and brought to its ultimate ideological and formal conclusions through many elaborations." The poetry of the first three collections cannot be read, therefore, as "a language that . . . wishes to celebrate its own rites within an idea of style" but must instead be seen as representing the search for "its own justification . . . and its own continuance in an open confrontation with an eventual notion of reality."[60]

According to my reading of the earlier Montale, that justification is found in process itself (defined as the marginal), in the importance of private and unique memories, and in the lay miracle, especially as embodied in the beloved of *La bufera e altro.* These are all very personal

124
Eugenio
Montale:
Poet
on
the
Edge

realities that serve to fill the void created by Montale's lack of certainty concerning the real and to sustain his dedication to poetic creation. In *Satura* we see their gradual erosion, until in *Diario* and *Quaderno* they have all but disappeared, to be replaced with the poet's explicit insistence on the *primum formale* of these new poems.[61] Here the phenomenology of language takes over as the poet's central preoccupation, the issue of content having been effectively rendered null by Montale's belief that there is really nothing that can be written of, nothing real that is capable of being captured in words. Or to turn this around, everything can be written of—any experience, notion, insight, opinion—precisely because all is nothing, all equally grist for the word mill. Almansi and Merry call this attitude Montale's recourse to "that obsessive, over-exploited *nulla / tutto* oxymoron"[62] found throughout *Diario* and *Quaderno.*

The sheer number of poems (two hundred) that make up *Diario* and *Quaderno*, more than the first three collections combined, and the lack of any organization according to section titles or suites as in the first three and, to a certain extent, in *Satura*, highlight their lack of thematic unity. Trying to find some organizational principle in their presentation is akin to searching for the needle in the haystack: it may be there, but it is so overwhelmed as to make such a search a lesson in frustration and futility. The final poems of *Diario del '71 e del '72* are both superficially closural: "p.p.c." ("per prendere congedo," or "in order to leave") from its title to its valedictory message is presented as an ultimate farewell; "Per finire" (To End) is a sort of literary will in which the poet asks that his "facts" and "nonfacts," all that has made up his life as expressed in poetry, be consigned to the flames of "a beautiful bonfire." Yet both are falsely teleological: the ending they suggest is belied by the outpouring of poetry that follows. They are necessary, however, because the collections that have no thematic or organic unity must end somehow, and the strongly final tone of both signals the arbitrary nature of those ends.

Thus theme cannot be pursued, and we must turn instead to the elaboration of a theory of language. In Jacomuzzi's sensitive study entitled "L'Elogio della balbuzie" (In Praise of the Stutter) we are provided with one of the essential elements upon which that theory is built: the stutter. Stuttering is generally considered to be a defect of speech and those afflicted by it to be handicapped. It is defined variously as speech characterized by "continued involuntary repetition

125
The
Retrobottega:
Readings
of the
Last
Voice

of sounds or syllables owing to excitement, fear, or constitutional nervous defect" and by "blocks or spasms interrupting the rhythm."[63] The word *balbuzie* first appears in poem 11 of "Xenia I." Celia, the Philippine girl, calls to find out how Montale's ailing wife is doing. When she realizes that Mosca is dead "una balbuzie / impediva anche lei" (a stutter / impeded her also). It appears again in *Satura* proper in the poem "Incespicare" (To Stammer), where the poet writes: "Incespicare, incepparsi / è necessario / per destare la lingua / dal suo torpore. / Ma la balbuzie non basta . . ." (To stammer and stumble / is necessary / in order to awaken language / from its torpor. / But stuttering is not enough). In *Quaderno* we find the term in an untitled poem that begins: "Chissà se un giorno butteremo le maschere / che portiamo sul volto senza saperlo" (Who knows if one day we might not throw off the masks / we wear on our faces without knowing it). Here Montale proposes a hypothetical savior who would be able to tell us "la parola / che attendiamo da sempre" (the word / we have always been waiting for), were it not for the fact that even he would be ignorant of his privileged status. The poet concludes: "Chi l'ha saputo, se uno ne fu mai, / pagò il suo dono con balbuzie o peggio" (He who knew it, if there ever was such a person, / paid for his gift with stutters or worse).

It is not so much the term itself, however, but the way in which the concept of repetition, spasms, and the like forms the principle of these poems that is of great interest to those who seek to understand Montale's theory of language. To speak, and to write poetry, is to stutter, to express oneself hesitantly and repetitiously, not only because the defect is in the user but also because it is in the very medium itself: language. Not only is content thus debased and rendered essentially without meaning, but the form of language too is attacked for its essentially flawed nature. According to Montale language as a phenomenon is completely human, although in "La lingua di dio" (God's Language) in *Diario* a divine origin is posited: "Se dio è il linguaggio, l'Uno che ne creò tanti altri / per poi confonderli . . ." (If god *is* language, the One who created so many others / in order to confuse them). Language is therefore vulnerable to the same uncertainties and weaknesses as any human element. It is called in "Un tempo" (Once) in *Quaderno* "this mad god / who does not lead to salvation because it knows / nothing of us and obviously / nothing of itself." It is approximate—"qualche cosa che approssima ma non tocca" (something that approximates but does

126
Eugenio
Montale:
Poet
on
the
Edge

not touch); unillumined—"pietà per chi . . . brancola nel buio / delle parole" (pity for those who grope about in the dark / of words); reflective of the nullity of the world and of the mind—"Se il mondo ha la struttura del linguaggio / e il linguaggio ha la forma della mente / la mente con i suoi pieni e i suoi vuoti / è niente o quasi e non ci rassicura" (If the world has the structure of language / and language has the mind's form / the mind with its fullnesses and its voids / is nothing or just about and does not reassure us).[64] As Jacomuzzi asserts in "L'Elogio" (p. 154) this attitude toward language becomes a sort of "negative theology within the sphere of human language," a theology that I believe to be in close correspondence with Montale's more inclusive negative theology as expressed in the poem "The Black Angel."

The poet whose poetry is most intimately bound to a theology of language and for whom theological and linguistic considerations could not be separated is of course Dante. As remote from him as the Montale of this last season may appear to be, a brief reconsideration of Dante's fundamental tenets regarding language, reality, and the role of poetry should nonetheless prove pertinent. The comparison is not predicated on some sort of direct line of inspiration traceable from Dante to Montale; but I am convinced that the modern poet's preoccupations are comparable to those of Dante, at least in the sense that for both poetry involves the meaning of history, the possibilities open to human reason, and the link between the experiential and the epistemological in the search for significance and validation. Montale himself suggests his ties to Dante, in a purely schematic and undeveloped way to be sure, in his essay "Dante Yesterday and Today," where he states: "Dante *is not* modern . . . the fact of which cannot hinder us from understanding him, at least in part, and of feeling him to be strangely close to us. But in order that this occur it is necessary to reach another conclusion: that we are no longer living in a modern age but rather in a new Middle Ages of which we are not yet capable of spotting the salient traits." This new Middle Ages, he goes on to say, can be seen either negatively as "a new barbarity" by those who believe in "the complete triumph of scientific-technical reason," or it can be seen as a positive development by those, among whom Montale would number himself, "who do not believe in the nonsense of reason unfolding ad infinitum." It could be understood in this sense as a revolutionary "disturbance of the very notion

127
The
Retrobottega:
Readings
of the
Last
Voice

itself of civilization and culture."[65] Montale's latest poems may in fact be read as moving toward this disturbance. Dante's theology of language and his concept of history were positive while Montale, living in a new Middle Ages, is assailed by profound doubts concerning both the effectiveness of language and the progressive nature of historical events. The points of contact between the two poets' visions might best be thought of as analogous to the relationship of the negative of a photograph to the print itself—a sort of unity in contrasts. For Dante there is a radical discontinuity between human language and revealed Truth, as represented by the *Logos.* Presumption was at the root of the Fall from grace and is also the cause of the second Fall, the loss of the primordial unified language as recounted in the story of the Tower of Babel. At the same time language, fallen or not, is exclusively human and signals the mediate position of man between the unspeaking animal, purely bestial and incapable of reason, and the Divine, the superrational perfection of angelic intellection and therefore unneedful of speech. Language is a powerful instrument of mediation between the human and the divine realms. In his treatise on language, *De vulgari eloquentia,* Dante outlines the lineaments of his search for a redeemed language, a language that is the equivalent of the intermediate state of mankind as it moves from the Fall toward plentitude, a progression made possible by Christ's mediation between the perfect Creator and his tainted creatures. Dante calls this language the "volgare illustre" (illustrious vulgar tongue). The etymological root of the adjective in the word *light* (lux) is central to our understanding of the phrase. The language is not only illustrious—that is, noble and learned—but more importantly it reflects the final source of light—God or the sun—and lights the way for others struggling out of the darkness of spiritual confusion. The *volgare illustre* is pursued like a panther through the wilderness of Italian dialects; but it is not to be captured, for it is as elusive as a fragrance that "spreads its perfume everywhere and appears nowhere." This is the case because it is not an embodied reality but rather an essence that exists *in potentia,* actualized only partially and imperfectly in the writings of the best poets. The implication is that Dante himself will bring it to life within the context of his *Commedia,* which has as its theme the ultimate redemption of man. A redeemed poetic language will speak of a redemptive view of history, and the instrument of expression will thus directly

128
Eugenio
Montale:
Poet
on
the
Edge

reflect the content of the poem. There is at stake in the *Commedia*, then, not only the truth of the salutory message it carries to its readers but also the very status of poetic language as a possible vehicle for that truth. If Dante was aware of the fraudulent, obfuscating qualities of language, as Giuseppe Mazzotta argues most convincingly in his book *Dante, Poet of the Desert*,[66] it is also nonetheless true that his essential faith in the absolute reliability of God's plan as it unfolds throughout history extends to his final faith in poetry as a vehicle for revelation of that plan. Language can reflect the essence of both experience and knowledge, of history and the teleology of the fullness of time outside of history, because it is the instrument of man, who is both within and ultimately without the world. Dante's belief that the world can be read like a book and that God's signs are everywhere and within the grasp of the rational mind sustained his poetic enterprise; his historical and literary views were determined by his a priori assumption of order, cohesion, and progression, and his unshakable belief in the possibility of reunion with perfection made possible and accessible to man by Christ's coming.

Dante's poetics go far beyond aesthetics; inherent in his poetry are the vaster issues of reason, faith, the meaning of history and of the individual within it, and salvation—the final meaning of both larger events and private, unique lives. Montale's latest poetry is similarly imbued with extraliterary concerns but seen from the perspective of a modern poet for whom the certainties that nourished Dante's vision have been irrevocably lost. In spite of the darkly humorous, playful, and even totally self-referential aspects of his recent poetry, his sense of this loss endows it with great moral seriousness. I am not implying that Montale should be read as some sort of latter-day prophet or that we should seek the essence of his poetry in some sense of mission that might have guided him throughout his career.[67] Precisely the opposite is true: Montale is representative of the modern mind and sensibility because he eschews prophecy, cohesion, and transcendental order. Yet in rejecting these certainties he consistently shows his awareness of their existence as personal, historical, cultural, and spiritual keystones around which the most enduring art has always been built. In these recent poems he returns to the issue of the connection between language and revelation, the temporal and the timeless, but he does so in a humiliated style very much in keeping with the times. Dante's goal was a re-

129
The
Retrobottega:
Readings
of the
Last
Voice

deemed literary language that would accurately reflect his faith in God's plan; Montale's goal is the creation of a poetic idiom that reflects the collective loss of such faith and the tragic dilemma that has resulted.

A somewhat analogous vision is expressed in the recent poetry of James Merrill, who in his *Divine Comedies* and subsequent volumes alludes to Dante not only in the choice of title but also in the attempt to turn poetry away from solipsism toward a verse that can accommodate both the individual soul and the universal spirit of today.[68] Merrill's long poem is based on a totally irrational *point de départ*—communication with spirits from the beyond via the Ouija board—but is utterly permeated with a reasoning, nonmystical mind seeking to probe present-day realities and future results of the contemporary reliance on science as the new God. I am not suggesting that the two modern poets are alike in terms of style, sensibility, or tone. Yet Montale would understand Merrill's recourse to the eccentric in his search for some transcendent value; for Montale too, our salvation rests not in reason but in irrational deviations from the norm, in so-called mistakes, in lay miracles rather than in the Dantesque fullness of time. Truths are still sought, therefore, but they are of necessity partial, even contradictory truths that can be expressed only in the flawed, stammering speech of the contemporary poet.

It is this more inclusive dimension of the recent poetry of Montale that I see as its positive core. In these stuttering poems he is tackling the very issue of communication itself, having moved away from the literary hermeticism of the earlier stylistic adventures into the realm of a more open confrontation with language and its potential. Like Dante, who used Italian rather than the more valid literary idiom of his day, Latin, in order to create his great poem, Montale has chosen to use language that, although permeated with the estranging qualities of all literary discourse, is nonetheless the speech of everyday, accessible to an audience generally unprepared or unwilling to read more traditionally poetic verse. The paradox is that what it so directly communicates is the final impossibility of meaningful communication, and the knowledge it shares is that unequivocal knowledge is beyond the reach of the human mind. But even this paradox can be seen as positive not only for this poetry but for future poetry as it fights for some raison d'être. In openly and uncompromisingly embracing limitations and ambiguities as its

130

Eugenio
Montale:
Poet
on
the
Edge

motifs and motives poetry will show what Jacomuzzi calls "solidarity with life," and its continuance will be "in the crucial assumption and in the conscious practice of this uneliminable statute."[69] Poetry must reflect the poet's *coscienza* (awareness) and *conoscenza* (knowledge, consciousness), not in some sort of hierarchical relationship with experience but in a coextensive perception of the essential role of critical awareness and conscience in both life and art. This attitude toward the function of literary discourse is positive not because it privileges literature by placing it beyond human vulnerability to error and chance but because it assigns to it a critical function that lies squarely within the risky enterprise of living. And as Montale writes in "Il trionfo della spazzatura" (The Triumph of Trash): "Essere vivi e basta / non è impresa da poco" (To live and nothing more / is no small undertaking).

As Montale's most recent poetry moves beyond the hermeticism of his earlier verse it becomes vulnerable to the degradation of any more public entity. As usual Montale foresees the danger and uses irony in an attempt to forestall it. In the poem entitled "L'obbrobrio" (Opprobrium) in *Quaderno* Montale writes: "Non fatemi discendere amici cari / fino all'ultimo gradino / della poesia sociale" (Don't make me descend dear friends / to the very last step / of social poetry). With his customary skepticism the poet continues: "Se l'emittente non dà che borborigmi / che ne sarà dei recipienti?" (If the emittor gives forth only intestinal rumblings / what will become of the recipients?). Social poetry is thus implicitly equated with these embarrassing rumblings; both are humiliating expressions of the baser aspects of the human animal. Nor are they aesthetically pleasing. Here the definition of the title word proves illuminating: "having to do with works that offend the aesthetic sense; aesthetically deplorable."[70] In a certain sense this definition applies to the recent poems, which are often opprobrious in comparison with works of more traditional lyrical decorum and grace. They are filled with unpoetic words; they reject the rhythms and musical sonorities of the Italian language; they refuse the flow of the hendecasyllabic line: in short they are jarring and somehow disturbing rather than seductive and beautiful. Montale's poetry has always sought to pit itself against the lure of simple auditory enchantment, a difficult battle given the undeniable musicality of the Italian tongue; but the results are still a music permeated with a full and unforgettable beauty. One need only think of poems such as "The Sunflower," "The Customs House," or

131
The
Retrobottega:
Readings
of the
Last
Voice

"The Eel" for the melodies to return and enrapture. Now we are assailed by words such as *dentifricio* (toothpaste), *emmerdant* (a pain in the ass), *vada a farsi f——* (go get screwed), and many other foreign, dialectal, slang, and obscene words. As Montale writes in the poem "Torpore primaverile" (Spring Torpor) in *Quaderno*, "la nostra civiltà batte il suo pieno / scusate il francesismo rotte le museruole / le lingue sono sciolte non hanno freno" (our civilization is in full flower / pardon the Gallicism broken the muzzles / languages are loosed they have no control). Indeed in *Diario* and *Quaderno* it is difficult to find any poem that does not include an unpoetic word, a jerking rhythm, or an image of a decidedly prosaic, quotidian, or timely nature.

Lyricism has all but disappeared from these pages, replaced by poetry that is willfully querulous, degraded, or even slightly obscene and a poet who is unstintingly self-deprecating. "The eagle cannot be born / of the mouse" Montale announced in "Thrust and Parry I," from *Satura,* and the self-examination carried out in the next two collections seconds this conclusion: "Tentai di essere / un uomo e già era troppo / per me" (I tried to be / a man and that was already too much / for me), from "Il cavallo" (The Horse); "Non sono un Leopardi . . . Vissi al cinque per cento" (I am not a Leopardi . . . I lived at a 5 percent level), from "Per Finire" (To End); "Non amo / chi sono, ciò che sembro" (I do not love / who I am, what I seem), from "Mezzo secolo fa" (Half a Century Ago); "Noi uomini forniti di briquet, / di lumi no" (We men furnished with lighters, / with lamps no), from "I ripostigli" (The Storerooms).

All of these humiliated and humiliating tactics add up to poems that seek to convince rather than enthrall, and as Almansi and Merry so correctly point out, poetry is "convincing only if it is also incantatory."[71] We are generally enchanted by that which is capable of capturing our most private feelings; we are convinced more often by that which has attained public and collective recognition. In lowering the tone of his poetry, in presenting himself entirely "in bourgeois clothes," as he writes in *Satura*'s "Phone Tap," Montale has, perhaps necessarily, brought down his vision from its earlier literary hermeticism into the piazza.[72] The new idea of poetry subtending this strategem is vital and potentially positive; but the poetry itself is, for the most part, to use the rather harsh phrase of Almansi and Merry, "too clever by half."[73] Montale's irony concerning more public social poetry shows that he is

132
Eugenio
Montale:
Poet
on
the
Edge

perfectly aware of its potential weaknesses, but such awareness does not serve to protect the poetic results from negative criticism.

In another attempt to forestall any harsh assessment of the new poetry Montale turns his weapon of irony against his public. In the poem "I travestimenti" (The Disguises) of *Quaderno* he writes:

Basta un'occhiata allo specchio
per credersi altri.
Altri e sempre diversi
ma sempre riconoscibili
da chi s'è fatto un cliché
del nostro volto.

A glance in the mirror is enough
to believe oneself another.
Another and always different
but always recognizable
by those who have made a cliché
of our faces.

In these lines Montale presents himself as an astute self-observer. The flamingo of the final poem of *Satura* is also astute for hiding its head under its wing in order not to be seen. Language itself is similarly characterized by "le sue astuzie" (its astuteness) in the poem "La lingua di Dio" (God's Language) in *Diario*. This is a richly ambivalent term, for it can refer to the positive qualities of skill, adroitness, and discernment or to the negative ones of cunning and deceptive trickery. Montale is asking that we see his new poetry as being on the one hand discerning and sagacious and on the other hand tricky and cunningly deceptive. He implies that if we fail to do so, we will be guilty of having made a cliché of him based on our expectations originating in the "Montalian" Montale of the first three collections. But with whom does the cliché truly originate now? Are we wrong to hear certain turns of phrase—the *tu* imperative, the oxymora, the anaphoric repetitions—as well-worn devices, echoing and yet no longer equaling their earlier power? Or are they in fact to be read as astute indications of the poet's own awareness of their emptiness not only now but throughout his poetry from *Ossi* to the last lines of *Quaderno*? In either choice or both there is a negative result, for in this case the operation of negating a negative does not pro-

133
The
Retrobottega:
Readings
of the
Last
Voice

duce a positive but rather simply reiterates the basic negativity of the whole.

Montale's ironic stance, his own *astuzia*, distance the reader from any naïve, direct reading of the new collections. Jacomuzzi correctly asserts that we are finally the objects of Montale's wily tactics in that "the poet's irony is not practiced only or even to any great extent on the object of discourse, but rather on the expectations and the deciphering of the readers."[74] Yet in spite of the fact of our being read by Montale, the poems remain unprotected by their extremely skillful ploys from our reading of them as poems. Poetry may, as he writes in "Poetry" from *Satura*, "with horror / . . . refuse / the scholiasts' glosses," but we, the readers of it, can also refuse its glosses on us, especially if they imply that the worth of poems rests in our understanding of or response to them rather than in their own autonomous excellence. Montale may insist that his poetry "will end up with all the rest"[75] in chaos and oblivion, but this resolves nothing in regard to its excellence or mediocrity, an issue that must concern anyone for whom the value of art is of any import.

Is it possible to follow a course of banalization—theoretical, linguistic, and philosophical—and avoid writing banal poetry? This is the daring and the risk of Montale's recent poetry. The poems contained in the last three collections are certainly not uniformly banal, but they are rarely completely realized poems. Instead they tend to contain isolated fragments, bits and pieces that engage the ear and enchant the heart or simply tickle the viscera. They also go a bit too far in the destruction of Montale's own poetic myth. When the poet spreads all of his wares in full view, when he writes that "Celia was turned into a skeleton by termites / Clizia was consumed by her God / who was she herself," that Mosca is "some bones / and a few trinkets," that he himself "does not like / to be thrust into history / because of a few poems or little more" because "it has all been / a quid pro quo," how can we not feel somewhat cheated of the magic of the great poems that represent the enduring contribution of this poet?[76] Montale has truly taken a palinodic stand, if we consider that the term originally meant in Greek the recantation (literally the resinging) of an ode—the correction, therefore, of a former belief or attitude. Usually the palinode represents a conversion away from erroneous, faithless statements to the Truth as embodied in God and Christ.[77] In Montale's case we have just the opposite: a retro-

134
Eugenio
Montale:
Poet
on
the
Edge

spective consideration of the tenuous faith in words, love, and the positive knowledge made available through poetry has resulted in a rejection of this faith and a final cynicism expressible only in humiliated language.

I have suggested a possible reading of this last season that might not exclusively emphasize either its historical, extrinsic importance as radically new poetry or its status as a self-referential, negative gloss on Montale's own earlier production. The many implicit and explicit comments on poetry to be found throughout the last three collections indicate that Montale is deeply interested in this art form's past, present, and future. The ironic, corrosive operation on his earlier poetry, however, shows that the new season is also irrevocably bound up with the self-enclosed microcosm of Montale's unique poetic vision. There is no sharp dichotomy between these realms, just as there should be no one critical approach to the poems that excludes either. Montale's greatest accomplishment in this last season is the complete merging of shared and public preoccupations and the unique, private elements of his poetic universe. They are brought together in a metaphoric space that is neither here nor there but that alludes to both: the space of the marginal. Jacomuzzi use phrases such as "a perpetual oscillation" and "unstable equilibrium" in describing the discourse of Montale's latest poetry.[78] These terms can be extended to describe the overall status of poetry as implied by Montale throughout his career.

I have explained my use of the word *marginality* as a critical metaphor and have said that the space it defines is metaphoric. A metaphor is a rhetorical figure, perhaps *the* figure of all poetic activity; it is also a concept involving the question of knowledge, the operations of the human intellect upon experience, and its expression in language. *Metaphor* is itself most commonly defined in metaphors as a bridge, a vehicle, a link between two words or images that brings into being a new truth originating in the comparison.[79] It is therefore understandable as an edge term, much as *marginal* has been proposed as such.

In his article entitled "Art and Life: A Metaphoric Relationship," Richard Shiff speaks of the dynamism inherent in artistic activity, locating it on "a metaphoric bridge between a perfected art and an evolving life."[80] In his argument there exists the basic awareness of both life and art as process, the seeking of finalization, completion, knowledge, and revelation that provides the impetus for the continuation of both.

135
The
Retrobottega:
Readings
of the
Last
Voice

In *Diario* and *Quaderno* Montale is writing a poetry of *oltrevita*, of survival; he presents himself and his poems in the past tense as summations of a life already lived. Yet paradoxically the very existence of these late poems denies the death inherent in such finalizations by rejecting true enlightenment. As Shiff further points out, "we continue to live because we remain ignorant of the absolute truth which would end our passage through the experience of life."[81] Montale's acceptance of ambiguity, ignorance, the permanent oxymoron of both life and art is not therefore a passive pessimism, a relinquishing of vitality, a death. But to remain in the realm of perpetual oscillation so essential to any understanding of Montale's poetics, while providing proof of his assertion, "he [Montale] did not die," by continuing to write, the poet destroys the possibility of clinging to a notion of his earlier poetry as revelatory, as fixable or fixed truth. In a sense he kills off the Montale that was in order to go on being the Montale that is.

In spite of the great risks he has taken in transforming his voice at this stage in his career, in spite of his awareness of the precariousness of all art, in spite of his inability to accept traditional reassurances of meaning and transcendence as he approaches his own death, Montale remains tenaciously and even perversely optimistic. As he wrote in *Diario* in the poem "My Optimism," "Il tuo ottimismo mi dice l'amico / e nemico Benvolio è sconcertante" (Your optimism says my friend / and enemy Benvolio is disconcerting). It is disconcerting because it does not depend on hope or expectations of ultimate clarification by the great Artificer. Nor should we expect any final settling of accounts by this artificer of words. He refuses to present his poetry as the truth concerning the lack of truth, as the unambiguous assertion of ambiguity's hegemony. Not even this positive negativity is available to us if we take to heart the essential message of Montale's last season. After all, he told us many years ago that "tenacious endurance is nothing but extinction." However we are not the ones to light the bonfire that will consume Montale's poetry, for it has lit its own fire from within and has fulfilled the prophecy contained in *La bufera* that states: "a story only endures in ashes." Within these ashes there still persists that "spark that says / everything is beginning when everything seems / to char."[82]

4
Prose Glosses: Is Poetry Still Possible?

IN his career as a journalist Montale wrote innumerable prose pieces, some of which have already been anthologized in *Auto da fé* and *Sulla poesia,* others of which have still to be gathered.[1] He has published two collections of short prose: *Farfalla di Dinard,* which is made up of stories and prose pieces, and *Fuori di casa,* which consists of his travel pieces.[2] In her exhaustive and invaluable *Bibliografia montaliana* Laura Barile lists under the heading of "prose" these additional texts: *Il colpevole* (a republication of a story written in 1947 for the one and only edition of the Triestine review *Ponte Rosso*); *Lettere: Montale-Svevo; La poesia non esiste* (a small collection of short pieces on poetry and art published by Vanni Scheiwiller); *Seconda maniera di Marmeladov* (another small printing by Scheiwiller); *Nel nostro tempo* (a collage of various previously published pieces); *Trentadue variazioni* (a collection of pieces *fuori commercio*); and "È ancora possibile la poesia?" (Montale's Nobel Prize acceptance speech).[3] All of these prose writings deserve serious critical

137
Prose
Glosses:
Is
Poetry
Still
Possible?

attention, perhaps not in a context entirely separated from the poetry but certainly with the primary goal being the description and evaluation of Montale as critic, short-story writer, and cultural commentator. This, however, would be the occasion for another book and is not my goal in this chapter. Rather, I should like to concentrate attention on a few texts that are particularly revealing of Montale's poetics and of his beliefs concerning the function and meaning of poetry. These prose pieces are not necessarily explicit or direct commentaries on individual poems or collections of poetry, although as Cesare Segre and others have shown, this is a legitimate and profitable way of using the prose.[4] However, these pieces do provide us with further insight into Montale's attitudes toward life and art and can be considered, therefore, as *ancilla poesis*, leading to a deeper understanding of his poetry's origins and goals.

The short essay-story "La poesia non esiste" (Poetry Does Not Exist) was originally published in *Corriere della Sera* on October 5, 1946. It is directly tied to the war, which was an immediate reality in the Italy of 1944, the year in which the story takes place. The setting of the story, Montale's apartment in Florence, draws into its walls the dangers assailing the world outside while containing the more truly interior preoccupations of the poet concerning poetry and its function within the collectivity of people to whom its existence matters. The setting serves as a frame that comments ironically on the dialogue, the former being realistic, very much down-to-earth, and fraught with a sense of the immediate contingencies of personal threat—of the war, in short—while the latter is of the much less tangible realm of intellectual, philosophical discourse, abstract and remote from the battles raging outside. The two are played off one another in a vivacious, even humorous manner, but the essential seriousness of both cannot be ignored.

The season is "the dark winter" of 1944.[5] The narrator has opened his home to those Italians who are being sought by the German army for their partisan activities. These guests include Brunetto, a friend, and several others whom Montale calls, in English, "flying ghosts," men who come and go each evening and whose identities remain unknown to their host. The evening in question is being passed by the radio and the electric heater when suddenly the concierge calls up to warn the men of the arrival of a German soldier. The moment is tense, and the tension is heightened by such phrases as "there was no time to waste";

138
Eugenio
Montale:
Poet
on
the
Edge

"what would the friends do?"; "perhaps the German wasn't alone."
The frightened guests hasten to hide in a darkened room as their host
moves slowly toward the door. He opens it to find a young German offi-
cer, "a youth of little more than twenty years of age, almost two meters
tall, with a hooked nose like a bird of prey, and two eyes, both timid and
wild, under a disordered, brushlike lock of hair." He is holding a roll of
paper, which he points toward the narrator as if it were a "colubrina" (a
sort of musket). Up to this point in the story we are in the world of action, threat, and uncertainty. The scene might be likened in impact to
the opening shots of Rossellini's *Città aperta* (*Open City*), a film concerning the partisan fight, which depicts men in a situation analogous
to that of the three men in Montale's narrative. These first few paragraphs are in fact cinematographic in style. There is sparse descriptive
detail, only enough information about the men and the room as is min-
imally necessary to establish a picture of them. Then come several swift
movements or pans: the answering of the telephone, the men's disappearance, the host's quick switching of radio stations, the sound of the
doorbell, the unbolting of the door. There is no dialogue. The reader's
attention is completely fixed on the opening door and the figure stand-
ing at the threshold.

The description of the German, whose appearance reminds the narrator of a "bird of prey" and who points a threatening-looking object at
the host, is a masterful cliché in either film or fiction: the climax of suspense, the moment in a movie when the music would swell dramatically
and the camera fix on the frightened face of the Italian. The suspense is
broken in a most unorthodox fashion by the German's first words: "I
am a literary, and I bring you the poems you asked me for." In its tense
context this declaration takes on a humorous aspect, so completely inappropriate and unexpected is it. Not only has the German brought
poems rather than guns, but he has introduced himself incorrectly as a
letterario, a "literary." The narrator immediately comments: "Certainly
he meant a man of letters." The absurdity of the moment is intensified
by this correction, for even in a state of fear the narrator hastens to correct in a mental note the German's bad Italian. This is our first glimpse
of the host's dry wit, which becomes more obvious as the story ad-
vances. We must now begin to reorient ourselves, just as the narrator
must do, for the classic wartime drama has taken a decidedly original
turn.

139
Prose
Glosses:
Is
Poetry
Still
Possible?

All of this is accomplished in a page and a half; Montale's prose, like his poetry, tends to the understated, using the swift stroke, the minimal. The dialogue, introduced by the German's words, continues in the host's response. "Very flattered," he remarks that the young man's name is not unknown to him: "This is a great honor for me. How might I be of service?" At this point begins a long paragraph, the essential one, constructed entirely of description and "indirect free discourse." We learn that the German, Ulrich, had written to the narrator several years before concerning his translations of some Italian poetry, and the narrator had in turn asked that the young man send him a collection of Hölderlin's lyrics that were not available in Italy at that time. Ulrich never answered his request but, ironically, has turned up two years later and under the most inappropriate of circumstances with a typed copy of some three hundred pages of the poetry. He apologizes for having based his transcription on the Zinkernagel edition rather than on that of Hellingrath but is confident that "sein gnädiger Kollege" (his esteemed colleague) will be able to order the poems correctly with a few months' work. Ulrich asks for nothing in return, except perhaps for copies of some Italian poems. The irony of the situation is by now rampant; the two scholars are politely exchanging notes while Montale remarks in parentheses that he is in a cold sweat, "and not only in view of the hard work" of selecting appropriate "illustrious moderns" for the eager young German.

The visitor settles in to tell his life story. He says that he arranges concerts on the piazza of the Italian city where he is now stationed; he himself is a musician who plays, the narrator vaguely recalls, "the bugle or the fife." Before the war he was a student of philosophy, dedicated to finding and explaining "the essence of Life" and to disproving the assertion that philosophic speculation is a vicious circle that "bites its own tail, a whirling of thought around itself." He had been disillusioned in his search, however, for the professor under whose tutelage he explored the possibility of the *Dasein*, the "existential I in flesh and blood," took a dislike to him and kindly showed him the door. What was left to him was poetry, which however proved equally disenchanting. A brief if devastating survey follows: Homer was not a man, "and everything that departs from the human results as extraneous to man." The Greek lyrics are hopelessly fragmentary; Pindar's mythical, musical world is no longer ours; Latin oratory is equally out of our reach. Dante,

140
Eugenio
Montale:
Poet
on
the
Edge

whose name is brought up by the narrator in what one must imagine as a hesitant question, is "grandissimo," but one reads him as a *pensum*; Shakespeare is too natural, Goethe not natural enough. So much for the entire Western poetic tradition. "And the moderns?" the narrator asks, as he pours out the last of the Chianti that has accompanied their conversation. The young man dismisses them with equal dispatch: "They never give the impression of stability; we are too much a party to them to be able to evaluate them." He concludes: "Believe me, poetry doesn't exist . . . and then, then . . . a perfect poem would be like a philosophic system that completely satisfies, it would be the end of life, an explosion, a collapse, and an imperfect poem is not a poem. Better to struggle . . . with the girls."

With these words Ulrich stands, wishes his host a good digestion of Hölderlin, while Montale tells us that he hadn't the courage to reveal that he had stopped studying German two years before, and takes his leave. The narrator then goes into the darkened room where the men have been hiding, and Brunetto asks: "Has your German gone away then? And what did he have to say to you?" The answer is succinct: "He says that poetry doesn't exist." Brunetto's response to this is a simple "ah," accompanied by Giovanni's snores; the two men are sleeping, we are told, "in a very narrow bed."

This story is surely one of the most original and striking illustrations of the dichotomy between art and life as well as a subtly humorous depiction of the ironic relationship of the active to the contemplative life. The evaluation of poetry is presented through several filters: the wartime setting, the tense realities of the apartment hideout, the German's youth and naïveté, the narrator's essential silence, and the partisans' reactions to the German's conclusion that poetry does not exist. Had Montale presented these thoughts on the existence or nonexistence of poetry in a straightforward essay, as in fact he has done elsewhere to some degree,[6] our reception of them would have been entirely different. Here we see the vacuity of the discussion, given the very real issues and threats assailing the men and given Ulrich's extreme youth and idealism. Yet we also understand the human import of the meeting; the enemy is a twenty-year-old boy who has made the trip to the narrator's apartment not to conquer him and his concealed guests but rather to bring him Hölderlin's poetry and perhaps simply to find a kindred

141
Prose
Glosses:
Is
Poetry
Still
Possible?

soul with whom to discuss those things most real and most essential to him. In spite of Ulrich's negative conclusions concerning the life of poetry, the story shows just how persistently poetry does in fact exist, not certainly as a perfected abstraction, "un'esplosione,"[7] but as an eccentric, unexpected, even inappropriate gift emerging out of the darkness of the Florentine evening and disappearing back into it. Nor does poetry in any way alter the reality surrounding it, a reality that turns its back and begins to snore. There is good reason for this indifference: Brunetto and Giovanni have no reason to care about the existence of poetry when their lives are at stake. There are no grand gestures here, no clearly defined heroes or villains. The narrator is a gracious host to the Italian partisans and to the German alike. He is neither a hero nor a coward but quite simply a man capable of seeing the inadequacies of both life and art. The story is a perfect example of Montale's very basic belief in daily decency and a masterful dramatization of his self-portrait as expressed in "Intervista immaginaria": "I have lived my time with the minimum of cowardice that had been allowed to my weak powers, but there are those who did more, much more, even if they did not publish books."[8]

Montale rarely wrote poems as explicitly tied to the war as this prose piece, although "Finisterre" and *La bufera* are deeply imbued with the horror and tragedy of the war years. There is, however, a poem in *Quaderno*, written in 1975, which harks back to the First World War, in which Montale saw action. In "L'eroismo" (Heroism) the poet reveals his dreams of glory, encouraged by his beloved Clizia: "Clizia mi suggeriva di ingaggiarmi / tra i guerriglieri di Spagna . . ." (Clizia suggested that I might enlist / with the guerrilla fighters of Spain). But no such glory was his, and he remembers little of his actual military experience except for "futile exertions," "the irksome / clicking of the gunners." He also recalls "Un prigioniero *mio* / che aveva in tasca un Rilke e fummo amici / per pochi istanti" (*My very own* prisoner / who had Rilke in his pocket and we were friends / for a few instants). Ulrich and the prisoner are spiritually one and the same. Both men emerge from the generalizations of war as sparsely sketched and yet unforgettable human beings, one lugging around his three-hundred-page typescript of Hölderlin and the other his small Rilke. This is where poetry exists not only for Montale but for anyone who recognizes that, as Montale

142
Eugenio
Montale:
Poet
on
the
Edge

writes in "The Truth" in *Quaderno*, existence is often nothing more than "una tela di ragno" (a spider's web), infinitely tenuous, subjective, and minimal.

The essay "Tornare nella strada" (To Go Back to the Street) was first published in 1949. It is not, like "Style and Tradition" or "The Solitude of the Artist," usually singled out as an important statement by Montale worthy of translation and redistribution; yet I believe that it is highly revealing of Montale's attitude toward art and art's continuing life. The piece is in part a polemic against what Montale calls "current art," which is characterized by its rejection of form and its attachment to the concepts of immediacy, the ephemeral, and the solipsistic. In contrast Montale offers a conservative view of art, which is fully incarnated in form and which truly exists only when it attains "its second and greater life: that of memory and of individual, small circulation.[9]

The essay consists primarily of a definition of this second life as proposed by Montale. He begins by emphasizing the necessity of created art: "The uncreated work of art, the unwritten book, the masterpiece that could have been born and was not born are mere abstractions and illusions." But art does not end with the creation of works, for a work does not fully live until it is "received, understood, or misunderstood by someone: by the public." This public can consist of only one person, "as long as it is not the author himself." Furthermore, the success of art does not depend on the immediate consumption or enjoyment of the work of art "with an instant relationship of cause and effect," but rather "its obscure pilgrimage across the consciousness and the memory of people, its complete reflux back into life whence art itself drew its first nourishment." Montale states, "It is this second moment, of minute consumption and even of misunderstanding, that makes up what interests me the most in art."

The poet then goes on to give several examples of this phenomenon in his own experience: Svevo's *Zeno* always comes to mind when he sees a group of indifferent people following a funeral procession or when the north wind blows; he always sees a face of Piero or Mantegna or thinks of Manzoni's line "era folgore l'aspetto" (her face was a lightning flash) when he meets Clizia or other beloved ladies; Paul Klee's *Zoo* comes to mind when he thinks of strange animals, "zebra or zebu." The issue is not that of easy memorability, for if this were the case "Chiabrera would beat Petrarch, Metastasio would outsell Shakespeare," but of art,

143
Prose
Glosses:
Is
Poetry
Still
Possible?

which can give to someone a sense of "liberation and of comprehension of the world." What Montale believes in is the essential importance of the "incalculable and absurd existence" of art, which is not necessarily equal to "an objective vitality and importance of art itself." Another series of examples follows: someone can face death for a noble cause while whistling "Funiculì funicolà"; Catullus can come to mind in an austere cathedral, and conversely a religious aria of Handel can accompany a "profane desire"; we can remember a poem by Poliziano "even in days of madness and slaughter." Montale concludes that "everything is uncertain, nothing is necessary in the world of artistic refractions; the only necessity is that such refraction sooner or later be rendered possible."

The essay was written for a newspaper and not as a fully developed excursus on art; I do not therefore want to inflate its content or the depth of its argumentation. It is written well, alternating between discursive prose and striking concrete examples of what Montale himself has experienced as the second life of art. It reveals Montale's readiness to engage in polemics, his ability to take a stand and unequivocally argue its virtues. But what he is arguing here is also very much tied to the values at work in his equivocal, understated poetry: the importance of the marginal, the individual, the incalculable in art as well as in life. These eccentric and minimal qualities must, however, be fully expressed in artistic forms and cannot have meaning if they remain in the realm of the abstract or the mystical. Emotions and virtues or vices are highly abstract things, as are general concepts such as Life and Art, but they can be concretized not in order that their true essence be fixed once and for all but rather to enable them to be shared by others living through them. Given Montale's views on the unreliability of language and his uncertainty concerning history, either individual or collective, it is not surprising that he clings to this essentially minimal life of art, which can be as fraught with "misunderstandings" and contingencies as any communicative act. The central concern is that one be committed to the possibility of some sort of exchange in spite of the necessarily partial and imperfect nature of it.

Montale's own poetry has itself taken on this second life. His flora and fauna (the sunflower, the eel, the mouse, the butterfly); his locales (the customs house, the garden, the seashore); his talismanic objects (the ivory mouse, the shoehorn, the earrings); his beloved women (Cli-

144

Eugenio
Montale:
Poet
on
the
Edge

zia, Dora Markus, Gerti, Mosca, Annetta): all these and many more have entered into the psyches and hearts of his readers. I for one experience them as as much a part of my life as actual people, places, and things I know firsthand. They all serve as points of contact; they have taken hold and have thus reentered the cycle of life from which they emerged. They have the power to inform life because they themselves live in poems that make them matter. An indifferent or mediocre rendering of any individual experience or insight will condemn it to death no matter how intensely meaningful it might have been for the author. All people take with them to the isolation and silence of the grave the vital diversity and uniqueness of their own lives unless they are communicated and passed on through words and acts that transcend the death of the body. Like all great artists Montale leaves behind an indelible mark: his art, which is thoroughly imbued with "that ultimate hypothesis of sociality that an art born from life always has: to return to life, to serve man, to count as something for man."

"Farfalla di Dinard" (Butterfly of Dinard) is a very brief story that provides the title of the collection of stories first published in 1956. It is the final story of the collection, and its last sentence is beautifully closural: "I bent my head and when I lifted it again I saw that on the vase of dahlias the butterfly was no more."[10] Given the symbolic value of the butterfly in Montale's poetry—in "Vecchi versi" and "Omaggio a Rimbaud" especially but implicitly in the figure of Clizia, who is herself a creature of flight—the disappearance of this butterfly signifies much more than is expressed on the simple denotative level. The story is both allusive and concrete, as Cesare Segre has pointed out in his article "Invito alla 'Farfalla di Dinard.' " It seems almost a poem in prose in its movement from the initial "horizontality" of the opening lines to the "rare and expressive adjectives" and "unexpected metaphors" of its development.[11] But it is also rooted in the terra firma of prosaic irony and the common sense of the waitress who sees no butterfly at all. The story relates the following: A "little saffron-colored butterfly" has visited the narrator each day at his table in a café in Brittany. On the eve of his departure he is seized with the desire to know if it is a sign from his beloved, a "secret message." He decides to ask the waitress if she will check to see if the butterfly continues to appear after his departure, writing him a simple yes or no. "Stuttering," he explains that he is "an amateur entomologist" and asks the favor. The waitress responds in

145
Prose
Glosses:
Is
Poetry
Still
Possible?

French: "A butterfly? A yellow butterfly?" and adding in Italian, "But I see nothing. Look closer." The butterfly is nowhere to be seen.

The butterfly can be interpreted on many levels: it is a secret message, a mysterious connective link between distant persons, hope, nostalgia, love, poetry. It is also simply a butterfly, a purely coincidental presence that is as meaningless, and eventually as nonexistent, as the waitress's casual comments indicate. This mixture of the real and the imaginary, of tenuous and unironic hope and ironic deflation, is the essential tenor of Montale's poetry from the very first. "Farfalla di Dinard" can therefore be read as a sort of summation in miniature of a poetics centering around a search for some tangible, sure reality to which emotions and images can be attached.

The reality in question is that of the butterfly itself, which might be "*la* farfalla," or "*the* butterfly" (Montale's italics); the search is posited in clearly defined terms of yes and no. The narrator calls the problem "il punto da risolvere" (the point to be resolved). This point concerning the butterfly's existence is related to other points in Montale's poetry: "Ricerco invano il punto onde si mosse / il sangue che ti nutre" (I search in vain for the point whence was moved / the blood that nourishes you); "Una tabula rasa; se non fosse / che un punto c'era, per me incomprensibile, / e questo punto *ti riguardava*" (A tabula rasa; if it weren't / for the fact that there was a point, incomprehensible for me, / and this point *had to do with you*); "A un soffio il pigro fumo trasalisce, / si difende nel punto che ti chiude" (At a puff the lazy smoke quivers, / but persists at the point that hides you), of which Montale wrote in a letter to Bobi Bazlen, "It is clear that *at the point* can have two meanings: *at the moment in which* and *at the place in which*, both legitimate. For Landolfi, this doubt is horrible; for me it is a richness."[12] In the recent poem "A questo punto" (At This Point) in *Diario del '71* the phrase "a questo punto smetti" (at this point stop) is repeated three times and then resolved in the final lines, "A questo punto / guarda can i tuoi occhi e anche senz'occhi" (At this point / look with your own eyes and even without eyes). Certainly not all of these usages of the word are identical, but they are all joined by their essentiality, their use as a term of either temporal or spatial quiddity or as the desired resolution of some tension or doubt. But the point cannot be resolved in the story; an unequivocal answer is not possible, perhaps because the butterfly exists only for Montale, perhaps because

146
Eugenio
Montale:
Poet
on
the
Edge

it flew away before the waitress could note its presence. Its very existence is put in doubt, and the essential question of the meaning of its presence is thus vitiated and rendered unanswerable.

As Segre points out in his article, *Farfalla di Dinard* as a collection provides us with "a precious hermeneutical instrument" in our comprehension of Montale's poetry, in part because the "motive-occasion" for what will eventually be elaborated into poetry is almost always explicitly given in the stories.[13] In the title story we are told about the butterfly and its importance to the poet in an open manner that helps us determine its symbolic significance in the less accessible poems. This is the only kind of biography that can provide meaningful illumination of the poetry. In his explanation of the "Motet" that begins, "La speranza di pure rivederti" (The hope of even seeing you again) Montale also provides some information as to the autobiographical origins of the highly elusive series.[14] He was forced to do so given the erroneous critical attempts to explain so many elements in the poems, especially the "two jackals on a leash" of the above mentioned "Motet." The jackals that Montale actually saw in Modena he experienced as "an emblem, an occult citation, a *senhal,*" just as the butterfly of the story is felt to be an omen, the immediate reason for such a reaction being the fact that "Clizia loved odd animals." Montale bewails the "mental torpidity" of critics not because they did not come up with the correct explanation of the "Motet" but because they asked the wrong questions. He admits that there may have been too much "concentration" in his poetic rendering of the experience but counters:

> In the face of this poem criticism acts like that visitor at an art
> show who, looking at two paintings, for example a still life of
> mushrooms or a landscape with a man who is walking along hold-
> ing an open umbrella, might ask himself: How much do those
> mushrooms cost per kilo? Were they gathered by the painter or
> bought at the market? Where is that man going? What's his
> name? Is the umbrella made of real silk or a synthetic?

Montale concludes the article arguing for a *juste milieu* between understanding nothing and understanding too much, for "on either side of this mean there is no salvation for poetry or for criticism."

Taking off from this defense of the so-called obscure "Motet" Claire Huffman asked Montale if the reader must "limit his response to

147
Prose
Glosses:
Is
Poetry
Still
Possible?

the poems to the connotative and Montalian levels of poetic meaning, or is there a middle ground? Can one assign a referential value to the 'ideological phantasmata,' and perhaps even to the 'facts, situations and things' of the poetry?" Montale answers that "an explanation is always possible as long as one does not go as far as chronicle. (Who was Clizia? Who was the Fox? Who was the girl of 'After a Flight'?) I myself could not say, since they were transformed unbeknownst to them."[15] The point is to ask questions pertinent to the poetry and not to the satisfaction of extraliterary curiosity concerning the life of the poet. In this sense "Butterfly of Dinard" provides us with essential directives in our approach to the poetry, for the disappearance of the butterfly—of the real, seen butterfly, that is—is inevitable and even necessary to its elaboration into poetic symbol. The butterfly, Clizia, the Fox, even Mosca are all part of a stylistic adventure; and although they, like unnumerable other figures, places, and occurrences in the poems, were no doubt real and directly experienced, they all took flight away from chronicle and toward the realm of a lyrical existence. This is an opposite, although not opposing movement from the one described in "Tornare alla strada": there art was seen as feeding back into life; here life feeds into art. The space of conjunction must be understood as betwixt and between the two, in that zone in which both the radical disjunctions and the vital links between life and art can be sought out, expressed, and nourished.

Montale's Nobel Prize speech "È ancora possibile la poesia?" (Is Poetry Still Possible?) was made on December 12, 1975.[16] It is a curious piece, lacking the organized and cohesive quality of so much of Montale's critical writing. This can be explained, at least in part, by the fact that it was written in some haste and in the emotion of the moment. The poet writes in it that he had thought of entitling the talk "Will Poetry Be Able to Survive in the Universe of Mass Media?" and this interest in the world of today with its plethora of mass media is evident throughout the speech. But it also looks back to the poetry of the past and to Montale's conception of the origins of poetry.

Montale begins with the assertion that the world may soon experience "a historic shift of colossal proportions." This change, he insists, will signal not the end of man but rather the end of communal and social systems as we know them. What the result of such a change will be for mankind is not clear, although Montale suggests that the "age-old diatribe as to the meaning of life" may well cease, at least for a few cen-

148
Eugenio
Montale:
Poet
on
the
Edge

turies. He does not develop these thoughts any further, being "neither a philosopher, sociologist, nor moralist." He turns rather to his own area of competence: poetry, "an absolutely useless product, but scarcely ever harmful and this is one of its claims to nobility." In response to the judgment of his own production as being meager, he counters that "fortunately poetry is not merchandise." But what is it then? Originally it was the result of the desire to join a vocal sound to the beat of primitive music; "only much later could words and music be written down in some way and distinguished one from the other." So poetry is first sound; then it becomes visual, with "its formal schemes" having much to do with its "visibility." After the invention of printed books poetry can be defined as that which is "vertical" and does not fill up all the "blank space" (as Montale insists, "even certain empty spaces have a value"), unlike prose, which fills up all the space of a page and gives no indications as to its "pronounceability." Around the end of the nineteenth century the established forms of poetry no longer satisfied either the eye or the ear, and the crisis of form began, extending into all of the arts. Montale wonders what "rebirth or resurrection" might arise out of the so-called death of art, art that has become "consumer items, to be used and then thrown away."

The next section of the talk begins with a critique of the negative effect the contemporary attitudes of despair, confusion, and immediate gratification have had on art, which today, Montale asserts, has become "a show . . . that performs a kind of psychic massage on the spectator or listener or reader." This art is "sterile"' and shows "a tremendous lack of trust in life." What can be the place of poetry, "the most discreet of the arts . . . the fruit of solitude and of accumulation?" Poetry has kept up with the times, insisting on its purely visual or purely auditory nature; it has also broken down the old barriers between itself and prose. Montale insists that there are innumerable roads open to this "mainstream" poetry but that it will no doubt be ephemeral, producing few works that will survive the test of time. There will also be created an art, however, that is "control and reflection," a marginal art that "refuses with horror the term *production*; that art that rises up almost by a miracle and seems to fix an entire epoch and an entire linguistic and cultural situation." This poetry will be capable of surviving its own time and even of returning many years after its birth to influence the art of the future.

149
Prose
Glosses:
Is
Poetry
Still
Possible?

Montale next cites a poem by Du Bellay that found in Walter Pater its interpreter, and thus in a certain sense its life, centuries after its composition, proving that "great poetry can die, be reborn, die again, but it will always remain one of the highest accomplishments of the human spirit." The poet concludes that many contemporary books of poetry "might endure through time," yet there is still the question of what that endurance will mean. Will these books be able to bring anything meaningful to the future? The answer not only for poetry but for all art is directly tied to "the human condition." For Montale the destiny of art must be seen as analogous to the destiny of mankind, the ultimate question remaining whether "the people of tomorrow . . . will be able to resolve the tragic contradictions with which we have struggled from the very first day of Creation."

This speech is disturbing and unsatisfactory in many ways: first because it shows Montale at his most querulously conservative; second because it raises questions and issues that are not answered in any truly illuminating manner. It is clear that Montale does not like contemporary experiments in art, which he considers for the most part to be empty and self-indulgent. This is certainly his prerogative. I take issue not with his view but rather with the way in which he presents it. Either a satiric or parodic portrait of the contemporary artist or a full-fledged, developed critique would have been much more effective. What we have instead are potshots—brief sallies and equally swift retreats from the subject at hand. For example, Montale speaks of the "portrait of a mongoloid" on display in an art show, "a subject *très dégoutant*," and even more so when it was discovered to be not "a portrait at all, but the unfortunate one in the flesh." The poet ironically comments, "But why not? Art can justify anything." The poet also criticizes contemporary music that is "solely noisy and repetitive" and appeals to young people who "come together in order to exorcise the horror of their solitude." These examples of the degradation of art are the kind that bring knowing and even complacent nods of recognition and agreement from certain members of the audience but that do not push the implications of their assertion far enough. Why should we refuse to accept such portraits and such music as art? The ironic "art can justify everything" means its opposite of course; but if art does not justify anything and everything, who determines its limits, who polices its borders? If experimentation is disallowed, might not the very vitality of art be destroyed?

150
Eugenio
Montale:
Poet
on
the
Edge

In playing devil's advocate I am myself committing the very sin of which I accuse Montale in not offering answers to these and other fundamental questions raised in his speech. Yet I believe that the criticism stands: having decided to confront such vast issues as the present and future status of art and the survival of poetry in today's and tomorrow's world of mass communication, Montale ought to have equivocated less and provided more than the very general, although not untrue, conclusion that great art is always privileged and "rises up almost miraculously."

These last comments point to the essential defect of the speech. It is an example of what is atypical of Montale, both in his prose writings and his poetry: that is, an inclusive, panoramic theme and the epigrammatic, generalizing style that results. Thus the Nobel speech is a sort of negative reinforcement of that which is strong in and vital to Montale's work: the specific, the minimal, the concrete, the eccentric. The first three prose pieces I have discussed are all excellent examples of these virtues on both a thematic and a stylistic level. They all treat circumscribed topics using either fictional or discursive particulars that illustrate convincingly the issues in question. They are all brief, concise, and minimal, not in the subjects or experiences they deal with but in the presentation of them. Perhaps sensing the momentous quality attached to the Nobel speech, Montale sought to universalize his usually very particularized tone, with less than convincing results.

This criticism pertains to the last collections of poetry also; the poems in *Diario* and *Quaderno* that are least successful are those in which Montale gives in to a sententious, moralizing tone and encapsulates his thoughts in aphoristic verses. Irony and flashes of lyricism save the collections from this tendency, but in this essay such elements are missing. It is understandable that the poet should feel the push to summarize; the weight of more than sixty years as a poet and his tremendous reputation conspire toward that end. In the recent interview with Claire Huffman Montale was asked: "What things (or questions) interest you the most? What things don't interest you at all?" He laconically answered: "Practical issues, concerning survival (material survival). The fortunes of humanity are outside my area of competence."[17] In the speech just discussed he says he is no philosopher, no moralist. Both of these assertions are somewhat contradicted by Montale's recent poetry, his comments on his work, and the Nobel speech. I have chosen to criti-

151
Prose
Glosses:
Is
Poetry
Still
Possible?

cize the speech in particular not because it has some sort of eminent position in Montale's prose, although I fear that many people will read it in isolation and thus assign special weight to it, but because it represents those philosophizing, moralizing strands in the late Montale that do not lead to felicitous artistic or critical products.

There are many provisional conclusions concerning Montale's prose that can be offered even after limiting the discussion to only a few examples of his fiction and critical writings. One important point is that Montale must be seen as a European writer, both as poet and critic, rather than as a regional or even an Italian one. When *Ossi di seppia* first appeared there was a tendency to see it as a volume that fit into a Ligurian tradition, but it was soon recognized that such an approach was much too limiting, if not erroneous. Already in the first collection Montale's ties to a much wider poetic and philosophical tradition were evident, in spite of his undeniable interest in writing of his place of birth, the sea, and the particular local landscape of which he later wrote in "Dov'era il tennis" (Where the Tennis Court Was) in *La bufera e altro*: "It is strange to think that each of us has a landscape like this, even if very different, that will have to remain *his* own immutable landscape."

Le occasioni and *La bufera* made it even more evident that Montale was a cosmopolitan poet participating in a much broader tradition than simply the Italian one, a fact explicitly pointed out by the poet himself in his choice of epigraphs for these collections from Spanish, English, and French literature as well as in his mention of the French symbolists, Gerard Manley Hopkins, Keats, and others in his explications of certain of the poems contained therein. His *Quaderno di traduzioni* (Translation Notebook) also reveals his very active interest in the poetry of other Western traditions, as do his many pieces on poets from Valéry and Prévert to Ezra Pound, Auden, Roethke, and T. S. Eliot. The prose pieces discussed here are typical in the range of interests they reveal: German poetry in "La poesia non esiste"; travel in France in "Farfalla di Dinard"; modern painting and music in "Tornare nella strada"; contemporary art in "È ancora possibile la poesia?" Even more so than in the poetry it is in the prose that we see the eclectic and wide-ranging culture of Montale, which inevitably feeds his verses and gives his work a frame of reference far beyond the confines of Italy. The Italian lyric tradition is of course an extremely rich and varied one, ranging from

152
Eugenio
Montale:
Poet
on
the
Edge

Dante to Petrarch to the Baroque poets to Leopardi and the great triumvirate of Carducci, Pascoli, and D'Annunzio, not to mention the moderns—futurists, crepuscularists, hermeticists, and so on. I am not suggesting that Montale has divorced himself from this tradition or that he did not make use of it in elaborating his own poetry. But what is so clearly evident, especially in his autobiographical, fictional, and critical writings, is his assimilation of other linguistic, literary, and cultural materials and his constant view of artistic activity as transcending national boundaries.

This cosmopolitan orientation is no doubt motivated in part by temperament and purely personal tastes. In a general sense Montale's recourse to other traditions and cultures is also tied to what he has called "an unfittedness . . . a maladjustment both psychological and moral" that from the first made him feel in disharmony with his immediate environment.[18] In a more specific sense we can see in his view of the Italian language another source of discontent, for he says of it, "I wanted to wring the neck of the eloquence of our old aulic language," using interestingly enough a Verlainian turn of phrase. He further comments on his attitude toward Italian that "in the new book [Occasions] I continued my battle to dig out another dimension from our heavy polysyllabic language, a language that seemed to me to refuse an experience such as mine . . . I have often cursed our language, but in it and through it I came to recognize myself as incurably Italian: and without regrets.[19] Here is evident a combative resistance to Italian, Montale's native language, as well as a final capitulation without regrets to its inevitable hegemony.

A humorous piece included in the collection *Farfalla di Dinard* reveals Montale's rather shamefaced admiration of the English style. I say "shamefaced" because the self-parody is rampant, and yet the very real attachment to such a style is equally evident. The story is entitled "Signore inglese" (English Gentleman), and this gentleman practices a new sport: that of being a "fake Englishman."[20] He does this in Switzerland because an Englishman in England is nothing special and because he needs a neutral space in which to carry out his fiction. Montale writes that he has been trying for years to emulate the man but without success. What follows is a merciless depiction of English habits: the renunciation of any athletic activities, the daily consumption of tea and cakes, the maintenance of a stoic silence broken only by some *chiù* (a clipped

153
Prose
Glosses:
Is
Poetry
Still
Possible?

"thank you") if anyone should speak to him or do him some small service. Montale concludes that "in an imaginary club of fake Englishmen the presidency would be his and the vice-presidency would be mine." The story is entirely humorous but it has its origins in the poet's real fascination with and admiration for the laconic, absolutely un-Mediterranean English style.

If Montale can be associated with a European perspective, it is very much an old-world one—that is, of a culture and style particular to the nineteenth- and early-twentieth-century intellectual.[21] The new world, America, held great interest for many Italian writers of the thirties and forties, especially Cesare Pavese, and that interest resulted in the translation of American classics, in travel books, and in the general elaboration of a myth of America. Although Montale translated some American literature, both prose and poetry, and spent a few days in New York,[22] he never shared this American fever, a fact entirely consonant with his conservative and deeply old-world character. The world and culture in which he feels most at home are those of the people evoked in the poem "Lettera" (Letter) in *Satura:* "i veri e i degni avant le déluge" (the true and the deserving *avant le déluge*). This may seem at odds with his modernity as a poet, but I do not believe that we must see a contradiction here, for his conservatism has always been tempered with a most acute awareness of the present moment. Montale does not express a belief in the superiority of the good old days but rather points to and seconds certain fundamental values and styles as timeless and therefore universally valid. His distrust of and even disdain for contemporary manifestations of power, immediacy, speed, and self-gratification show by contrast his sustained belief in the minor virtues of patience, painstaking care in and dedication to one's craft, awareness of one's limits, and daily decency. There is undeniably a bit of the snob in Montale, but he has never sought to hide this facet of his personality. His prose works display his European, cosmopolitan, conservative, and even slightly aristocratic tastes and interests. In them we see a mind that has certain affinities with the poetic genius behind the collections of verse; we also learn much from them of the man behind the hermetic, ironic poetic *I*.

In his fictional-autobiographical prose in the collections *Farfalla di Dinard* and *Fuori di casa* Montale reveals his penchant for satire, irony, and humor, a voice that is fully developed poetically in the latest

154
Eugenio
Montale:
Poet
on
the
Edge

poems. In his journalistic and critical writings he shows his constant involvement in the past, present, and future of art in the Western world. It is clear that his greatness lies in his poetry, for although he is an accomplished raconteur and a perceptive critic, he is not exceptionally gifted as either. This is understandable, for sustained and rich prose demands a synthetic vision of a believed and believable reality—not realism necessarily but the ability to build a complete world. Montale's description of the stories of *Farfalla* as "culs-de-lampe" (vignettes) is apt.[23] They are *occasioni*, more discursively presented than in the poems of course but nonetheless brief and sketchy pieces that find their total meaning in their collectivity and in their interrelationship with the poetry they directly or indirectly gloss. The poet's critical writings also tend toward the sketch, the single insight, the unsystematic presentation of the opinions and insights of a cultivated but not especially privileged reader of both texts and events. This emphasis on the seemingly minimal in both his poetry and prose is perhaps the most essential aspect of the Montalian voice. Thematically, stylistically, and philosophically his writing is the expression of a long dedication to the value, and indeed necessity, of what is individual and unique in both art and life. For Montale, if poetry is still possible it is because it is born, lives, dies, and is born again through wars, great social, cultural, and even spiritual upheavals, not as an essential issue or as a force for change and final revelation but as "an entity of which we know very little."[24] This phrase could well be applied to the human race itself, so convinced are we of our central and superior position, "our certainty or illusion of believing ourselves to be privileged,"[25] when in fact our salvation, and poetry's, lies instead in the courageous recognition of how minimal is our self-knowledge, how deeply marginal and inevitably ambiguous is that which we seek to make essential and unequivocal: our own existence.

Conclusion

IN any study of the
work of a particular poet essential questions are inevitably implied that
concern all poetry: its origins, its function, its survival, its relationship
to other art forms and to life. These questions generally remain secondary to the more explicit ones that are directed toward the specific poems
under examination; but they are nonetheless present and sooner or later
reveal their undeniable importance not only in the realm of criticism
but also in the poems themselves. This is especially true in the study of
modern and contemporary poetry, which, like other areas of recent artistic endeavor, has shown itself to be highly self-conscious. We read
poems and novels, look at paintings and sculpture, attend plays and re-
citals—in short, we perceive art that is by and large already perceiving
itself as art and asking the question we ask of it: "What am I doing
here?"[1] This questioning is not new with the art of our century, though
certainly the emphasis on self-questioning is greater and more explicit
than ever before. Montale's poetry is representative of this modern em-

phasis not only in its constant attention to its own status, potential, and limitations as poetry but also in the answers it openly or implicitly provides to these fundamental questions. However Montale continually refuses the finality of definitive conclusions or the authority of stable certainties while nonetheless structuring his poetry around an endless search for them. This refusal must therefore be kept in mind if we are to remain true to the essential message of this poet. Montale himself has provided us with the appropriately ambiguous description of his conclusions on poetry: they are "provisional conclusions," as partial, open ended, and conditioned by doubt as the poetry from which they emerge.

Montale has written that poetry "is not born at all and therefore / has never been born. It *exists* like a rock / or a grain of sand."[2] He has also asserted that "technique is present in every work of art but it is not art and does not make art . . ."[3] He insists in the first statement on the ontological essence of poetry as opposed to any historically determined birth; he sees its origins as ultimately unfindable or at least indefinable in historical or even personal terms. Something or someone produces poetry just as something creates a rock or a grain of sand, but we cannot know for sure what or who that generative force is. The second assertion reiterates in a different manner this same stance in terms of artistic creation. Technique is not art; therefore any attempt to define and understand art that limits itself to a consideration of technique—and by extension any attempt to make art by technique alone—is doomed to failure. If neither historical nor formalistic explanations of art are adequate, it becomes necessary to look elsewhere. And this is precisely what Montale does. In speaking of his own poetry Montale uses the words *instinctive* and *adherent.* He underlines the separateness of art from life when he writes, "I thought early on, and I still think, that art is the form of life of those who do not really live: a compensation or a surrogate,"[4] This assertion tends toward a psychologistic view of why artistic activity exists, a view that is certainly not in complete opposition to one that recognizes the importance of context—the artist within a certain life—or one that concentrates on the formal results of the surrogate life. But this insistence does imply again that neither history nor form is adequate to explain art. At this point the letter must give way to the spirit, the concatenation of events and words to the incantation of the intangible that is at the heart of all human cre-

Conclusion

ativity. In a poem dedicated to Benedetto Croce, "A un grande filo-
sofo" (To a Great Philosopher) in *Diario del '72*, Montale wrote:

> Lo spirito non è nei libri, l'avete saputo,
> e nemmeno si trova nella vita e non certo
> nell'altra vita. La sua natura resta
> in disparte . . .[5]

> Spirit is not in books, you knew it,
> nor is it to be found in life and certainly
> not in the other life. Its nature remains
> apart . . .

Not in books, life, or the beyond, but *in disparte:* this is the metaphorical space in which the true nature of the human spirit resides. Given
this conviction it is inevitable that Montale should reject any one sure
definition of the origins, function, or meaning of art, for such a definition would have to rest on a belief in the manifestation of art's essential
nature through culture, history, form, or myth, and this would be a belief utterly alien to Eugenio Montale.

As is evident not only in these assertions but also throughout Montale's poetry, he relies greatly on the *via negationis* in seeking to arrive at
any conclusion. Poetry is *not* born; art is the form of life of someone
who does *not* really live; technique is *not* art; the spirit is *not* to be
found in books, life, or the afterlife. Montale established this approach
as basic to his way of thinking very early on. In the "Osso" that begins,
"Do not ask of us the word," he openly states that the only clearly definable message available to his poetry is a negative one: "ciò che *non*
siamo, ciò che *non* vogliamo" (what we are *not*, what we do *not* want).[6]
This attitude, which I have followed through its elaborations in the six
collections of poetry, can be understood as the essential determinant of
those qualities of ambiguity, understatement, and marginality so typical
of and constant in Montale's poetry.

As Kenneth Burke has convincingly argued, we can locate "the specific nature of language in the ability to use the Negative."[7] The general
point is that there are no negatives in nature; everything that exists is,
and it is only linguistically that we endow the world with negativity,
usually by means of a comparison or contrast. One inevitable result of
negative assertions is ambiguity or inconclusiveness: if for example I say

that Mary is not nice, the question still remains as to what in fact she *is*, for inasmuch as she exists, she is something. The natural assumption following on the assertion that she is not nice is that she is the opposite of nice: she is disagreeable, unpleasant, and so on. But this assumption is just that—an assumption—for it is conceivable that Mary is not nice because she is better than nice: saintly, exceptionally generous, kind, and thoughtful. Generally such an ambiguity would be resolved in everyday conversation by means of a shared context, by an implicit agreement as to the true nature of the person in question, or by the addition of a positive statement that would complete or clarify the negative one: "Mary is not nice. She is always bad tempered"; or "Mary is not nice. She is simply the most selfless, giving person I know." Montale's constant recourse to the negative does not resolve itself positively in such straightforward ways. The result is an equivocal poetry that remains in the realm of unresolved tensions and uncertainties, in the realm of essential linguistic ambiguity. I have already discussed the negativity of "Non chiederci la parola" as it functions at a linguistic level and the way in which the poem's message is carried entirely in its structure. Although oxymora, dubitative forms such as *forse* and *non sapere*, and other stylistic elements in Montale's poetry are not all purely linguistic negatives, they do all result directly or indirectly from a negativistic source that is basically linguistic in origin and nature. In other words, ambiguity and the negative can both be understood as distinctive marvels of human speech, originating in particularly human feelings and perceptions of what is an ontologically unambiguous, positive natural reality. Our modern sense of the chasm that ultimately divides man from his world is thus captured in all its inevitability in Montale's poetry, which is without question "more a means of knowledge than of representation."[8] The poet's tool—language—is itself incapable of representation, given its negativistic, unnatural status.

The etymological background of the term *ambiguity* is pertinent to our understanding of Montale's ambiguous verse. It is derived from the Latin word *ambages*, meaning "circumvention," "digression," "evasion." This term therefore originally indicated a physical avoidance of a direct route and was destined only later in its development to take on the psychological and linguistic meanings it now bears. In Burke's dramatistic theory of the development of the negative in human speech there is a similar insistence on the physical origins of the basic hortatory function of the negative. According to his theory words with admonitory connotations such as *beware* or *caution* are posited as the result of a desire to communicate the necessity of avoidance or evasion of a danger; even though they themselves are not negative expressions, they prepare the way for the later emergence of true linguistic negations such as "Don't go there," or "Don't take another step." From these negative imperatives gradually grew the negative indicative (He does not go there. She does not take another step.), although the latter are still endowed with some of the original admonitory force.[9]

Even if one does not accept this dramatistic explanation of the birth of the negative in speech, I think that its implicit ties to the ambiguous in speech can, at least in part, be understood in terms of some concept of evasion. In everyday usage ambiguity is often criticized as being an unwelcome evasive tactic; we are expected to make ourselves clear and to aim for precise, unequivocal assertions. A similarly critical response is also often elicited by the use of negative phrases that remain open to several possible interpretations of the sort exemplified in "Mary is not nice." If we say, "It isn't that," we are expected to complete and clarify our thoughts with a positive assertion of what it is. Poetry functions in a different way; poetic ambiguity is by now generally accepted as an enriching aspect, a positivity that is not only not to be avoided but indeed to be sought out as adding to the wealth of poetic achievement.[10] Merely decorative or ingenious ambiguities are not, of course, representative of the truly positive aspect of poetic creation. But when the polyvalence of words, and through them of experience, is an important part of the effects and meaning of a successful poem, we do feel the positivity of the unresolved and unresolvable ambiguities into which the text has plunged us. Poetry of this sort permits us to enjoy and to learn from what most other areas of experience do not: deliberate and willful equivocality.

In the case of Montale's poetry ambiguity is in great part the result of the poet's primary desire for evasion. Montale himself insisted on such a goal, stating for example that one of his basic motives is "evasion, the flight from the iron chain of necessity."[11] As I argued, this evasion can be understood as the search for some breakthrough to absolute expression, which, as Montale recognized, is an unreachable goal but which nonetheless has sustained his art throughout his long career. This may seem to be an absurd commitment: to acknowledge from the

Conclusion

very beginning that a goal can never be reached. But as Simone de Beauvoir has written, "The notion of ambiguity must not be confused with that of absurdity."[12] Her comments on the art of painting clarify this dynamic aspect of ambiguity that is inherent in art as in life: "Painting is not given completely either in Giotto or Titian or Cézanne; it is sought through the centuries and is never finished; a painting in which all pictorial problems are resolved is really inconceivable; painting itself is this movement towards its own reality . . ."[13] It is clear that these words are eminently applicable to poetry as well and second very convincingly the decidedly unabsurd quality of Montale's commitment to an unreachable but essential artistic end. Evasion understood in this nonutopian sense is a profoundly powerful and positive characteristic of art the ambiguity of which is one of its most constant characteristics. It says no to conclusiveness, engages us in continuing dialogues, is threatened by oblivion, by changing tastes, by political and social realities, and yet paradoxically it does not disappear even in the most scientifically and rationally oriented societies. Montale may believe that his own attempt to evade the iron chain of necessity was a failed one; but his poetry, in rooting itself firmly in the ground of the negative and ambiguous, asserts the positive and certain victory of great art. This is perhaps its final and most paradoxical ambiguity.

Montale's poetry has enjoyed a remarkably enthusiastic reception, from the earliest appearance of *Ossi di seppia* through the latest poems of *Satura, Diario,* and *Quaderno.* This is not to say that he is a popular poet but rather that he did not suffer long years of being ignored and unread before being discovered by either a critical or a general public. From the retrospective position of almost sixty years beyond the publication of *Ossi,* it is difficult to imagine a time when Montale was not called Italy's greatest living poet; yet Montale was once a neophyte, his poetry once new and unencumbered by the many layers of critical responses, subsequent collections and reevaluations, and the passage of time itself that has brought him fame and the ultimate recognition of the Nobel Prize. I and many others have insisted on the understated quality not only of Montale's poems but of his participation in the cultural and political life of Italy throughout two world wars, innumerable isms, and astounding innovations, inventions, improvements, and disintegrations in the world at large. How has a poet who has always stayed on the edges and whose poetry has always emphasized its own inade-

Conclusion

quacies come to occupy a mainstream position most clearly, although certainly not exclusively, in Italian culture? What made possible this movement from the solitary to the public, from the margins to the forefront of the ranks of those generally recognized to be the great twentieth-century poets? This movement is best understood not in general historical or literary historical terms, but rather in terms of the critical metaphor of marginality.

In order to understand better the position of Montale's poetry in modern Italian letters it is helpful to consider the understated style that characterizes both it and the poet who created it. In the essay "Style and Tradition" written for the journal *Il Baretti* in 1925 Montale outlined a modest program for his generation of writers. This early piece is itself an understated plea for the acceptance of limited and reasoned goals in literature in implicit opposition to the then prevailing tendency to "elevate into laws and imperatives our most uncontrollable impulses."[14] Montale insists that there is no "literature at once civil, learned, and popular" in Italy just as there is no real "middle class . . . with a general well-being and intellectual comfort without highs but also without great lows." The inevitable result of this lack is that the Italian writer must "work in solitude, and for few" with as a constant goal "the creation of a tone, of a mutually intelligible language that would unite us with the crowd for whom we work, even if that work is ignored; a language that would concede to us the use of understatement and of allusion, and the hope of collaboration; the creation of a center of resonance that would permit poetry to constitute once more the dignity and the pride of Italy rather than some solitary, individual shame."

Clinging to past glories is not the answer, but the poets who reject all traditions and achievements in favor of a new messianic urge will produce little of lasting value. Montale's hope lies instead in what he calls "a superior kind of dilettantism, saturated with human and artistic experiences," which would contribute to the creation of a "cordial ambience, of allusion and of understanding, in which could arise, without misunderstandings, an expression of art, even if modest." He concludes the essay with a plea for recognizing the worth of the quiet commitment of "wise and shrewd disenchanted ones, conscious of limits and humble lovers of their art more than of the remaking of the [Italian] people," whose most positive contribution would be to "safeguard what has up to now been realized." In this "shared minimum of a program"

Conclusion

is to be found the work of an entire generation of poets to come. The words *modest, disenchanted, humble, minimum,* and so on all point to Montale's rejection of grand gestures or bombastically important goals in favor of a commitment to individual excellence that might eventually result in the new "center of resonance."

Unlike many writers who shared Montale's convictions at a moment in Italian history when such a stance was both artistically and politically motivated, Montale himself has stayed true to this minimum throughout his long career. He has not associated himself with any movements, refused to pontificate, clung to his basic conservatism even when strongly criticized for it; in short, he has remained on the edges of official and officious institutionalized culture. The positive reception of his poetry throughout the last sixty years is eloquent testimony to the lasting value of a dedication to modest yet worthwhile goals. Inevitably though, given the difficult and complex nature of his poetry and his insistence on the necessity for solitude and detachment in creating lasting art, Montale has often been accused of intellectual and political ivory-towerism, the worst brand of bourgeois separatism and passivity, by those intellectuals and artists who believe that the artist's responsibility does not end with his art but rather must extend actively into the political and social life of his country and the Western world. It is not a question of either-or of course; engagé artists have coexisted with more private and detached ones throughout history. What is clear however is that Montale's consistent stance has, at least in his own career, proven to be a successful and fruitful one. Yet it is equally clear that he has not been able to avoid the contentious and often obfuscating whirlwind of mainstream cultural concerns and reactions into which his own poetry has been swept. The poet's survival strategy has been one of ironic detachment, of astute maneuvering among the sharp rocks of fame—a strategy most evident in his latest poetry, in which Montale cannot ignore the institution he has become.

As I have sought to argue throughout this study, marginality represents a positive and dynamic quality of both life and art; conversely the fixed center is fraught with the dangers of rigidity, canonization, and solipsism, a kind of turning about itself that allows for no real freedom and accomplishment. Edgar Wind posits that "art has been displaced from the center of our life not just by applied science, but above all by its own centrifugal impulse."[15] I would argue that the centripetal im-

Conclusion

pulse is more responsible for the widely shared perception of art as somehow separate and exclusive unto itself and its own concerns. When art is felt to be the expression of an individual who by definition is marginal to centralized and institutionalized groups or movements or is seen as eccentric, feisty, resistant to safe generalizations, then it does touch the center of our life. But when as is commonly the case it is embalmed in mystifying rhetoric as to its loftiness or parceled out in controlled doses in museums or expensive productions it takes on the cold and unpleasant aspect of a duty much like all the other structured duties that make up our social life. This is not necessarily the fault of art but rather the result of a response to art as structure more than as movement and struggle. Sartre commented in reference to social facts that "structures are created by activity which has no structure, but suffers its results as structure."[16] Perhaps this is an inevitable result of artistic as well as of social activity; but those artists who seek to demystify their production and who insist on the marginal position of art are really keeping it more in the center of our life than those who would propel it there by aligning it with great forces, be they political, social, or cultural, that unavoidably tend toward codification and fixedness. Montale's poetry has been assimilated into the official structure of Italian culture and literary history, but it always insists on its own eccentricities—and I use this word in both its common and etymological meanings—on its continuing irresolvability: on its marginality.

Montale's poetry came to represent the attitudes, feelings, and aspirations of an entire generation not only because of the poet's quiet commitment to his own personal search for absolute expression but also because the time was ripe for a poet "in bourgeois dress,"[17] whose steadfastness and unassuming, decidedly unmessianic voice found a public disillusioned with more exuberant assertions of poetry's powers and yet in need of values and beliefs that give some sense to an increasingly senseless and chaotic world. Montale's understated voice is indicative of an entire attitude toward self, the world, and language that found an audience in harmony with that attitude. To realize that inadequacies, limits, and uncertainties could nonetheless provide the basis for a compelling poetic vision was heartening to those whose eyes were open wide enough to see that with progress and increasing social and personal well-being did not come a corresponding spiritual clarity or conviction.

Conclusion

By remaining unremittingly aware of the precariousness of any absolute assertions, be they of an artistic, political, or personal nature, and by providing through his poetry and his life an example of the positive worth of daily decency, Montale made more clear to his fellow artists and readers than many more openly declamatory poets the very basic need for clarity, minimal faith, and a sense of meaning and direction that continues to make itself felt in even the most disillusioned and faithless of times. He has succeeded in doing so not by shouting his truth but by whispering his and our perplexities in a subdued, doubt-ridden voice that is nonetheless fully endowed with affirmative power: it speaks the yes of all great art. The critic Pier Vincenzo Mengaldo has called this aspect of Montale's achievement "that dialectic between negativity of message and affirmativity of form that had been Leopardi's as well as Baudelaire's and that is one of the great ways of being of modern poetry."[18] This problematic modus vivendi of modern poetry finds one of its most unforgettable expressions in the poetry of Eugenio Montale. He tells us "I am no Leopardi, I leave little to burn."[19] But we have come to know that even one small spark, if patiently fanned, is enough to catch fire and blaze forth into a limitless, unquenchable flame. It is true that a new time is upon us and that poets continue the search for poetry in ways other than those of Montale's generation. But it is equally true that Montale's poetry goes far beyond its temporal and national boundaries, itself the fuel of present and future fires both artistic and critical. It remains engaging, demanding, and eloquent, thus maintaining its precarious yet invigorating position on the edge.

Notes
Bibliography
Index

Notes

Introduction

1. What follows is a partial list of some of the most important American and English contributions. TRANSLATIONS: *Eugenio Montale: Selected Poems*, introduction by Glauco Cambon (New York: New Directions, 1965); *Provisional Conclusions: A Selection of the Poetry of Eugenio Montale*, trans. Edith Farnsworth (Chicago: Henry Regnery Co., 1970); *Selected Poems of Eugenio Montale*, trans. George Kay (Baltimore: Penguin Books, 1969); *Eugenio Montale: New Poems*, trans. and intro. G. Singh, with an essay on *Xenia* by F. R. Leavis (New York: New Directions, 1976); *The Butterfly of Dinard*, trans. G. Singh (Lexington, Ky.: University of Kentucky Press, 1971); *Poet in Our Time*, trans. Alastair Hamilton (New York: Urizen Books, 1976). ARTICLES: By Glauco Cambon: "Eugenio Montale's Dantesque Style," in *Dante's Craft* (Minneapolis: University of Minnesota Press, 1969); "Eugenio Montale's 'Motets': The Occasions of Epiphany," *PMLA*, 82, no. 7 (1967), 471–484; "Ungaretti, Montale, and Lady Entropy," *Italica*, 4 (1960), 231–238. By Claire Licari Huffman: "The Poetic Language of Eugenio Montale," *Italian Quarterly*, 47–48 (1969), 105–128; "Structuralist Criticism and the Interpretation of Montale," *The Modern Language Review*, 72, no. 2 (1977), 322–334.

168

Notes
to
Pages
1–4

BOOKS: Guido Almansi and Bruce Merry, *Eugenio Montale: The Private Language of Poetry* (Edinburgh: Edinburgh University Press, 1977); Glauco Cambon, *Eugenio Montale* (New York: Columbia University Press, 1972); Joseph Cary, *Three Modern Italian Poets: Saba, Ungaretti, Montale* (New York: New York University Press, 1969); Arshi Pipa, *Montale and Dante* (Minneapolis: University of Minnesota Press, 1968); G. Singh, *Eugenio Montale: A Critical Study of His Poetry, Prose, and Criticism* (New Haven: Yale University Press, 1973).

2. Charles Wright has recently published his translation of the complete volume *La bufera e altro, The Storm and Other Poems* in the Field Translation Series (Oberlin, Ohio: Oberlin College, 1978). I have had the opportunity of reading in manuscript form William Arrowsmith's excellent translation of the same collection and can only hope that it will appear soon in book form (individual poems will appear in various journals). New Directions published G. Singh's translation of the latest collection, *Quaderno di Quattro Anni*, under the title *It Depends: A Poet's Notebook* (New York: 1980).

3. I have used most the one existing biography of Montale by Giulio Nascimbeni, entitled *Eugenio Montale*, Gente Famosa Series (Milan: Longanesi, 1969). I have also culled information from interviews with Montale, now published in his *Sulla poesia* (Milan: Mondadori, 1976), pp. 557–607, and from biographical outlines in Almansi and Merry, Singh, Cary, and others, and from discussions with the poet.

4. Montale uses the words *fatti* and *nonfatti* in the closing poem of *Diario del '72*, "Per finire" (To End), in which he writes: "I recommend to my posterity / (if there will be any) in the literary world, / the existence of which remains improbable, to make / a nice bonfire out of all that which might have to do with / my life, my events, my nonevents . . ." I translate from the original Italian, p. 580 of *Tutte le poesie* (Milan: Mondadori, 1977). The comment on life as a labyrinth is translated from an interview with Montale conducted by Enzo Biagi, included on pp. 186–193 of his book *Dicono di lei* (Milan: Rizzoli, 1978).

5. "In chiave di 'fa' " is on pp. 57–60 of *Farfalla di Dinard* (Milan: Mondadori, 1969); the quotation is from p. 60.

6. "Intenzioni: Intervista immaginaria" was first published in the journal *La Rassegna d'Italia* (1946) and is now available in *Sulla poesia*, pp. 561–569. The original Italian reads: "L'esperienza mi fu utile: esiste un problema d'impostazione anche fuori del canto, in ogni opera umana" (p. 562).

7. This comment appears as a note to the fifth edition of *Ossi di seppia* (Turin: Einaudi, 1942). I have taken it from Laura Barile, *Bibliografia montaliana* (Milan: Mondadori, 1977), p. 9.

8. The introduction is now available in *Letteratura italiana del Novecento* (Florence: Le Monnier, 1958), pp. 453–457.

9. From Montale's "Testimonianza" in *Firenze: Dalle Giubbe Rosse all'Antico Fattore*, ed. Marcello Vannucci (Florence: Le Monnier, 1973), pp. 51–53.

10. *Firenze: Dalle Giubbe Rosse*, p. 9.

11. Montale speaks of this "maladjustement" (*sic*) in "Confessioni di scrittori (Interviste con se stessi)" in *Sulla poesia*, pp. 569–574.

12. "Intervista immaginaria," in *Sulla poesia*, p. 566.

13. Pp. 181–186 of *Farfalla di Dinard*.

14. The title of Guido Almansi and Bruce Merry's penetrating study of Montale's poetry is *Eugenio Montale: The Private Language of Poetry* (Edinburgh: Edinburgh University Press, 1977).

15. "Intervista immaginaria," in *Sulla poesia*, p. 567.

16. "The princes have no eyes with which to see these great marvels; their hands no longer serve but to persecute us."

17. *Eugenio Montale: The Private Language of Poetry*, p. 4.

18. The poet made these comments in his Nobel Prize acceptance speech, "È ancora possibile la poesia?" (Is Poetry Still Possible?), given in December 1975 and now available in *Sulla poesia*, pp. 5–14. The comments I quote are on p. 9.

19. Beginning with certain poems of *Satura* and increasing in much of *Diario* and *Quaderno* is the tendency toward self-explication. See the third chapter of this study for a discussion of this ironic self-consideration.

20. I rely greatly on the following books by the anthropologist Victor Turner in elaborating and applying concepts relating to his term *marginality: The Forest of Symbols: Aspects of Ndembu Ritual* (Ithaca: Cornell University Press, 1967); *The Ritual Process: Structure and Anti-Structure* (Chicago: Aldine Publishing Co., 1969); *Dramas, Fields, and Metaphors: Symbolic Action in Human Society* (Ithaca: Cornell University Press, 1974).

21. The first two quotations are from Montale's Nobel Prize speech, "È ancora possibile la poesia?"; the second two are from his "Intervista immaginaria," *Sulla poesia*, p. 562 and p. 569.

22. Almansi and Merry, *Eugenio Montale: The Private Language of Poetry*, p. xi.

I. The Marginal: Readings of the First Voice

1. Unless otherwise indicated, all quotations of poetry are from *Tutte le poesie* (Milan: Mondadori, 1977). This chapter is based in great part on my article "The Marginal Concept in *Ossi di seppia*," *Italica*, 55 (Winter 1978), 402–417.

2. From "Ho scritto un solo libro," an interview with Giorgio Zampa first published in *Il Giornale Nuovo*, 27 June 1975, now available in *Sulla poesia* (Milan: Mondadori, 1976), pp. 601–607.

3. From "Le reazioni di Montale," in *Eugenio Montale: Profilo di un autore*, ed. Annalisa Cima and Cesare Segre (Milan: Rizzoli, 1977), pp. 192–201.

4. From "Intenzioni: Intervista immaginaria," first published in 1946, now available in *Sulla poesia* pp. 561–569.

5. From "Introduzione a *Ossi di seppia*," first published in 1933 with the

title "Introduzione a Eugenio Montale," now available in Gianfranco Contini, *Una lunga fedeltà: Scritti su Eugenio Montale* (Turin: Einaudi, 1974), pp. 5–16.

6. These are the opening lines of the first poem of the fourth collection, *Satura*, entitled "Il *tu*." The poet himself has, however, referred to the *tu* using precisely the term he rejects in this poem: "Il 'tu' delle mie poesie . . . non è mai rivolto a me stesso: è un 'tu' istituzionale, l'antagonista che bisognerebbe inventare se non ci fosse" (The *you* of my poems . . . is never directed to myself: it is an institutional *you*, the antagonist that would have to be invented if it did not exist). In Giulio Nascimbeni's biography *Eugenio Montale* (Milan: Longanesi, 1969), p. 74.

7. Guido Almansi and Bruce Merry, *Eugenio Montale: The Private Language of Poetry* (Edinburgh: Edinburgh University Press, 1977), p. 7.

8. Almansi and Merry, *Eugenio Montale: The Private Language of Poetry*, p. 9.

9. I say *her* as it is generally thought that this early presence is associated with the beloved of later poems. Like the majority of Montale's unnamed *you's*, *she* is also *we*, the readers. Emerico Giachery points out the openness of the reference in "In Limine": "Si potrebbe aggiungere che il perplesso eroe negativo . . . demanda questa possibilità positiva al 'tu,' a un'alterità supponibilmente femminile . . . anche se lasciata imprecisata e perciò anche identificabile col lettore, un lettore immaginato più ricco di ventura che non l'autore" (One could add that the perplexed negative hero . . . displaces this positive possibility to the *you*, to an otherness supposedly feminine . . . even if left imprecise and thus identifiable also with the reader, a reader imagined as more endowed with good fortune than the author). In Emerico Giachery, "Metamorfosi dell'orto," *Atti e Memorie dell'Arcadia*, 3rd ser., 7, fasc. 1 (1977), 35–60.

10. The literary garden is most typically associated with escapist literature, but it can also be seen as emblematic of highly self-conscious literature. In Giuseppe Mazzotta's "The *Decameron*: The Marginality of Literature," *University of Toronto Quarterly*, 42, no. 1 (1972) 64–81, we find an excellent application of the term *marginality* to Boccaccio's masterpiece; of the garden setting of the *Decameron* Mazzotta writes: "Far from being an evasion into frivolity, the retreat to the garden is a dramatic strategy which enables Boccaccio to reflect on history and to find, in this condition of marginality, of provisional separation from the historical structures, a place for secular literature" (p. 64). These words, *mutatis mutandis*, are applicable to Montale's garden retreat.

11. Maggi Rombi includes a *spoglio* of the word *orto* in her study *Montale: Parole sensi e immagini* (Rome: Bulzoni, 1978), pp. 167–168. See Glauco Cambon's "La forma dinamica dell'orto di Montale," in *Omaggio a Montale*, ed. Silvio Ramat (Milan: Mondadori, 1966), and Emerico Giachery's "Metamorfosi dell'orto," 35–60, for useful discussions of the *orto*. The choice of this term rather than the more traditionally poetic *giardino* serves to emphasize the

171

countereloquent insistence in Montale's poetry: an *orto* is a vegetable or fruit garden of the homiest, least formal variety.

12. Note 35 of Giachery's article "Metamorfosi dell'orto."

13. The etymological explanation of the term states that it is "that which is behind, or in front of, the *murus.*" In John T. White, *The White Latin Dictionary* (Chicago: Follett, 1948), p. 474. Both *limbo* and *lembo* derive from the Latin term *limbus,* meaning "a border that surrounds anything; a hem, edging." In *The White Latin Dictionary,* p. 250.

14. The description of *limbo* is found in Canto 4 of the *Inferno.*

15. Silvio Ramat, *Montale* (Florence: Vallecchi, 1965), p. 16.

16. Giachery, "Metamorfosi dell'orto," p. 40.

17. From Montale's speech "Dante ieri e oggi," first presented as the final talk at the "Congresso per il settimo centenario della nascita di Dante," 24 April 1965, now available in *Sulla poesia,* pp. 15–34.

18. In the collection *Farfalla di Dinard* (Milan: Mondadori, 1969), pp. 156–160.

19. D'Arco Silvio Avalle uses this most appropriate phrase in the introduction to his *Tre saggi su Montale* (Turin: Einaudi, 1972), p. 13.

20. There is a basic difficulty in finding terms descriptive of the general concept of marginality, given its particular emphasis on essential ambiguity. The phrases *betwixt and between, neither-nor, interstitial,* and so on, which I use throughout my study, are borrowed from Victor Turner, who in turn has used them throughout his studies. Although working in the area of cultural anthropology, Turner has provided many seminal ideas for the study of literature in his books *The Forest of Symbols: Aspects of Ndembu Ritual* (Ithaca: Cornell University Press, 1967), *The Ritual Process: Structure and Anti-Structure* (Chicago: Aldine Publishing Co., 1969), and *Dramas, Fields, and Metaphors: Symbolic Action in Human Society* (Ithaca: Cornell University Press, 1974), and my debt to him is both explicitly and implicitly evident in my application of these ideas.

21. "Intenzioni: Intervista immaginaria," in *Sulla poesia,* p. 562.

22. In his "Intervista immaginaria" Montale writes that he felt he was living "sotto a una campana di vetro" (under a bell jar); see *Sulla poesia,* p. 565. In "Confessioni di scrittori (Interviste con se stessi)" he speaks of his sense of "totale disarmonia con la realtà" (total disharmony with reality), and of "un inadattamento" (lack of adjustment), a moral and psychological "maladjustement" (*sic*); see *Sulla poesia,* p. 570.

23. "Intervista immaginaria," *Sulla poesia,* p. 564.

24. Turner, *The Forest of Symbols,* p. 97.

25. Montale states: "I miei motivi sono semplici e sono: il paesaggio (qualche volta allucinato, ma spesso naturalistico: il nostro paesaggio ligure, che è universalissimo); l'amore, sotto forma di fantasmi che *frequentano* le varie poesie e provocano le solite 'intermittenze del cuore' (gergo proustiano che io non uso) e l'evasione, la fuga dalla catena ferrea della necessità, il miracolo, diciamo così, laico"—"My motives are simple and are: the landscape

172

(sometimes hallucinated, but often naturalistic: our Ligurian landscape, which is most universal); love, under the form of phantasms that *frequent* the various poems and provoke the usual 'intermittences of the heart' (Proustian jargon I don't use) and evasion, the flight from the iron chain of necessity, the lay miracle, let's put it that way." From a letter to P. Gadda Conti in Alvaro Valentini, *Lettura di Montale: Ossi di seppia* (Rome: Bulzoni, 1971), p. 11.

26. Turner, *The Forest of Symbols*, p. 94.

27. Gaston Bachelard, *The Poetics of Space*, trans. Maria Jolas and with a foreword by Etienne Gilson (Boston: Beacon Press, 1969), p. xxiii.

28. Valentini, *Lettura di Montale*, p. 11.

29. Valentini, *Lettura di Montale*, p. 11. The italics are Montale's.

30. *Attendere* may signify either "to wait for" or "to dedicate oneself to; to serve." Both meanings are applicable to the experience of love understood as a patient commitment to what no longer is or is yet to be.

) 31. This critical awareness permeates all Montalian criticism from the earliest readings of Contini through Ramat's first monograph in Italian to the recent work of non-Italian critics such as Almansi and Merry and Singh. Therefore I shall not attempt to single out any one passage as more representative than innumerable others. The poet himself plays with his own concept of the miracle, of salvation, in recent poems such as "L'angelo nero" (*Satura*) and "Quel che più conta" (*Diario del '72*), discussed in some detail in chapter 3.

32. In Valentini, *Lettura di Montale*, p. 11.

33. In *Sulla poesia*, p. 565.

34. Etienne Gilson, *Painting and Reality* (Princeton: Princeton University Press, 1957).

35. Hugo Friedrich, *La lirica moderna*, trans. Piero Bernardini Marzolla (Milan: Garzanti, 1961), p. 181. The English translation is mine.

36. In Montale's note to the *Ossi di seppia*, now in *Tutte le poesie*, p. 709.

37. Montale wrote these words to Paola Nicoli in a letter dated August 24, 1924; quoted in Giachery, "Metamorfosi dell'orto," p. 38.

38. Silvio Ramat judges "Crisalide" to be a poem that "suffers from a complex construction (soffre di una costruzione macchinosa) and attributes its weakness to Montale's desire to maintain an "emphatic tone" that at times becomes "turbid" (*Montale*, p. 71). Marco Forti states that we find in "Crisalide" "una situazione simile a quella di 'Arsenio' ma non altrettanto drammaticamente e simbolicamente matura" (a situation similar to that of "Arsenio" but not as dramatically and symbolically mature), in his book *Eugenio Montale: La poesia, la prosa di fantasia e d'invenzione* (Milan: Mursia, 1973–1974), p. 111.

39. Almansi and Merry, *Eugenio Montale: The Private Language of Poetry*, p. 53.

40. Joseph Cary, *Three Modern Italian Poets: Saba, Ungaretti, Montale* (New York: New York University Press, 1969), p. 268.

41. Most critics are, however, aware of the complexities of any autobiographical explanation of the figure of Arsenio. Ramat writes that "one speaks,

173

as could be expected, of the autobiographism of this poem," but he immediately adds that if "usually Montale makes his autobiography vibrate with a vitality that is unknown to the Arsenio in question, then we are in the face of a case of extremely pitiless self-criticism ("un caso di autocritica spietata oltremisura"); see *Montale*, p. 69. Cary notes that "Arsenio might also be considered a 'version' of Eugenio Montale, who has been known to sign letters with that name. Other sardonic self-appellations: 'Eusebius'—the name given by Robert Schumann to the gentle, dreamy, contemplative and 'poetic' side of his 'split' personality; 'Tiresias'—the passive prophet-androgyn resuscitated by Eliot; 'Mirco'—the lovelorn shepherd . . ." (*Three Italian Poets*, p. 278).

42. Gianfranco Contini wrote of "a myth in Montale that becomes quite central to his poetry: more than the sea; and it is the noon hour" (l'ora del meriggio), in his "Introduzione a *Ossi di seppia*" now available in *Una lunga fedeltà*, p. 12. He calls the storm "the privileged moment of the later phenomenology of Montale" (l'istante privilegiato della più tarda fenomenologia di Montale), in "Dagli *Ossi* alle *Occasioni*," *Una lunga fedeltà*, p. 25.

43. As Ramat has insisted, Montale's sallies into the future are always "incrinati da dubbi" (flawed by doubts); see *Montale*, p. 23. In "Arsenio," as in many other poems with a strong impetus toward a future understood as possible escape, the *dubbi* are concretely expressed in the many dubitative forms (*if* clauses, the adverb *forse*). See my discussion in chapter 2.

44. In Montale's poetry the verb *discendere* (to descend, go down) almost always indicates a movement that is spiritual or psychological as well as physical. It can be either positive (toward deeper self-knowledge) or negative (toward more profound chaos and / or despair). See my discussion of the "Mottetti" in chapter 2.

45. Marco Forti mentions this sense of creative potentiality thus: ". . . the usual . . . elements of the Ligurian topography . . . are [as if] loaded with a sense and metasense [senso e sovrasenso] of analogical imminence, of metaphoric potentiality . . ." He further writes that "everything here can suggest a creative unquiet [inquietudine creatrice] . . . the possibility of a qualitative leap conjured up from who knows where . . ." (*Eugenio Montale*, p. 107).

46. Turner, *The Forest of Symbols*, p. 102.

47. Turner, *The Ritual Process*, p. 103.

48. Almansi and Merry, *Eugenio Montale: The Private Language of Poetry*, p. 52.

49. I am of course referring to Smith's book *Poetic Closure: A Study of How Poems End* (Chicago: The University of Chicago Press, 1968), especially the chapter entitled "Closure and Anti-Closure in Modern Poetry," pp. 234–260.

50. Almansi and Merry, *Eugenio Montale: The Private Language of Poetry*, p. 52.

51. *Eugenio Montale*, p. 108.

52. Giachery notes that the title "indicates without a doubt the potential winged being" (l'essere alato in potenza); he points to a confirmation of this in

the autograph variant of the poem, which contains the line "forse non sorgerà dalla crisalide / la creatura del volo" (perhaps it will not rise up from the chrysalis / the creature of flight), in "Metamorfosi dell'orto," p. 46. As Giachery indicates, the earlier version is now available in *Autografi di Montale*, ed. Maria Corti and Maria Antonietta Grignani (Turin: Einaudi, 1976), pp. 15–21. This book lists the autograph material now available at the University of Pavia, to which Montale has given all of his manuscripts, letters, and so on. In writing this book I have not, unfortunately, had the opportunity to make use of this invaluable source.

53. Bachelard, *The Poetics of Space*, pp. 136–137.

54. Alvaro Valentini also notes the importance of the verb, stating that its ambiguity is "particularly felicitous," for it emphasizes that the barge is not only that but also "the particular magic word that is awaited and waits in its turn"; in *Lettura di Montale: Ossi di seppia*, p. 179.

55. Martin Buber, *I and Thou*, trans. Ronald Gregor Smith (New York: Charles Scribner's Sons, 1958), p. 17.

56. Almansi and Merry, *Eugenio Montale: The Private Language of Poetry*, p. 53.

57. Cary, *Three Modern Italian Poets*, p. 272.

58. All italics are mine.

59. "Stato d'animo ansioso, sospeso, nell'attesa di un evento, fra le opposte sollecitazioni della speranza e del timore." In Giacomo Devoto and Gian Carlo Oli, *Dizionario della lingua italiana* (Florence: Le Monnier, 1971), p. 2548.

60. The most explicit tie between the beloved and the butterfly is to be found in the short story "Farfalla di Dinard" (Butterfly of Dinard) in the collection of short stories of the same name (Milan: Mondadori, 1969), pp. 240–241.

61. In his "Intervista immaginaria" in *Sulla poesia*, p. 566.

62. Contini writes of Montale's "poesia in fieri" (poetry in the making), which reflects "the very theoretical crisis in action" (la stessa crisi teoretica in atto), in his "Introduzione a *Ossi di seppia*" in *Una lunga fedeltà*, p. 12.

63. *The Forest of Symbols*, p. 97.

64. *Tre saggi su Montale*, p. 13.

65. "Intervista immaginaria" in *Sulla poesia*, p. 562 and p. 564.

66. In "Sul *Diario del '71 e del '72*," first published as a cover blurb to the volume, now available in *Una lunga fedeltà*, pp. 97–98.

II. Style as Tension: Love and the *Avventura Stilistica*

1. "I projected the Selvaggia or the Mandetta or the Delia (call her what you will) of the *Motets* onto the background of a cosmic and terrestrial war without goals and without reason, and I entrusted myself to her, lady or cloud, angel or stormy petrel." Montale is here speaking of the feminine figure as she is elaborated in the poems of "Finisterre" in *La bufera e altro*; see *Sulla poesia* (Milan: Mondadori, 1976), p. 568.

2. The note states that "Iride" had already appeared "also with the name of Clizia" in the third collection and earlier in "many poems of *Le occasioni:* for example in the 'Motets' and in [the poem] 'New Stanzas' "; see *Tutte le poesie* (Milan: Mondadori, 1977), p. 714. In his book *Il rovescio della poesia* (Milan: Longanesi, 1977) Mario Martelli seeks to sort out all of Montale's clarifications concerning the various feminine figures in his poetry. Martelli ultimately reaches the conclusion that the poet has willfully misled us and that the exact identification of the women is impossible. The poet himself has insisted to me that biographical exactitude is irrelevant.

3. "The little poems of Mirco, which then formed a series, an autobiographical novelette [which was] anything but gloomy, were born day by day." These words are in Montale's article "Due sciacalli al guinzaglio" (Two Jackals on a Leash) first published in 1950 in the *Corriere della Sera* and now available in *Sulla poesia,* pp. 84–87.

4. Montale wrote that the *Vita nuova* "gives a first form, already in itself complete, to that which will be the process of transhumanization of Beatrice"; in "Dante ieri e oggi" (Dante Yesterday and Today), now available in *Sulla poesia,* pp. 15–34. I am translating from page 22.

5. *The Random House Dictionary of the English Language,* ed. Jess Stein and Laurence Urdang (New York: Random House, 1967), p. 933.

6. "Dante ieri e oggi," in *Sulla poesia,* p. 21.

7. Franco Croce notes that "there is, it is true, a fundamental image that is somewhat an emblem of this zone of Montale's poetry, as light . . . was the emblem of the most typical 'Ossi,' and it is the image of smoke, fog, shadow" in his article "*Le occasioni*" in *La rassegna della letteratura italiana,* no. 203 (1966), 266. A list of the words *sera* (evening), *oscurità* (darkness), *notte* (night), *buio* (darkness), *ombra* (shadow), *tenebra* (shadow), and *fumo* (smoke) is included in my unpublished doctoral dissertation, "The Poetic Itinerary of Eugenio Montale," Yale University, 1974, p. 97.

8. The first quotation is from "Ho scritto un solo libro," in *Sulla poesia,* p. 604; the second is from "Le reazioni di Montale," in *Eugenio Montale,* ed. Annalisa Cima and Cesare Segre (Milan: Rizzoli, 1977), p. 194.

9. "Dante ieri e oggi," in *Sulla poesia,* p. 17.

10. There is of course Arshi Pipa's book-length study *Montale and Dante* (Minneapolis: University of Minnesota Press, 1968), in which many of the stylistic echoes of the *Commedia* are located and their significance discussed. Glauco Cambon has always been highly sensitive to the presence of Dante in Montale's poetry; see especially his article "Eugenio Montale's 'Motets': The Occasions of Epiphany," *PMLA* 82, no. 7 (1967), 471–484, to which I am greatly indebted, as well as his "Eugenio Montale's Dantesque Style," in *Dante's Craft* (Minneapolis: University of Minnesota Press, 1969), pp. 161–192. Among Italian critics Angelo Jacomuzzi and Giorgio Orelli have pointed out important affinities between Montale and Dante. Emerico Giachery's article "Ancora su Montale," *Atti del Convegno di Studi,* Casa di Dante, Rome (6–7 May 1977), pp. 291–296, is a most helpful review of these

critics' findings as well as Giachery's own further suggestions as to Montale's *dantismo*.

11. There is apparent chronological ordering in the last two volumes of poetry, *Diario* and *Quaderno di quattro anni*; but even there we can discern a tampering with time in the service of atemporal, ideal structure.

12 . I have in mind the analogous insistence in the *Divine Comedy* on the *ri-* prefix, first at the end of the *Inferno* (34.133–134 and 34.139)—"Lo duca e io per quel cammino ascoso / intrammo a ritorner nel chiaro mondo" and "e quindi uscimmo a riveder le stelle" (My guide and I by that hidden road / entered to return to the bright world . . . and thence we came forth to resee the stars)—and then even more intensely at the end of the *Purgatorio* (33.142–145)—"Io ritornai dalla santissima onda / rifatto sì come piante novelle / rinovellate di novella fronda, / puro e disposto a salire alle stelle" (I returned from the most holy wave / remade just like new plants / renewed with new foliage, / pure and disposed to climb up to the stars). Both here and in Montale's poem the emphasis is on a return that is also a reformation, or positive newness. Guido Almansi and Bruce Merry point out Montale's constant "recourse to the *ri-* prefix" throughout the "Motets" in *Eugenio Montale: The Private Language of Poetry* (Edinburgh: Edinburgh University Press, 1977), pp. 76–78, but they insist more on the aspect of reclamation of the past than on what I would see as the equally important motive of future renewal that a new understanding of past events might provide.

13. "Intervista immaginaria," in *Sulla poesia,* p. 566.

14. "Dante ieri e oggi," in *Sulla poesia,* p. 22.

15. Montale told me during one of our conversations that an earlier version of this line from "The Balcony" was "l'estro [the whim] di attenderti vivo." The change to *ansia* might be seen as a conscious or unconscious desire to tie the sunflower of the earlier poem to the lady of the "Motets."

16. "Due sciacalli al guinzaglio," in *Sulla poesia,* p. 85.

17. "Due sciacalli al guinzaglio," in *Sulla poesia,* p. 84.

18. The first quotation is from "Dante ieri e oggi," *Sulla poesia,* p. 21; the second is on p. 34.

19. Alvaro Valentini cites this phrase from G. Mariani, *Poesia e tecnica nella lirica del Novecento* (Padua: Liviana, 1958), in his study *Lettura di Montale: Le occasioni* (Rome: Bulzoni, 1975), p. 103.

20. *Eugenio Montale: The Private Language of Poetry,* p. 78.

21. *Eugenio Montale: The Private Language of Poetry,* p. 79.

22. "Due sciacalli al guinzaglio," in *Sulla poesia,* p. 84.

23. Glauco Cambon has pointed out this generalized *dantismo*, writing that "like the *Inferno*'s prologue, this 'Motet' consummates a catastrophe and ushers in the possibility of a renewal by way of a perilous quest which should lead the bewildered poet back to his Lady"; "Eugenio Montale's 'Motets': The Occasions of Epiphany," *PMLA*, 82, no. 7 (1967), p. 474.

24. "Lettere a Bobi Bazlen," in *Sulla poesia,* p. 96.

25. Mario Martelli cites the letter to Guarnieri, written by Montale in 1964, in which this information is given, in *Il rovescio della poesia*, p. 10.

26. Avalle insists (correctly I believe) throughout his studies of Montale's poetry that the poet relives his sources; be they Italian (Dante, Petrarch, D'Annunzio, Pascoli), French (Mallarmé, Rimbaud), or Anglo-Saxon (Hardy, Hopkins, Eliot), Montale makes them his and creates out of them his own unique experience, which is then transformed into poetry "in modo assoluta-mente moderno" (in an absolutely modern way); see D'Arco Silvio Avalle, *Tre saggi su Montale* (Turin: Einaudi, 1972), p. 114. In other words, Montale, like all great poets, creates his own predecessors.

27. "Due sciacalli al guinzaglio," in *Sulla poesia*, p. 86.

28. "Le reazioni di Montale," in *Eugenio Montale*, ed. Cima and Segre, p. 195.

29. "Lettere a Bobi Bazlen," in *Sulla poesia*, pp. 93–97.

30. Avalle states that "in the hardness and the cold splendor of the jewels are recognized the attributes [and] the very destiny of the absent one" (*Tre studi su Montale*, p. 45). He further asserts that the "transference of these ob-jects' [jewels'] properties to Iris-Clizia has a precise reason," that reason being that they represent the "precise existential condition" of the beloved (p. 46). Her jewels are not therefore mere ornaments of her person but rather symbols of her brilliance and strength, just as the many double-*l* words linked to her in Montale's poetry are not simple rhetorical or auditive poetic devices but essen-tial elements in the semantics of Clizia's poetic existence.

31. Although Montale makes this statement concerning the writing of his prose pieces included in *Farfalla di Dinard*, I believe that it is applicable to his poetry as well. See the preface to the English version, *The Butterfly of Dinard*, trans. G. Singh (Lexington, Ky.: University of Kentucky Press, 1971).

32. This section of the chapter is based in great part on my article, "Mon-tale's 'Forse': The Poetics of Doubt," in *Forum Italicum*, 13, (Summer 1979), 147–168.

33. Innumerable critics have spoken of Montale's poetry in these terms; I shall quote only a few representative examples. In his essay "Montale 1925" Sergio Solmi writes concerning *Ossi di seppia*: "An atmosphere of arid and re-flected desolation seems to gnaw at the material of this poetry from every side." See *Per conoscere Montale*, ed. Marco Forti (Milan: Mondadori, 1976), pp. 99–105; I am translating from p. 100 of this source. In the same collection of essays Gianfranco Contini, in "Montale e *La bufera*," written in 1956, com-ments that "in Montale's work the first phase is negative and destructive . . . the second phase is relatively positive or constructive" (p. 148). Almansi and Merry write of Montale's "irony which does not exclude but actually includes tragedy and despair" in *Eugenio Montale: The Private Language of Poetry*, p. xi. In defense of the positivity to be found in Montale's verse Joseph Cary comments: "I believe that critics have made too much of Montale as a waste-lander, a poet of desolation and despair. I do not mean that the mouse is an eagle, but if he knows he is a mouse then this is something—perhaps he is a

'lucky' mouse"; in *Three Modern Italian Poets: Saba, Ungaretti, Montale* (New York: New York University Press, 1969), p. 326.

34. The phrase is from the poem "Lettera a Malvolio" (Letter to Malvolio) in *Diario del '71*, included in *Tutte le poesie* (Milan: Mondadori, 1977), p. 521.

35. Hölderlin's assertion is quoted by Maurice Blanchot in his book *L'Espace littéraire* (Paris: Gallimard, 1955), p. 374.

36. These calculations were made before I had the opportunity to read the latest collection, *Quaderno di quattro anni*. See Luigi Rosiello's "Consistenza e distribuzione statistica del lessico poetico in Montale," in *Rendiconti*, fasc. 11–12 (September 1965), 397–421, for a computer-based study of Montale's lexicon.

37. In an earlier version of "Crisalide" now available in the archives at the University of Pavia there are several more *forse*'s that do not appear in the final version. The fourth stanza begins: "Forse non vincerete l'ombra oscura / che da ogni parte tenta di rinchiudervi; / forse non sorgerà dalla crisalide / la creatura del volo" (Perhaps you will not overcome the dark shadow / that from all sides tries to close you in; / perhaps will not rise up from the chrysalis / the creature of flight). The earlier version ends with the line: "E forse non m'è data" (And perhaps it is not given to me). This version is available in *Autografi di Montale* (Turin: Einaudi, 1976), pp. 14–21.

38. The definition is from *The White Latin Dictionary* (Chicago: Follett, 1948), p. 241.

39. *Forse* "indica il dubbio, la probabilità, l'approssimazione, l'attenuazione"; see Giacomo Devoto and Gian Carlo Oli, *Dizionario della lingua italiana* (Florence: Le Monnier, 1971), p. 935.

40. See my article "Montale's 'Forse': The Poetics of Doubt" for a complete listing of the word *forse* as it appears in all of the collections.

41. Antonino Musumeci has noted the significance of the *forse* appearing in an enjambment, writing that "this insistence on the dubitative adverb at the end of the line, detached from the object that grammatically is connected to it, creates an instant of silence that is pregnant with the lack of certainty of the poet himself" in his study "Silenzi montaliani: Note sull'*enjambement* nella poesia di Montale," *Forum Italicum*, 6 (December 1972), 497–514. Almansi and Merry also list a few of the usages of *forse* in *Eugenio Montale: The Private Language of Poetry*, p. 91.

42. In their analysis of the poem "Eastbourne" (*Le occasioni*) Almansi and Merry point out the significance of the parenthetical phrase contained there and comment that "the whole poem is articulated round this central 'perhaps,' even though it is contained inside one of the poet's rare and therefore significant parentheses"; *Eugenio Montale: The Private Language of Poetry*, p. 91.

43. See Glauco Cambon's "La forma dinamica di 'L'orto' di Montale," in *Omaggio a Montale*, ed. Silvio Ramat (Milan: Mondadori, 1966), pp. 168–174, and Emerico Giachery's "Metamorfosi dell'orto," in *Atti e memorie*

dell'Arcadia, 3rd ser., 7, fasc. 1 (1977), 35–60, for especially sensitive readings of this and other poems in which the *orto* appears.

44. Susanne Langer, *Feeling and Form: A Theory of Art Developed from "Philosophy in a New Key "* (New York: Charles Scribner's Sons, 1953), pp. 242–243.

45. "Intervista immaginaria," in *Sulla poesia,* p. 565, 567.

46. "Le parole e la musica," in *Auto da fé* (Milan: Il Saggiatore, 1966), p. 110.

47. "La musica aleatoria," in *Auto da fé,* p. 244.

48. "Le reazioni di Montale," in *Eugenio Montale,* ed. Cima and Segre, p. 193.

49. "È ancora possibile la poesia?" in *Sulla poesia,* p. 7.

50. Alvaro Valentini quotes both Solmi's and Gargiulo's early comments on the series in his book *Lettura di Montale: Ossi di seppia* (Rome: Bulzoni, 1971), pp. 127–128. Ramat's discussion of "Mediterraneo" is in his book *Montale* (Florence: Vallecchi, 1965), pp. 57–59. Marco Forti considers the series in his book *Eugenio Montale: La poesia, la prosa di fantasia e d'invenzione* (Milan: Mursia, 1973–1974), pp. 90–97.

51. "Intervista immaginaria," in *Sulla poesia,* p. 566.

52. "Le reazioni di Montale," in *Eugenio Montale,* ed. Cima and Segre, pp. 193–194.

53. *Sulla poesia,* pp. 562–567 *passim.*

54. The adjective *piccino* emphasizes the poet's childlike sense of inferiority in relation to the great father, the sea, for it is an adjective "con riferimento all'età infantile" (with reference to infancy) and carries a "tono accentuatamente spregiativo, meschino, gretto" (tone quite pejorative, mean, petty); see Devoto and Oli, *Dizionario della lingua italiana,* p. 1697.

55. *Potere* (to be able to) is also a noun in Italian meaning "power" or "force" and is related to the concept of potency or confident mastery. Montale's various negative usages of the word show how far he considers himself to be from assertive confidence.

56. Cf. "Solo quest'iride posso / lasciarti" (This iris alone am I able / to leave to you) of *La bufera*'s "Little Testament."

57. *Eugenio Montale: The Private Language of Poetry,* p. 100.

58. "È ancora possibile la poesia?" in *Sulla poesia,* p. 7.

59. In this regard see his poem "Lettera a Malvolio" of *Diario,* the fifth collection, in which the poet writes in ironic self-defense, "No, / non si trattò mai d'una fuga / ma solo di un rispettabile / prendere le distanze" (No, / it was never a question of flight / but only of a respectable / stepping back), thus showing an awareness of his "sins." See Pier Vincenzo Mengaldo's *"Lettera a Malvolio"* in *Eugenio Montale,* ed. Cima and Segre, pp. 134–167, for an excellent reading of the poem.

60. Umberto Carpi, *Montale dopo il fascismo: dalla "Bufera" a "Satura"* (Padua: Liviana, 1971); Arshi Pipa, *Montale and Dante* (Minneapolis: University of Minnesota Press, 1968); and other recent studies have contributed to

this politicization of Montale. I attempt to deal with some of the complexities of this issue in my final two chapters.

61. "Intervista immaginaria," in *Sulla poesia*, p. 564.

62. "Le reazioni di Montale," in *Eugenio Montale*, ed. Cima and Segre, pp. 192.

63. "Intervista immaginaria," in *Sulla poesia*, p. 568.

64. Maggi Rombi, *Montale: Parole sensi e immagini* (Rome: Bulzoni, 1978), p. 62.

65. As I have indicated, however, in the "Mediterraneo" suite the "poetics of fire" is already declared in the final lines of the final poem "Dissipa tu se lo vuoi": "Bene lo so: bruciare, / questo, non altro, è il mio significato." The word *bruciare* here can be seen as having both negative and positive connotations, as expressing both continued unfulfilled desire for the sea's wholeness and essentiality and a hopeful dedication to the search for them.

66. The importance of fire to the beloved's myth is already implicit in the poem "Elegia di Pico Farnese" (Elegy of Pico Farnese) in *Le occasioni*, where the troublesome word *didspori* appeared. As Luciano Rebay finally clarified in his article, "I diàspori di Montale" *Italica*, vol. 46 (Spring 1969), pp. 33–53, Montale had in mind the word *diospiro*, or *kaki*, because as the poet indicated, it is "frutto rosso, frutto di fuoco" (red fruit, fruit of fire); p. 46.

67. Angelo Jacomuzzi speaks of a negative and positive symbolic oscillation in images having to do with light and fire in his study "Per un 'omaggio' di Montale 'a Rimbaud,' " in *La poesia di Montale* (Turin: Einaudi, 1978), p. 114.

68. See "Per uno studio sulla religiosità nella poesia della *Bufera e altro*," in *La poesia di Montale*, pp. 34–57.

69. "Intervista immaginaria," in *Sulla poesia*, p. 568.

70. "Intervista immaginaria," in *Sulla poesia*, p. 568.

71. "Other is the figure in 'Ballad Written in a Clinic,' still other is she of the 'Flashes and Dedications' and of the 'Madrigals' "; see *Tutte le poesie*, p. 714.

72. Almansi and Merry, *Eugenio Montale: The Private Language of Poetry*, p. 113.

73. Montale provided a revealing note concerning the lady of the "Madrigali" in a letter to Silvio Guarnieri quoted by Giachery on p. 296 of his article "Ancora su Montale": "Here appears the AntiBeatrice as in the *Vita nuova*; like the 'donna gentile' whom Dante wanted to pass off on us as Philosophy while it is supposed she was something else, so much so that she awakened Beatrice's jealousy . . . But I don't know how this news might be of use to you. Sometimes you make me think of Isidoro Del Lungo who believed to have resolved every single problem in Dante when he discovered that Beatrice Portinari had really existed." Nor should we believe that every problem in Montale's "Madrigali" is resolved by the woman's name provided us in the acrostic of the poem "Da un lago svizzero" (From a Swiss Lake).

74. Italics throughout this passage are mine.

75. In *La poesia di Montale*, p. 54.

76. Sergio Antonielli wrote that "Montale . . . comes to tell us with *La bufera* that the essential aspect of the crisis of the twentieth century is for him that one which is religious," in "Clizia e altro," *Letteratura*, nos. 79–81 (1966), 106.

77. In *La poesia di Montale*, p. 56.

78. *Suscitare* is defined as "to make to rise up, to call forth, in a spiritual sense; to provoke an effect" (far sorgere, sollevare, in senso spirituale; provocare un effetto); see Devoto and Oli, *Dizionario*, p. 2408. The verb is perfectly suited to describe the sort of internal, spiritual activity in which the poetic speaker is involved.

79. Jacomuzzi states that Montale's poetry is "occupied by an energetic semantic and communicative decisiveness" that is not controlled by the "whimsical standard of content and feelings, but by the real [standard] of language and style" (non alla stregua velleitaria dei contenuti e dei sentimenti, ma a quella effettuale della lingua e dello stile); see *La poesia di Montale*, p. 56.

III. The *Retrobottega*: Readings of the Last Voice

1. From "Le reazioni di Montale," in *Eugenio Montale*, ed. Annalisa Cima and Cesare Segre (Milan: Rizzoli, 1977), pp. 192–193. The translation here and throughout is my own.

2. "Le reazioni di Montale," p. 193.

3. Montale states that the latest poems offer "the other side of the coin, the opening of the poet's back-shop," in the interview recorded in "Le reazioni di Montale," p. 192.

4. I refer to many of the articles on the recent collections throughout this chapter. Therefore I shall not list them here. Among the pieces to which I do not make direct reference are Glauco Cambon's review of *Satura* in *Books Abroad* (Autumn 1971), Paolo Milano's review of *Diario* entitled "Diario appena scritto" in the magazine *Espresso* (8 April 1973), and Giulio Cattaneo's article "I miniepisodi di Montale," in *Nuova antologia*, no. 2047 (July 1971), 331–333, in which he discusses the quotidian episodes that provide the material for the poems of *Satura*.

5. Viktor Sklovskij, an early Russian formalist, wrote of the process of estrangement, stating that "the goal of art is that of transmitting the impression of the object, as 'vision' and not as 'recognition'; the procedure of art is the procedure of 'estrangement' . . . art is a way of 'feeling' the becoming of the object, while the 'already accomplished' has no importance in art." This passage is my rendering of *Teoria della prosa*, trans. Cesare G. De Michelis and Renzo Oliva (Turin: Einaudi, 1976), p. 12. As far as I know, no English translation of this study exists.

6. As Montale wrote his Nobel Prize acceptance speech he considered the physical aspect of poetry and concluded that "poetry has become a literary genre with very precise characteristics: it has on the page a vertical appearance,

with frequent indentations on the right margin and many conventional 'new paragraphs.' [Poetry] differs from the narrative genre substantially because of its appearance." This passage is taken from Domenico Porzio's diary of the poet's trip to Sweden in order to receive the Nobel, *Con Montale a Stoccolma* (Milan: Ferro Edizioni, 1976), p. 16, in which are also several excellent photographs of Montale.

7. Gianfranco Contini, "Sul *Diario del '71 e del '72*," in *Una lunga fedeltà* (Turin: Einaudi, 1974), p. 97.

8. Montale himself stated that the title *Satura* "has three or four meanings. Excluding that of appetizing *avantgout*, I want it to keep all of them," in "Autointervista," first published in the *Corriere della Sera* (7 February 1971) and now available in *Sulla poesia* (Milan: Mondadori, 1976), pp. 599–600. I translate from p. 599. In another interview conducted on the radio, the poet said: "I have played a little on the equivocality of the title [*Satura*], but I would not exclude the possibility that it might mean satire also, even if the satirical poems are few, let's put it that way. Instead, as a presentation of poetry of a diverse kind, with diverse intonation and theme, then, might I dare to say, understood as 'miscellany' the word might work . . ." The original Italian is quoted in Marco Forti, *Eugenio Montale: La poesia, la prosa di fantasia e d'invenzione* (Milan: Mursia, 1973–1974), p. 352.

9. The definition is from G. Devoto and G. C. Oli, *Dizionario della lingua italiana* (Florence: Le Monnier, 1971), p. 2069.

10. Andrea Zanzotto calls *Satura* a word "della saturazione, del non-poterne più" (of saturation, of exhaustion) in his article "Da 'Botta e risposta I' a *Satura*," in *Montale*, ed. Cima and Segre, p. 122.

11. Montale made this comment in the radio interview mentioned in n. 8, now quoted by Maria Corti in her article "*Satura* e il genere 'diario poetico,'" first published in *Strumenti critici*, no. 15 (June 1971) and now available in *Eugenio Montale*, ed. Marco Forti (Milan: Mondadori, 1976), pp. 273–296.

12. In "Dante ieri e oggi," *Sulla poesia*, p. 30.

13. Montale writes of "i critici . . . / da me depistati" (the critics . . . / by me thrown off the track) in the first poem of *Satura*, "Il *tu* (The *You*) in *Tutte le poesie* (Milan: Mondadori, 1977), p. 325.

14. Corti, "*Satura*," pp. 292–293.

15. Corti, "*Satura*," p. 293.

16. This sense of surprise was based not only on the newness of tone and themes in *Satura* but also simply on the fact that Montale was seventy-five years old when it appeared. Even more surprising were the next two volumes, *Diario* and *Quaderno*, published untypically soon after *Satura*.

17. Montale stated this in his "Intervista immaginaria," first published in 1946; now in *Sulla poesia*, p. 564.

18. These comments are cited by Maria Antonietta Grignani in her article " 'Due prose veneziane': tra prosa e poesia," in *Letture montaliane in occasione dell'ottantesimo compleanno del Poeta* (Genoa: Bozzi Editore, 1977), pp. 335–369.

19. This phrase is used by Guido Almansi and Bruce Merry in their book *Eugenio Montale: The Private Language of Poetry* (Edinburgh: Edinburgh University Press, 1977), p. 131. They have taken it from Aldo Rossi's "Il punto su Montale dopo il quarto libro, *Satura,*" in *L'Approdo letterario,* no. 53 (March 1971), pp. 3–20.

20. See Angelo Jacomuzzi, "L'elogio della balbuzie: da *Satura* ai *Diari,*" in his book *La poesia di Montale* (Turin: Einaudi, 1978), pp. 146–173. I shall refer several times throughout my discussion to this excellent piece.

21. "Da 'Botta e risposta I' a *Satura,*" in *Montale,* ed. Cima and Segre, p. 121.

22. Zanzotto in *Montale,* ed. Cima and Segre, p. 122.

23. See Almansi and Merry, *Eugenio Montale: The Private Language of Poetry,* pp. 128–152, for a very perceptive critique of the weaknesses of *Satura.*

24. Oreste Macrì notes in his discussion of the poem "L'angelo nero" of *Satura,* in *Due saggi: Il demonismo nella poesia di Montale e teoria dell'edizione critica* (Lecce: Milella, 1977), p. 69, that "il mostro neologistico bisuffissale *inespungibile* [of that poem] fa parte del pullulio in *Satura* di aggettivi in -abile, -ibile, -evole . . ." (the neologistic monster with two suffixes *inexpungible* is part of the swarming in *Satura* of adjectives in -able, -ible . . .).

25. Corti, "*Satura,*" p. 276.

26. Corti, "*Satura,*" p. 291.

27. Corti writes in "*Satura,*" p. 294, that "in a time like the present, when rhetoric with its complex foundation of figures of thought and speech lives on the one hand prosperously at the service of the persuasion of advertising, and on the other hand is taken advantage of by the formal pomposity of writers with a Manneristic calling, Montale chooses a third road, that one opened to Italian literature in the far-off thirteenth century by writers such as Guittone [D'Arezzo], in whom rhetorical extravagance is turned into an instrument of ethical-political satire."

28. These words almost always appear at the end of a line, either in an enjambment or in order to complete a phrase. Because of this they stand out even more than they would were they embedded in the line.

29. The definition is found in S. Battaglia, V. Pernicone, *La grammatica italiana* (Turin: Loescher, 1963), p. 179.

30. Corti, "*Satura,*" p. 292.

31. In "Le reazioni di Montale," p. 192.

32. Montale has stated that "il 'tu' delle mie poesie non è mai rivolto a me stesso: è un 'tu' istituzionale, l'antagonista che bisognerebbe inventare se non ci fosse" (the *you* of my poems is never addressed to myself: it is the institutional *you* or the antagonist whom it would be necessary to invent if one were not to exist) in Giulio Nascimbeni's biography of the poet, *Eugenio Montale* (Milan: Longanesi, 1969), p. 74.

33. Almansi and Merry, *Eugenio Montale: The Private Language of Poetry,* p. 128.

184

34. Angelo Jacomuzzi, "Le stalle di Augìa," in *La poesia di Montale*, pp. 58–91.

35. In his study Martelli correctly points out also that many critics (Franco Croce, Jacomuzzi, Umberto Carpi, Pier Vincenzo Mengaldo, Andrea Zanzotto, Maria Corti) have spoken of the "stalle d'Augìa" (the Augean stables) of this poem as a "metaphor or, rather, an allegory of Fascism"; Mario Martelli, *Il rovescio della poesia* (Milan: Longanesi, 1977), p. 39.

36. In *Eugenio Montale*, ed. Cima and Segre, p. 115.

37. Servants often appear in Montale's poetry and prose; in the latest collections, Gina, Montale's housekeeper and companion of many years, makes several appearances, in "Il rondone" (The Swift) and "Al mio grillo" (To My Cricket) of *Diario* and "Il giorno dei morti" (The Day of the Dead) and "Appunti" (Notes) of *Quaderno*.

38. This last is a reference to the short story "Clizia in Foggia," in *Farfalla di Dinard* (Milan: Mondadori, 1969), pp. 103–109, in which Clizia dreams that she is a spider in Pythagoras' house.

39. See Antonio Musumeci's article "Il bestiario montaliano," in *Italica*, 55 (Winter 1978), 393–401, for a useful résumé and discussion of the many animals and birds in Montale's writings.

40. The beloved is assailed by icy winds in the "Motet" beginning, "Ti libero la fronte dai ghiaccioli" (I free your forehead of icicles); "Lui" appears in "La primavera hitleriana" of the "Silvae" in *La bufera e altro*.

41. Macrì, *Due saggi: Il demonismo nella poesia di Montale*; see especially pp. 3–20.

42. There is Montale's characterization of himself as a "povero Nestoriano" (poor Nestorian) in the poem "Iride" in *La bufera*; Nestorius' heresy was to insist too heavily on the essential humanity of Christ. In the poem "Vento sulla mezzaluna" (Wind on the Half-Moon) in *La bufera*, as well as in the short story "Sosta a Edimburgo" (Stop in Edinburgh) in *Farfalla di Dinard*, Montale implies that God is to be found here on earth, if at all. The beloved is clearly portrayed throughout *La bufera* as a bearer of divine strength and vision into this world.

43. I am thinking of Montale's typical insistence on multiple levels of meaning in his poetry. D'Arco Silvio Avalle, in the introduction to his book *Tre saggi su Montale* (Turin: Einaudi, 1972), cites one example—"Il mio prigioniero può essere un prigioniero politico; ma può essere *anche* un prigioniero della condizione esistenziale" (My prisoner can be a political prisoner; but he can *also* be a prisoner of the existential condition), Montale's words concerning his poem "The Prisoner's Dream" of *La bufera*—and calls this tendency "the equivocal structure" of the poet's explications (p. 13).

44. The proverbial "lupus in fabula" is the equivalent of the English "speak of the devil" idiom.

45. In an interview with Annalisa Cima, Montale stated that "Croce said: poetry is inside the heart of the poet, and that it is then written or not does not take away anything [from it]. Instead it is not true, it is not true at all, [for] if

one gets involved in writing, this internal phantasm changes, sometimes changes sex, age, weight, height, taste, smell." The original Italian is in *Incontro Montale*, ed. A. Cima (Milan: Vanni Scheiwiller, 1973), p. 18.

46. Montale uses the word three times in his poetry: first, in "Xenia II," poem 4, in which Mosca reveals "incredibili agnizioni" (amazing insights); next, in "Divinità in incognito" (Incognito Divinities) of *Satura*, where the poet writes of a "divinity, even of the lowest level" who might have touched him, but "l'agnizione mancava" (the realization was missing); last, in the poem "Annetta" of *Diario*, where the girl is called "un'agnizione / reale perché assurda" (a real agnition / because absurd).

47. Stefano Agosti, "Il testo della poesia in Montale: 'Sul lago d'Orta,' " in *Eugenio Montale*, ed. Cima and Segre, pp. 168–189; I translate from p. 170.

48. Agosti, "Il testo della poesia di Montale," p. 182.

49. There are many other examples of this attitude throughout the early and late poetry; the "Osso" that begins, "So l'ora" (I know the hour), contains the line, "la più vera ragione è di chi tace" (the truest account is of the one who is silent); in the "Osso" beginning, "Forse un mattino" (Perhaps one morning), the poet writes of carrying away his secret in silence (zitto); in *Satura* the poet asserts in "Incespicare" (Stammering) that because everyone speaks "il mondo / . . . è muto" (the world is mute); and Montale writes of a piece of coral that is superior to a human collective "perché non parla" (because it does not speak) in *Quaderno* in the poem that begins, "Siamo alla solitudine di gruppo" (We've come to group solitude).

50. *Sulla poesia*, p. 564.

51. The dialogue with Montale was first published in *Settimo Giorno*, ed. Bruno Rossi (5 June 1962) and is now available in the original Italian in *Sulla poesia*, pp. 592–599.

52. This piece first appeared in *Corriere della Sera* (7 February 1971) and is now available in *Sulla poesia*, pp. 599–600.

53. "Sul *Diario del '71 e del '72*," in *Una lunga fedeltà*, pp. 97–98.

54. "La pittura / da cavalletto costa sacrifizi / a chi la fa ed è sempre un sovrappiù / per chi la compra e non sa dove appenderla" (Easel painting demands sacrifices / from whoever does it and it is always *de trop* / for whoever buys it and doesn't know where to hang it). These are the opening lines of the poem "Poor Art" in *Diario*, *Tutte le poesie*, p. 475.

55. *Eugenio Montale: The Private Language of Poetry*, p. 154.

56. "Montale—la poesia giorno per giorno" first appeared in *Il Giorno* (April 8, 1973) and is now available in *Montale*, ed. Marco Forti (Milan: Mondadori, 1976), pp. 311–315.

57. *Una lunga fedeltà*, p. 98.

58. *Invito alla lettura di Montale* (Milan: Mursia, 1973), p. 146.

59. "Still and always, for the late Montale of *Diario*, the most reductive negation can be translated into metaphor and, as such, into affirmation: the regime is still that of perennial antinomies or, as the poet himself has said in *Diario del '71*, of the permanent oxymoron that is its rhetorical figure." My

translation of the original Italian, in *Eugenio Montale* (Milan: Mursia, 1973–1974), p. 491.

60. "L'elogio della balbuzie: da *Satura* ai *Diari*," in *La poesia di Montale*, pp. 146–173.

61. In the poem "Un poeta" (A Poet) in *Quaderno* Montale writes that in poetry "quello che conta non è il contenuto / ma la Forma" (that which counts is not the content / but the Form).

62. *Eugenio Montale: The Private Language of Poetry*, p. 154.

63. From *The Oxford Universal Dictionary* (Oxford: Clarendon Press, 1955), p. 2052.

64. From, respectively, "Domande senza risposta" (Questions without Answers), in *Quaderno*; "Il tuffatore" (The Diver), in *Diario*; and "La forma del mondo" (The Form of the World), in *Diario*.

65. "Dante ieri e oggi" in *Sulla poesia*, pp. 15–34.

66. This book (Princeton: Princeton University Press, 1979) is a most thought-provoking consideration of the themes of history and allegory in the *Commedia*.

67. Montale himself stated in his "Intervista immaginaria" that he never felt himself to be "invested with an important mission"; *Sulla poesia*, p. 569.

68. *Divine Comedies* (New York: Atheneum, 1977); *Mirabell: Books of Number* (New York: Atheneum, 1978) is the sequel to and completion of the earlier collection.

69. "L'elogio della balbuzie," p. 160.

70. "Spesso in tono scherzoso, a proposito di opere che offendono il senso estetico" (Often in a joking manner, concerning works that offend the aesthetic sense); definition appears in G. Devoto and G. C. Oli, *Dizionario della lingua italiana*, p. 1520.

71. *Eugenio Montale: The Private Language of Poetry*, p. 154.

72. Montale has stated that poetry "often . . . is called to a different destiny and people want to see it again in the piazza. But those who bite and who go down into the *agora* are soon booed"; "Intervista immaginaria," *Sulla poesia*, p. 564.

73. *Eugenio Montale: The Private Language of Poetry*, p. 159.

74. "L'elogio della balbuzie," p. 172.

75. This phrase appears in the poem "Asor" in *Diario*, *Tutte le poesie*, p. 554.

76. From, respectively, "Two Destinies," "In the Inhuman," and "Half a Century Ago," all in *Quaderno*.

77. A palinode is usually felt to be both existentially and poetically motivated: Petrarch turns away from Laura in poem 366 of the *Canzoniere* in order to accept the superiority of the *vera beatrice*, the Virgin Mary. But in his very choice of words the poet shows the poetic self-consciousness underlying his conversion, for as is immediately obvious, *beatrice* refers also to Dante's beloved and is thus an implicit criticism of his poetry as well as of Petrarch's own.

Thus even the most apparently sincere of palinodic gestures can be read as suspect and ultimately equivocal.

78. "L'elogio della balbuzie," p. 161. For my own part, I must admit to an oscillating response, sometimes positive, sometimes negative, to these latest poems. Perhaps the final positivity is to be found in the unstable equilibrium created in readers who cannot easily decide and argue once and for all for either their excellence or their failure; in short, in the continuing fascination we feel with these astute new poems.

79. I cannot begin to discuss the complexities surrounding the term *metaphor* but would simply suggest two good starting points for a reconsideration of them: the discussion of the term and the bibliography contained under *metaphor* in the *Princeton Encyclopedia of Poetry and Poetics*, ed. A. Preminger, F. Warnke, and O. B. Hardison, Jr. (Princeton: Princeton University Press, 1974), and the "Special Issue on Metaphor," in *Critical Inquiry*, 5 (Autumn 1978).

80. Richard Shiff, "Art and Life," *Critical Inquiry*, 5 (Autumn 1978), pp. 107–122.

81. Shiff, "Art and Life," p. 109.

82. The first two quotations ("tenacious endurance . . ." and "a story . . .") are from "Little Testament," the third is from "The Eel," both in *La bufera*.

IV. Prose Glosses: Is Poetry Still Possible?

1. *Auto da fé: Cronache in due tempi* (Milan: Il Saggiatore, 1966); *Sulla poesia*, ed. Giorgio Zampa (Milan: Mondadori, 1976). Neither *Auto da fé* nor *On Poetry* has been translated fully into English, although selected essays have appeared in various journals. A collection of Montale's articles on prose and music is being prepared by Zampa and should appear soon as *Sulla prosa*.

2. *Farfalla di Dinard* first appeared in 1956 in a limited edition published by Neri Pozza; expanded editions appeared in 1960 and 1969 published by Mondadori. G. Singh's English version, *Butterfly of Dinard*, was published in 1971 by the University of Kentucky Press. *Fuori di casa* (Away From Home) was first published in 1969 by Ricciardi and republished in 1975 by Mondadori. No English version exists.

3. Barile's *Bibliografia montaliana* (Milan: Mondadori, 1977) is an important contribution to the systematization of Montale's works.

4. In his article "Invito alla 'Farfalla di Dinard,' " first published in *I segni e la critica* (Turin: Einaudi, 1970), and now available in *Per conoscere Montale*, ed. Marco Forti (Milan: Mondadori, 1976), pp. 175–191, Segre shows how useful the stories are in understanding the elaboration of much of the same raw material into poetry.

5. All quotations in my discussion of "La poesia non esiste" are my own translations based on the 1969 edition of *Farfalla di Dinard* (Milan: Mondadori), pp. 187–191.

6. Scattered throughout the essays included in *Sulla poesia* are meditations on the existence and function of poetry; Montale's Nobel Prize accep-

tance speech, discussed later in this chapter, is entirely constructed around the fundamental question: Is poetry still possible?

7. Ulrich is, in fact, repeating some of Montale's own words concerning the limits of poetry and is in this sense an ironic alter ego of the poet. I am thinking particularly of Montale's assertion in his "Intervista immaginaria" that "absolute expression would be . . . an explosion . . ." (*Sulla poesia*, p. 565).

8. *Sulla poesia*, p. 569.

9. All quotations from "Tornare nella strada" are my own translations of the article from *Auto da fé*, pp. 134–138.

10. All quotations from "Farfalla di Dinard" are my own translations of the story from the 1969 edition of *Farfalla di Dinard*, pp. 240–241.

11. Segre, *Per conoscere Montale*, p. 190.

12. From, respectively, "Stanze" (Stanzas) in *Le occasioni*; "Xenia II," poem 1; and the "Motet" beginning, "Perché tardi?" (Why do you delay?). The letter to Bobi Bazlen is in *Sulla poesia*, pp. 95–96.

13. Segre, *Per conoscere Montale*, p. 190.

14. "Due sciacalli al guinzaglio," in *Sulla poesia*, pp. 84–87. All quotations are my own translations based on this source.

15. Claire Huffman, "Eugenio Montale: Questions, Answers and Contexts," in *Yearbook of Italian Studies* (1973–1975), pp. 218–233.

16. The piece is available in *Sulla poesia*, pp. 5–14. There is also available a small volume that includes the Italian text, and Swedish and English translations (Stockholm, Rome: Italica, 1975). I base my own translations on the first source.

17. Huffman, "Eugenio Montale: Questions, Answers and Contexts," p. 232.

18. In "Confessioni di scrittori (Interviste can se stessi)" in *Sulla poesia*, pp. 569–574.

19. In "Intervista immaginaria," *Sulla poesia*, pp. 565–567.

20. *Farfalla di Dinard* (1969), pp. 223–225. Translations are my own.

21. Arturo Loria (1902–1957) was a writer and a friend of Montale's during the thirties and forties in Florence. He kept a journal (1942–1943), now available in *Firenze: Dalle Giubbe Rosse all'Antico Fattore* (Florence: Le Monnier, 1973), in which we can read the following (in my translation): "October 11, 1942: the afternoon in Rovezzano with Eugenio Montale, very amusing during the return trip as he let loose on the topic of bel canto . . . When Montale talks about this subject, he says unexpected, very deep, and enchanting things . . . Montale could, with his taste and his advice, tame many beastly singers. I would love to see him suddenly transported square into the singing world with the duty of top 'trainer.' His 'man of the 1800s' side would get a strong push to reveal itself more openly. And his poetry, then? No, giving it a little thought, there wouldn't be any conflict: Montale's poetry, which I love and respect, ideally belongs to 1880" (pp. 128–129). Although I am not in agreement with

Loria's opinion of Montale's poetry, I completely second his insight into the nineteenth-century aspects of Montale's intellect, tastes, and character.

22. A trip described in "Andati e tornati in novanta ore" (Round Trip in Ninety Hours), in *Fuori di casa.*

23. See Montale's Preface to the English version of *Farfalla di Dinard* (G. Singh, *Butterfly of Dinard,* 1971), p. 5.

24. "È ancora possibile la poesia?" in *Sulla poesia,* p. 7.

25. "È ancora possibile la poesia?" in *Sulla poesia,* p. 14.

Conclusion

1. These are Montale's words from the poem "La poesia" (Poetry), in *Satura,* from *Tutte le poesie* (Milan: Mondadori, 1977), p. 375, in which words are personified: "Appena fuori / si guardano d'attorno e hanno l'aria di dirsi: / che sto a farci?" (Scarcely out / they look around and seem to ask themselves: / what am I doing here?).

2. Again these words are from a poem, "Asor," included in *Diario del '72,* from *Tutte le poesie,* p. 554.

3. Montale wrote these words in his essay on Croce, "L'estetica e la critica," first published in 1962 and now available in *Sulla poesia,* ed. Giorgio Zampa (Milan: Mondadori, 1976), pp. 128–143. My translation is from p. 140 of this source.

4. From Montale's "Intervista immaginaria," in *Sulla poesia,* p. 562.

5. The poem concludes: "Conosce il nostro vivere / (lo sente), anzi vorrebbe farne parte / ma niente gli è possibile per l'ovvia / contradizion che nol consente" (It knows our living / (feels it), would even like to be a part of it / but nothing is possible for it for the obvious / contradiction that does not consent to it).

6. This is the first poem of the "Ossi" series, written between 1921 and 1925.

7. *Language as Symbolic Action: Essays on Life, Literature, and Method* (Berkeley: University of California Press, 1966), p. 419. See also Burke's *The Rhetoric of Religion: Studies in Logology* (Berkeley: University of California Press, 1970), especially the epilogue, "Prologue in Heaven" (pp. 273–316), for a lively dialogue between God and Satan that centers in great part on the negative in human speech.

8. "Intervista immaginaria," in *Sulla poesia,* p. 564.

9. I am referring to Burke's ideas as discussed in the chapter "A Dramatistic View of the Origins of Language," in *Language as Symbolic Action,* pp. 419–425 *passim.*

10. William Empson's "seven types" of ambiguity as discussed in his book of the same title have helped readers to recognize the complexities of poetry, even though to limit ambiguities to a particular number of types seems to be a somewhat erroneous attempt at classification of what is not easily classifiable.

11. Montale wrote this in a letter to P. Gadda Conti, quoted in Alvaro Va-

Notes
to
Pages
159–164

lentini, *Lettura di Montale: Ossi di seppia* (Rome: Bulzoni, 1971), p. 11.

12. Simone de Beauvoir, *The Ethics of Ambiguity*, trans. Bernard Frechtman (New York: Philosophical Library, 1948); I am quoting from a reprint of pp. 129–155 of that book in *Contemporary European Ethics*, ed. Joseph J. Kockelmans (Garden City, N.Y.: Doubleday, 1972), p. 300.

13. De Beauvoir, *The Ethics of Ambiguity*, p. 300.

14. "Style and Tradition," in Eugenio Montale, *Auto da fé* (Milan: Il Saggiatore, 1966), pp. 15–19. All quotations in my translation are from this source.

15. *Art and Anarchy* (New York: Vintage Books, 1969), p. 18.

16. From the article "Itinerary of a Thought," in *New Left Review*, 58 (1969), 57–59. I quote from Victor Turner's reference to it in *Dramas, Fields, and Metaphors: Symbolic Action in Human Society* (Ithaca: Cornell University Press, 1974), p. 255.

17. This is Montale's self-descriptive phrase from the poem "Intercettazione telefonica" (Phone Tap), in *Satura*, from *Tutte le poesie*, p. 374.

18. Pier Vincenzo Mengaldo, "Fortini e i 'Poeti del Novecento,'" in *Nuovi argomenti* (January-March 1979), 159–177. The quotation is from p. 173 of this article reviewing Franco Fortini's *I poeti del Novecento* (Bari: Laterza, 1977).

19. In Montale's concluding poem of *Diario del '72*, in *Tutte le poesie*, p. 580, "Per finire" (To Conclude).

Works
by
and
about
Montale

Almansi, Guido, and Bruce Merry. *Eugenio Montale: The Private Language of Poetry.* Edinburgh: Edinburgh University Press, 1977.

Avalle, D'Arco Silvio. *Tre saggi su Montale.* Turin: Einaudi, 1972.

Barile, Laura, ed. *Bibliografia montaliana.* Milan: Mondadori, 1977.

Bettarini, Rosanna, and Gianfranco Contini, eds. *Eugenio Montale: L'opera in versi* (edizione critica). 2 vols. Turin: Einaudi, 1980.

Cambon, Glauco. *Eugenio Montale.* New York: Columbia University Press, 1972.

——— introd. *Eugenio Montale: Selected Poems.* New York: New Directions, 1965.

Cary, Joseph. *Three Modern Italian Poets: Saba, Ungaretti, Montale.* New York: New York University Press, 1969.

Cima, Annalisa, and Cesare Segre, eds. *Profilo di un autore: Eugenio Montale.* Milan: Rizzoli, 1977.

Contini, Gianfranco. *Una lunga fedeltà: Scritti su Eugenio Montale.* Turin: Einaudi, 1974.

Corti, Maria, and Maria Antonietta Grignani, eds. *Autografi di Montale.* Turin: Einaudi, 1976.

192

Works
by
and
about
Montale

Farnsworth, Edith, trans. *Provisional Conclusions: A Selection of the Poetry of Eugenio Montale.* Chicago: Henry Regnery Co., 1970.

Forti, Marco. *Eugenio Montale: La poesia, la prosa di fantasia e d'invenzione.* Milan: Mursia, 1973–74.

———— ed. *Per conoscere Montale.* Milan: Mondadori, 1976.

Giachery, Emerico. "Metamorfosi dell'orto." *Atti e Memorie dell'Arcadia,* 3rd ser., vol. 7, fasc. 1 (1977), 35–60.

Huffman, Claire Licari. "Eugenio Montale: Questions, Answers and Contexts." *Yearbook of Italian Studies* (1973–1975), 218–233.

———— "Structuralist Criticism and the Interpretation of Montale." *The Modern Language Review,* 72 (1977), 322–334.

Jacomuzzi, Angelo. *La poesia di Montale: Dagli "Ossi" ai "Diari".* Turin: Einaudi, 1978.

Kay, George, trans. *Selected Poems of Eugenio Montale.* Baltimore: Penguin Books, 1969.

Letture montaliane in occasione dell'ottantesimo compleanno del Poeta. Genoa: Bozzi Editore, 1978.

Macrì, Oreste. *Due saggi: Il demonismo nella poesia di Montale e teoria dell'edizione critica.* Lecce: Milella, 1977.

Martelli, Mario. *Il rovescio della poesia.* Milan: Longanesi, 1977.

Montale, Eugenio. *Auto da fé: Cronache in due tempi.* Milan: Il Saggiatore, 1966.

———— *Farfalla di Dinard.* Milan: Mondadori, 1969.

———— *Fuori di casa.* Milan: Mondadori, 1975.

———— *Quaderno di traduzioni.* Milan: Mondadori, 1975.

———— *Tutte le poesie.* Milan: Mondadori, 1977.

Musumeci, Antonino. "Il bestiario montaliano." *Italica,* 55 (Winter 1978), 393–401.

———— "Silenzi montaliani: Note sull'*enjambement* nella poesia di Montale." *Forum Italicum,* 6 (December 1972), 497–514.

Nascimbeni, Giulio. *Eugenio Montale.* Milan: Longanesi, 1969.

Pipa, Arshi. *Montale and Dante.* Minneapolis: University of Minnesota Press, 1968.

Porzio, Domenico. *Con Montale a Stoccolma.* Milan: Ferro Edizioni, 1976.

Ramat, Silvio. *Montale.* Florence: Vallecchi, 1965.

———— ed. *Omaggio a Montale.* Milan: Mondadori, 1966.

Rebay, Luciano. "I diàspori di Montale." *Italica,* 46 (Spring 1969), 33–53.

Rombi, Maggi. *Montale: Parole sensi immagini.* Rome: Bulzoni, 1978.

Rosiello, Luigi. "Consistenza e distribuzione statistica del lessico poetico in Montale." *Rendiconti,* fasc. 11–12 (September 1965), 397–421.

Singh, G., trans. *The Butterfly of Dinard.* By Eugenio Montale. Lexington, Ky.: University of Kentucky Press, 1971.

———— trans. and introd. *Eugenio Montale: New Poems.* New York: New Directions, 1976.

Works
by
and
about
Montale

———— trans. and introd. *It Depends: A Poet's Notebook.* By Eugenio Montale. New York: New Directions, 1980.

———— *Eugenio Montale: A Critical Study of His Poetry, Prose, and Criticism.* New Haven: Yale University Press, 1973.

Valentini, Alvaro. *Lettura di Montale: Ossi di seppia.* Rome: Bulzoni, 1971.

———— *Lettura di Montale: Le occasioni.* Rome: Bulzoni, 1975.

———— *Lettura di Montale: La bufera e altro.* Rome: Bulzoni, 1977.

Wright, Charles, trans. *The Storm and Other Poems.* By Eugenio Montale. Field Translation Series. Oberlin, Ohio: Oberlin College, 1978.

Zampa, Giorgio, ed. *Eugenio Montale: Sulla poesia.* Milan: Mondadori, 1976.

Index
of
Names

Index
of
Names

Index
of
Montale's
Poetry
and
Prose

198
Index
of
Montale's
Poetry
and
Prose

199

Index
of
Montale's
Poetry
and
Prose

200
Index
of
Montale's
Poetry
and
Prose